WHY NATIONS ACT

SAGE FOCUS EDITIONS

WHY NATIONS ACT

Theoretical Perspectives
for Comparative Foreign
Policy Studies

Edited by
Maurice A. East
Stephen A. Salmore
Charles F. Hermann

SAGE PUBLICATIONS   Beverly Hills/London

For information address:

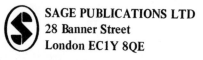

SAGE PUBLICATIONS, INC.
275 South Beverly Drive
Beverly Hills, California 90212

SAGE PUBLICATIONS LTD
28 Banner Street
London EC1Y 8QE

Library of Congress Cataloging in Publication Data

Main entry under title:

Why nations act.

   (Sage focus editions)
   Includes bibliographical references.
   1. International relations. I. East, Maurice A.,
1941– II. Salmore, Stephen. III. Hermann, Charles
F., 1938– IV. Series.
JX1395.W53   327   77-22119
ISBN 0-8039-0718-4
ISBN 0-8039-0719-2 pbk.

FIRST PRINTING

CONTENTS

dedicated to James N. Rosenau

ACKNOWLEDGMENTS

This book is one element in the research activities of the Comparative Research on the Events of Nations (CREON) Project. We hope that the theoretical perspectives developed here, which are central to research in the CREON Project, will prove to be of value to individuals who approach the study of foreign policy from various points of view. Although the pages that follow do not require familiarity with the CREON Project, it seems appropriate to mention its purposes here and to acknowledge those who have sponsored this undertaking.

The Comparative Research on the Events of Nations Project is a cross-national study of the foreign policy behaviors of 36 nations. CREON has two primary objectives: (1) to map and compare the range of foreign activities initiated between 1959 and 1968 by the nations under study, and (2) to seek explanations of foreign policy behaviors in terms of combinations of different theoretical perspectives. The effort is an interdisciplinary project based at multiple universities. Each of the contributors to this volume has particular debts to his or her own university community for its assistance, and these are acknowledged in the separate chapters. All of us, however, are indebted to the Mershon Center at Ohio State University, which has identified CREON as one of its programmatic projects and, since 1970, has provided continuous support from which we all have benefited. As will be evident in subsequent chapters, the Center's Director, Richard C. Snyder, has been an intellectual resource for the project, and administrative and financial assistance have been provided by the Center under his leadership.

We also wish to give prominent acknowledgment to the National Science Foundation for its simultaneous grants to the University of Kentucky (GS-40347), Ohio State University (GS-40356), and Rutgers University (GS-40348). The NSF grants have made possible vigorous inquiry at multiple university sites and have enhanced the collaborative dimensions of the undertaking.

Turning from the general CREON Project to the preparation of this book, we all have read and reread each other's chapters and made suggestions for revisions. Several project members made special efforts to comment on particular chapters and these are noted at appropriate points. All of us, however, wish to single out two individuals for their generous and extensive contributions to the task of preparing this book. One of our collaborators, Margaret Hermann, reread the entire manuscript several times in an effort to improve the continuity and save us from some of our errors in reasoning and grammar. Carole Jacobson not only typed the manuscript several times and researched the bibliography but also kept up our spirits with her positive example.

Finally, we wish to comment on our decision to dedicate this book to James N. Rosenau. Anyone familiar with the effort to develop foreign policy as an area of comparative inquiry will immediately recognize the prominent role that Jim Rosenau has played; his general contribution would suffice to explain why authors of a book in the area would wish to pay him tribute. Those of us affiliated with the CREON project, however, have a special association for which we are grateful. Jim Rosenau created the occasion that brought the original CREON investigators together to consider foreign policy. He was co-principal investigator on the project under which the first CREON variables were defined and data were collected. And what is more, his own ideas on the comparative study of foreign policy have been both points of departure and points of reference for our own efforts. We trust the following pages will reflect the influence of James Rosenau.

1

INTRODUCTION

Charles F. Hermann and Maurice A. East

We, the authors of this book, know little about you, the prospective reader. Presumably you have some interest in foreign policy, but it is difficult for us to estimate how much prior thought you have given to this topic. Obviously, your level of expertise and knowledge will be substantially greater if you are a professional analyst of foreign affairs than if you are a student with minimal prior training in the area. We hope that this volume will prove to be stimulating to both advanced analysts and fairly new students, and we have written it with these two groups in mind.

These comments are necessary at the beginning of this introductory chapter to alert you to what lies immediately ahead. Often when professionals address one another they assume considerable shared knowledge. Such behavior occasionally is inappropriate with students. We feel that, in writings on the comparative study of foreign policy, students are too frequently asked to accept certain assumptions without reflection. For example, the student may wish to ask why one should want to adopt a comparative approach and if it is reasonable to expect to discover patterns in the variables that influence foreign policy actions. Before turning to the specific orientation of this book, we shall devote several sections of this introductory chapter to addressing some of these issues in at least a preliminary fashion. We hope that the readers who have worked these matters through for themselves will bear with us and that those who have not done so before will be encouraged to take up the task.

THE COMPARATIVE PERSPECTIVE
ON FOREIGN POLICY

This book advances a set of theoretical perspectives for the comparative study of foreign policy behavior. By comparative we mean that the theoretical perspectives in the book attempt to provide interpretations of foreign policy behaviors that are applicable both cross-nationally (i.e., comparisons of multiple nations at a single point in time) and longitudinally (i.e., comparisons of one nation with itself across an interval of time). Given our extremely imperfect understanding of any one government's external behavior at even a single point in time, the question naturally arises: Why study foreign policy comparatively? Might not a better strategy be to develop a reasonably satisfactory explanation of one government's behavior for a brief period of time and then gradually expand our explanatory system to include other governments and longer periods of time? In other words, one must learn to walk before trying to run. One might even question whether the progression to systematic comparison was possible.[1]

Another challenge to a comparative approach would question the value of any cross-national comparative explanation even if it could be developed. What is the purpose of the comparative approach? Are not most of the major questions one might want to answer concerned with the foreign behavior of one actor over a relatively short period of time? This position could be summarized with the assertion that the primary questions, at least for our times, pertain to the actions of individual nation states. Clearly, the contributors to this volume take a different perspective, but the case for a comparative approach to the study of foreign policy should be carefully reviewed.

First, we believe that a comparative approach increases one's comprehension of a single actor. Cross-national and longitudinal comparisons of foreign policy behaviors will increase a person's ability to distinguish between the common and the unusual elements that contribute to a particular government's external behavior. On the one hand, comparative analysis can lead to the identification of important deviant cases—that is, those having unusual features. On the other hand, it can guard against unwarranted interpretations that suggest a particular nation's foreign policy can be explained in terms of unique features pertaining to that country when, in fact, comparison reveals that those same features exist in other nations manifesting different policies.

By way of illustration, consider the foreign policy behavior of the United States. American foreign policy has often been a topic of research and, just as often, results from such research have been generalized to other nations. With respect to many of the variables that frequently are regarded as important in explaining foreign policy (e.g., economic wealth, military capability, governmental complexity), the United States occupies what can be considered an extreme position—near one end of the distribution of all contemporary nations. If these variables are important in explaining foreign policy behavior, the extreme position of the United States on these variable distributions makes it appear unreasonable to expect other governments to behave in a manner similar to that of the United States. In short, even if we know how the United States acts, we do not automatically know how other nations will act. By giving the analyst some sense of one actor's position in relationship to others, comparative analysis makes it possible to avoid this error. It provides a means of investigating the differences among nations and the effects of such differences on foreign policy behavior. An assertion of unsubstantiated uniqueness also appears in interpretations of international affairs. For example, a single-minded unity of purpose and clarity of vision are often ascribed to the external policy of American adversaries such as the Soviet Union, even though such coordination and planning would be regarded as an almost impossible achievement for the government of the United States. It may be that Russian ideological fervor or unity of national experience justifies such a claim of unique behavior for the Soviet Union or it may be that post hoc examination of only one country's behaviors permits a false interpretation. Through some sort of comparative analysis such interpretations can be investigated.

A second reason for urging comparative analysis in the study of foreign policy stems from the rapidly changing environment in which we live in the latter part of the twentieth century. Much has been said and written about the major changes transpiring in world affairs: the increasing number of nations, the extreme economic inequalities, the enhanced interdependence, the transformation of the Cold War, the emergence of important nonnational actors, and so on. By using a comparative approach, we can learn about the effects of such changes. Thus, by examining units at intervals over time (longitudinal comparison), we can establish what phenomena are actually changing, at what rate, and with what effects. By examining multiple units at one point in time (cross-national comparison), we can explain the differential impact of such changes on the foreign policy behavior of various nations.

Let us look at some of the interpretations of foreign policy behavior in the post-World War II era in order to illustrate this particular point. Frequently such interpretations were based on a series of more or less explicit assumptions that we will call the "Cold War" model. Although the Cold War model may never have been completely satisfactory, it did provide a framework for explaining much of the foreign behavior of many nations. For example, the model was useful in determining the nations that would receive economic and military assistance, the composition of opposing coalitions, and the perceived sources of external threats. However, the appropriateness of the Cold War model has clearly declined today as comparative analysis would probably show. A cross-national comparison of nations would reveal that a substantial proportion of them are not members of either of the major alliance blocs and thus do not "fit" into the Cold War model. Moreover, those nations that continue to be members of the major alliance blocs no longer operate according to the assumptions of the model. Longitudinal comparative analysis would demonstrate, for example, that the relations between the United States and France or between the Soviet Union and China have changed significantly since the 1950s. Using the information generated by longitudinal and cross-national comparative analyses, we need to forge other, more adequate models for explaining the behavior of nations.

The first two reasons for adopting a comparative approach to the study of foreign policy should appeal to anyone concerned with world politics and foreign policy regardless of the particular methods or type of explanatory system they employ. Our third reason for the comparative study of foreign policy stems from our commitment to one means of gaining insight and understanding—the scientific method. A number of thoughtful statements concerning the role of comparison in scientific inquiry have been written by individuals interested in the comparative study of foreign policy (e.g., McGowan, 1975; Raymond, 1975; Rosenau, 1975), in comparative politics (e.g., Merritt and Rokkan, 1966; Przeworski and Teune, 1970; Holt and Turner, 1970), in other social sciences (e.g., Bendix, 1963; J. W. M. Whiting, 1969; Naroll and Cohen, 1970), and in the philosophy of science (e.g., Nagel, 1961; A. Kaplan, 1964). The roles of comparison in scientific inquiry are many—for discovery, for control against error, for determining parameters and degree of generalizability. Examination of the issues associated with these and other scientific uses of comparison is beyond the scope of this essay. In making a summarizing observation, however, we can do no better than to quote McGowan and Shapiro (1973: 25): "Scientific method uses comparison very heavily whenever hypotheses are checked against data; and since all sciences are empirical at some point, they all use comparison."

At this point an important qualification is necessary, one that often is overlooked by those who enthusiastically advocate a comparative and scientific approach to foreign policy. To assert that comparative analysis is an integral part of any scientific inquiry provides by itself neither a justification nor a guarantee of feasibility for cross-national and longitudinal comparisons of foreign policy. With regard to the general feasibility of doing such analyses, we point to anthropology and, more recently, to sociology for evidence of the progress these disciplines have made by using scientific cross-national and longitudinal comparisons. As to the desirability of such comparisons, we refer the reader back to the first two arguments. Moreover, we list a series of questions, susceptible to scientific inquiry, that can only be answered by cross-national and/or longitudinal comparisons. Do rich and poor nations have different perceptions of their problems? Can democratic nations have effective foreign policies? How have the relations among East and West bloc nations changed since the 1950s? Is the United States more or less warlike than other nations? This list of questions could be expanded almost indefinitely. Our position should be clear by now. Because interesting foreign policy questions such as the above cannot be adequately answered by improved comprehension of a single nation's foreign behavior, and because such work is feasible, comparative analysis of foreign policy is needed.

THE SEARCH FOR EXPLANATIONS OF FOREIGN POLICY BEHAVIOR

Following K. W. Deutsch (1968: 82-86), it is useful to view the foreign policy behavior of governments as resulting from a mix of random elements and discernible regularities. By random elements we mean factors influencing foreign policy behavior whose likelihood of occurrence is so unpredictable that they must be regarded as accidents in accounting for foreign affairs. Events such as the sudden death of a world leader or the canceling of a summit meeting because of a domestic riot may be regarded as accidents with respect to foreign policy. They appear random for a number of reasons, including the complexity of their antecedents, their remote linkage with foreign affairs, and their infrequency or irregularity of occurrence. As our comprehension of various aspects of our world increases, some elements that now seem accidental may become predictable. It seems safe to conclude, however, that foreign policy behavior will always be influenced—sometimes in very substantial ways—by forces that we can only regard at the time as random.

In contrast, other factors influence foreign policy with some regularity. These factors recur and have such consistent effects that they create patterns and regularities in foreign affairs. Such regularities can be detected through systematic analysis. Moreover, their influence on foreign policy behavior can be explained. For many persons concerned with foreign policy—including those committed to the development of the field through the methods of scientific inquiry—a basic task is the identification and formation of explanations of these regularities. For example, Knorr (1956) has identified some of the important factors that regularly influence a nation's ability to wage war and has described their effects.

Despite numerous efforts, including the contributions of scholars ranging from Plato to Karl Marx and from Charles Beard to Lewis Richardson, it seems fair to say that the discovery and description of the role of these presumed regularities in foreign affairs have been exceedingly difficult. Why? Some may believe the answer is that few, if any, such regularities exist. There are, however, alternative interpretations, rejecting the rather pessimistic conclusion that foreign policy is almost exclusively the result of totally unique and unpredictable forces. One such interpretation suggests that the previous lack of success in accounting for regularities in foreign policy results from the simplicity of our earlier attempts at explanation.

Many early explanations of foreign policy activity can be characterized in either of two ways. A first group of attempted explanations was based on single and often highly generalized determinants such as power, geophysical location, social class, elite or group interest, leader personality, and national interest. Moreover, the effects of these key determinants were often seen as uniform, direct, and singular. Although it would seem a reasonable strategy to begin with single-factor explanations of foreign policy, more and more individuals engaged in foreign policy analysis have concluded that most single-factor explanations of foreign affairs are unsatisfactory. Such explanations seem limited to those foreign policy occasions when the emphasized factor predominates. Moreover, single-factor explanations can only account for a wide range of policies if the behavior pattern to be explained is defined in extremely broad and general terms or if the explanatory terms are actually used in different ways simultaneously—as happens, for example, with the concept of power.[2] The resultant loss of rigor and imprecision of meaning forms inadequate basis on which to expand our knowledge.

A second group of early explanations of foreign policy suffered from almost the reverse of the disability experienced by the first. Rather than attempting to account for foreign policy in terms of a single factor, analysts in the second group offered an indiscriminant list of numerous elements that presumably influenced foreign policy. Although alerting us to the variety of factors that could contribute to foreign policy (e.g., Thompson and Macridis, 1962), too frequently these efforts became little more than "shopping lists." Occasionally, items were identified only by broad concepts (e.g., public opinion, technology, polarity) without specification of either the boundaries or discrete variables that were supposed to be included. Little or no attention was given to how these various properties affected foreign policy or to the conditions under which their impacts might be great or negligible. Nor was any thought given to the manner in which such variables were interconnected with one another to amplify, abate, or transform their isolated effects. In sum, this checklist approach to foreign policy explanation greatly enlarged the number of possible variables but contributed little to improved explanation.

In the face of such conclusions, there has been an increasing recognition of the need for more complex explanations of foreign policy behavior. An early step in the development of more complex explanatory systems was the construction of a framework in which to organize and locate the numerous factors that might regularly influence foreign policy. Snyder et al. (1954) offered a decision-making framework for this purpose more than two decades ago. Allison (1969) has moved us further in the direction of complex explanations by his persuasive demonstration that one can arrive at strikingly varied interpretations of the same occurrence when focusing on different sets of explanatory variables from different frameworks or perspectives.

The framework that the analyst adopts suggests a certain set of explanatory variables and, in turn, a certain kind of interpretation of foreign policy. In addition to the analyst's perspective, the particular context or condition can affect the appropriateness of a particular foreign policy explanation. As Rosenau (1966) has argued, the explanatory mechanisms of primary importance for interpreting the foreign policy behavior of one type of nation may prove far less relevant for interpreting the foreign policy behavior of another type of nation.

In sum, the search for satisfactory explanations of foreign policy behavior has led to the conclusion that interpreting recurrent influences on foreign policy will probably require (a) more complex explanatory systems with a larger number and variety of variables and (b) increased awareness of the limiting conditions under which such variables operate.

BASIC ORIENTATIONS IN CREON

We have now stated the position of the contributors to this book on several important issues in the study of foreign policy. We have indicated that we favor comparative analysis and the search for more complex explanations of the recurrent influences operative in foreign affairs. Although no consensus exists on these matters, our views are similar to those of a number of others engaged in the study of foreign policy. During the course of our collaboration on the Comparative Research on the Events of

Nations (CREON) Project that generated this volume, we have come to share certain other orientations toward the study of foreign policy that are not as commonly held as the more general interpretations reviewed in the previous sections. The reader's ability to understand and evaluate subsequent chapters may be enhanced by a discussion of these CREON orientations. CREON is an interdisciplinary, multiuniversity research project focusing on the comparative study of foreign policy behavior.[3] Knowledge concerning five of the CREON orientations is important for interpreting our work.

First, we are committed to the development of multicausal explanations of foreign policy behavior that are susceptible to empirical investigation. This general point has been developed in the previous section and is a fairly widely accepted point of view. However, we now want to elaborate several ideas that may create consternation for some readers. Despite the important reservations raised by many about the concept of "cause," we find it a valuable theoretical device. According to Blalock (1961: 9): "If X is a cause of Y, we have in mind that a change in X produces a change in Y and not merely that a change in X is followed by or associated with a change in Y." We find the notion of a multiple set of variables "producing or forcing" a change in another set of variables (e.g., foreign policy behavior) a useful aid in theory development, particularly if we have aspirations for eventually producing something of value for policy formulation. Having said this, we acknowledge that causal laws can never be definitively demonstrated empirically in the open system of world politics. However, even if the empirical investigation of causality is limited, some of the implications that the notion of causality has for the study of foreign policy behavior can and, we believe, should be explored. Thus, our multicausal explanations must generate relationships between variables that can be explored by systematic empirical investigation.

One other point needs to be made concerning our commitment to multicausal explanations. We see this orientation leading to a different set of questions than those raised by Rosenau (1966) in his widely read pre-theories article. Rosenau's pre-theory statement leads one to ask: Under what conditions will one set of variables be relatively more potent or decisive in explaining foreign policy than another set? The macro question of our multicausal orientation is: Under a variety of conditions, how do various explanatory variables combine to provide a more complete explanation of foreign policy behavior? Whereas the Rosenau pre-theory emphasizes the relative ability of each type of explanatory variable to account for foreign policy behavior, the multicausal orientation views explanatory variables not as in competition with one another in accounting for foreign policy behaviors but as combining to produce a more adequate explanation than any one variable or cluster of closely related variables could do alone.

A second CREON orientation involves the conviction that we need to develop explanatory logic for the underlying causal mechanisms that relate hypothesized explanatory variables to foreign policy behavior. In our judgment we have progressed beyond the point where it is a useful contribution to our understanding of foreign policy simply to identify potential elements that somehow may influence foreign policy behavior. Indeed, we believe it is now essential to move beyond descriptive hypotheses that do little more than assert the existence of a relationship between two or more variables. McGowan and Shapiro (1973) have assembled an extensive propositional inventory that nicely demonstrates that considerable numbers of such descriptive hypotheses do exist in the comparative study of foreign policy. The next step in the development of multicausal explanations involves the careful explication of reasons for expecting variables to influence one another. The articulation of this explanatory logic is consistent with and required by the commitment to multicausal explanation. Development of the explanatory logic will aid in defining the parameters or conditions under which a given type of relationship can be expected. It will also increase the benefits that are derived when an expected relationship is not verified empirically. When the explanatory logic underlying an hypothesized relationship is explicit, an unexpected finding invites one to explore anew the underpinnings for the initial expectations, thus pushing theoretical development ahead.

The emphasis on explanatory logic has an important implication for the variables and theoretical perspectives that are examined in the CREON Project and, more specifically, in this book. No attempt is made in this book either to be exhaustive with respect to all theoretical perspectives that conceivably could influence foreign policy behavior or to comprehensively include all variables that could be enumerated within a given perspective. Instead we have selected both perspectives and variables for which we could develop an explanatory logic. Thus, when we move on to the empirical exploration stage, the clear possibility exists that not only our hypotheses but also our underlying interpretations can be falsified. In effect, we are putting our explanations "on the line."

The third CREON orientation concerns the locus of foreign policy activities. Essentially, we view foreign policy as being the product of individual decision makers operating in an organizational context. Furthermore, for the purposes of CREON research, we delimit that organizational context to national governments. Conceptualizing foreign policy in terms of individual decision makers is a well-established approach (e.g., Snyder et al., 1962). We build on this tradition for several reasons. As developed in chapter 3, we believe differences in the personal characteristics of political leaders can influence foreign policy behavior under certain conditions. Moreover, by conceiving of foreign policy as a human decision process, the CREON investigators establish the conceptual basis for a discrete unit of foreign policy behavior—the political level decision. We will develop this point in the next chapter.

Several aspects of the decision-making perspective deserve special comment because they have been the source of misunderstandings in the past. First, our conceptualization of decision making includes not only the actual choice process but also the antecedent conditions and the potential implementation or execution. Decision making, as we use the concept, does not stop with the making of one or a series of choices but includes as an integral part the process of translating the decision into action or inaction. The emphasis placed on the decision and on behavior is sometimes referred to as the behavioral approach, which leads to a second point to be noted. Some might assume that a behavioral approach precludes the analysis of institutions. That need not be the case, and with respect to CREON it certainly is not so. Foreign policy officials in virtually all contemporary national governments behave in the context of various organizational and institutional structures. As will be argued in several of the subsequent chapters, these structures can have a significant influence on foreign policy behaviors.

Although CREON limits its examination of foreign policy to decision making in national governments, we are not asserting that these are the only units that initiate purposeful external behaviors in attempts to influence others. In fact, in global politics today there are many more intergovernmental and nongovernmental organizations initiating such behaviors than national governments. What is more, some of these nonnational organizations, such as the giant multinational corporations, are exerting considerable influence—whether measured in terms of scope, domain, intensity, or rate of success. CREON, however, is confined to the foreign policy behaviors of national governments for both theoretical and practical reasons. On the theoretical side, we share the conclusion of Nye and Keohane (1971) that national governments are still the single most influential type of actors in world politics. It seems reasonable, therefore, to devote considerable research effort to better understanding the influences operating on these dominant actors. On the practical side, our resources for research are relatively modest. At the present time, data on the external behaviors of many intergovernmental and nongovernmental actors are far less accessible than data for national governments. As with any research strategy, it is necessary to place clear limits on the subject matter to be investigated. For the reasons outlined above, confining ourselves to a study of the foreign policy behaviors of national governments appeared to be an appropriate design.

A fourth CREON orientation involves our commitment to attempt to explain different kinds of foreign policy behaviors. Given that the study of foreign policy, at least since World War II, has been dominated by American scholars (a regrettably restrictive condition), it is understandable that a concern with the Cold War and potential nuclear war would influence the type of foreign policies studied. Many, if not most, studies that have dealt with a particular type of foreign policy in any systematic way have concerned war and peace or such related properties as friendship and hostility. We would not deny for a moment the importance of attempting to explain such governmental behaviors. However, continued emphasis on such foreign policy behavior could be extremely misleading. It is simply not accurate to describe the majority of the foreign policy behaviors of most governments only in terms of conflict and cooperation. In adopting such an emphasis, much of the variation in external behavior is ignored. To cite just one example, many conflicts have substantive issues at their core. To generalize about the affective dimension without examining the basis of the conflict results in discarding information that could be important in understanding the dynamics of the conflict and the forces that influenced its occurrence and termination. The almost exclusive attention to problems of war and peace is also being challenged by scholars from other nations as they begin to do research on foreign policy. These scholars make clear that for people in many parts of the world other issues may be more important in foreign policy than war and peace. For some governments, problems such as economic development, social justice, and access to essential resources have the highest priority because of their centrality to basic values and survival. The map of major foreign policy activities and the theories designed to account for them are in danger of becoming badly out of line with what governments are actually doing in foreign affairs if we continue to focus only on conflict and cooperation. Thus, CREON has made an effort to measure and examine a broader spectrum of foreign policy.

There is a fifth CREON orientation that the reader may already have discerned from our attempts to distinguish between general references to foreign policy and the subject of CREON investigations—foreign policy behavior. This point is so fundamental to the way our research is organized that it will be developed in greater detail in chapter 2.

LAYING THE CORNERSTONE:
DEVELOPING THEORETICAL PERSPECTIVES

In the preceding sections of this chapter, we have raised a number of issues relevant to the comparative study of foreign policy and, in particular, to the CREON research effort. Not all these issues will be developed or discussed in subsequent chapters, although we do attempt to be consistent with the views that have been outlined. The task of this book is to establish a cornerstone for future analysis, namely, the theoretical perspectives. By theoretical perspective we mean a general research orientation that posits the importance of some specified and interrelated set of variables for explaining foreign policy behavior and that provides an explanatory logic relating the set of variables to foreign policy behavior. Each of seven theoretical perspectives will be developed in one of the ensuing chapters, but the following descriptions offer an initial characterization.

1. **Personal Characteristics of Political Leaders.** This perspective is concerned with how individual differences among decision makers can affect foreign policy behavior. Under certain conditions, political leaders' beliefs, motives, decision styles, and interpersonal styles can influence their governments' foreign policy behavior.

2. **Decision Structures and Processes.** This perspective focuses on the ways in which the organizational machinery used by a government in addressing a particular issue impacts on foreign policy behavior. Many kinds of decision structures ranging from single individuals to large bureaucracies can be engaged in reaching and implementing foreign policy decisions. These different types of decision structures invoke different kinds of processes for coping with uncertainty, handling conflict among participants, and making and executing choices. These processes, which can change from problem to problem as well as from government to government, can affect foreign policy behavior.

3. **Political Features of Regimes.** This perspective deals with how differences in governmental structure, both those resulting from changes in regimes within a nation and those observed in the cross-national comparison of governments, can influence foreign policy behavior. Whereas the decision structures and processes perspective described in (2) concerns changes that vary from one type of decision to another, the political regimes perspective identifies features that vary from one government to another. A regime's freedom of action, determined by such variables as its internal coherence and degree of accountability to constituencies, is one important regime factor that can affect foreign policy behavior.

4. **National Attributes of Societies.** This perspective recognizes the impact on foreign policy of differences between societies. Certain relatively stable attributes of societies—such as cultural homogeneity, territorial size, and level of economic development—become important in determining how salient international matters are to the government, what external issues a government attends to, and the kinds and amounts of resources that are committed to foreign affairs.

5. **Properties of the International System.** This perspective incorporates those factors arising from the relatively stable patterns of international interaction that have a global context and that affect foreign policy. International system variables that may influence foreign policy behavior include the distribution of goods, values, and resources in the system and the complexity of the system as measured by its size, the range and scope of issues dealt with, its level of organization, and its degree of polarity.

6. **Prior Foreign Behavior.** This perspective relates the present foreign policy behavior of a government to the prior behavior that other actors addressed to it and the nature of its own prior behavior toward other actors. In other words, this perspective emphasizes the importance of the historical experience of particular interacting nations. A government can be expected to respond differently to action addressed to it by a traditional adversary than to action by a nation whose prior behavior has been marked by support. A government's foreign policy behavior is shaped by its prior interactions with other external entities.

7. **Transitory Qualities of the Situation.** This perspective directs attention to those transitory elements inside or outside of a society that become the stimuli for foreign policy decisions. Transitory qualities of the situation become occasions for decision when decision makers perceive them as affecting their government's goals and, thus, as creating problems for their government. How decision makers define or characterize the problem can affect their government's foreign policy behavior.

Although these seven theoretical perspectives incorporate many of the most popular explanatory variables used to account for foreign policy behavior, no claim is made that the set is comprehensive. Those who seek to explain foreign policy in terms of capitalist economies, public opinion, interest groups, or any number of other types of variables may find their preferred explanation treated only tangentially or perhaps not at all. There are two reasons for these omissions. First, a practical constraint stemming from the skills and predispositions of the authors must be acknowledged. These seven perspectives represent the theoretical interests of the CREON investigators. Second, the number of possible perspectives was limited by our own conviction that any proposed perspective should be based on an underlying explanatory logic that could be explicated in such a way as to generate hypotheses capable of empirical testing.

We should hasten to add that no empirical investigations will be presented in this book. Furthermore, multicausal explanations involving the integration of these perspectives will be discussed only in the concluding chapter. Although both of these tasks must be done and are underway within the CREON Project, we hope others also will pick up the challenge and pursue these tasks independently.[4] As a necessary precursor to such efforts, this book examines each perspective individually in a separate chapter. The objective is to determine how plausibly each perspective by itself can account for foreign policy behaviors. One way to view this objective is by analogy to the physical stress tests performed on proto-types of new airplanes to assess their structural features. Just as the wing of a plane may be stressed in a test situation until it breaks, so by pushing each perspective to its limit as an explanation of foreign policy behavior can its strengths and weaknesses be put in sharp relief. By examining the individual perspectives independently, the reader is likely to become more sensitive to the critical role that the assumptions play in linking the key variables to foreign policy behavior. One can more easily judge whether or not these assumptions seem reasonable. In those instances where the assumptions seem inconsistent with one's understanding of foreign policy, they can be altered or relaxed by the introduction of qualifying conditions from the other theoretical perspectives. In the concluding chapter we present an initial effort at integrating the perspectives, revealing that they are not always related directly to foreign policy behavior and that in some cases they are related mainly to one another. Thus, some perspectives assume the role of antecedent or mediating conditions for other perspectives.

As noted, these integrative efforts will be deferred to the final chapter. We believe, however, there is another issue of major proportions that must be addressed before we can begin the separate examination of the seven theoretical perspectives. Earlier we indicated that one of the distinctive CREON orientations concerned the conceptualization of foreign policy behavior, that is, the phenomena we propose to explain by means of the theoretical perspectives. It is to this too often neglected aspect of foreign policy analysis that we now turn.

NOTES

1. For a philosophical challenge concerning the feasibility of scientific compara-tive politics, see MacIntyre (1973).

2. See Sullivan (1963) for illustrations from basic textbooks of how power has been asserted to be a single explanatory concept while implicitly within the same books it has been used in multiple different ways.

3. CREON also is the name of an events data set that we developed to facilitate our research in foreign policy behavior (see C. F. Hermann et al., 1973). Some individuals (e.g., Zinnes, 1976) have concluded that CREON is only a data-gathering and storage activity. Our own perceptions, however, are strongly at variance with this view, as we hope to make clearer in this and other publications.

4. One such independent effort that appears to follow closely the CREON conceptualization is reported in Andriole et al. (1975). Less directly parallel to CREON, but still advancing in the general directions outlined here, is the research program of Brecher and his associates (see Brecher et al., 1969).

2

FOREIGN POLICY BEHAVIOR: THAT WHICH IS TO BE EXPLAINED

Charles F. Hermann

THE NEGLECTED CONCEPT OF FOREIGN POLICY

One of the most remarkable features of the post-World War II study of foreign policy is the scant attention given to the general concept of foreign policy and the dimensions and categories into which it can be profitably arrayed. Most textbooks on the subject, if they define the concept at all, appear satisfied to provide a simple paragraph or two devoted to a general definition. For example, Irish and Frank (1975) devote two pages; Coplin et al. (1974) offer about a page; but others (e.g., Westerfield, 1963; Spanier and Uslaner, 1974), including the most widely used comparative foreign policy text (Macridis, 1976), offer no explicit definition. Such abbreviated consideration fails to establish a sufficient basis for serious inquiry, yet advanced studies seldom provide much more development of the concept. The authors of the present volume contend that this neglect has been one of the most serious obstacles to providing more adequate and comprehensive explanations of foreign policy. Indeed, the need for defining foreign policy seems as inescapable as the neglect of it seems startling. In order to attempt to understand, explain, or forecast something, one must first be clear about what that something is. Given the apparent necessity for the development of the foreign policy concept, why has the task been so meagerly attended to for so long?

One answer may be that most people dealing with the subject have felt confident that they knew what foreign policy was and that others presumably shared their conceptualizations, removing the need for explication. After all, everyone talked in terms of diplomacy, trade, war, and the other forms of foreign policy. Thus, the essay on foreign policy in the *International Encyclopedia of the Social Sciences* (Cohen, 1968) offers no definition. In a collaborative essay seven years later, the same author acknowledges both the apparent consensus about a definition and its lack of development:

> While a reasonable consensus obtains among analysts regarding the general nature of foreign policy—it is a set of goals, directives, or intentions, formulated by persons in official or authoritative positions, directed at some actor or condition in the environment beyond the sovereign nation state, for the purpose of affecting the target in the manner desired by the policy makers—to have said that is not to have said *very much*. [Cohen and Harris, 1975: 383]

Another reason for the limited attention given to the concept is that most specialists in foreign policy devote their attention to one subpart or category of the general phenomena. Thus, research and writing tend to address particular aspects of foreign policy such as deterrence, intelligence, or diplomatic activities or to examine a particular policy in the context of some setting such as a military alliance, the United Nations, or a common market. Given this narrow focus, the analyst does not need to ask what are the characteristics of the general phenomena of which his or her study is a particular instance. Even analysts who survey the foreign policy of one country, a dyad, or geographical region use categories of policy or adopt procedures that minimize the need to develop the basic concept. Some study a particular instance or narrow series of foreign activities (e.g., SALT I, the Marshall Plan), others examine the role of specific institutions (e.g., the press, Congress, the CIA), whereas still others describe the general process among the policy-making elements. Those who have attempted to consider the entire scope of a country's foreign policy have often followed a historical chronology and have used as the boundaries for describing foreign activities the labels offered by policy makers themselves (e.g., the Brezhnev Doctrine, containment, Alliance for Progress). Such labels may help tag a certain policy or program, but they hardly establish categories useful for systematic comparison and theory construction. In short, all these approaches emphasize parts rather than the whole and make it possible to leave largely undefined the basic character of foreign policy.

Until recently, part of the difficulty could be attributed to the lack of interest on the part of any substantial number of foreign policy specialists in applying the methods of science to their chosen field of inquiry. As has been suggested, the important, but distinctive, tasks of description and prescription could proceed without the careful delineation of the field of inquiry. Those who early developed a scientific consciousness and sought the opportunity to conduct empirical investigations in the domain of foreign policy found a lack of data susceptible to treatment by the scientific method. The temptation arose among those scholars to define foreign policy in terms of the limited data available. In addition to the presence of little usable data, limited concern with scientific analysis, and primary attention to only one category or process of foreign activity, the concept of foreign policy is also difficult to cope with due to the troublesome concept of goals. As will be examined in more detail below, definitions of foreign policy have generally introduced the concept of the actor's purposiveness, goals, or motives.

It would be incorrect to say this neglect continues unnoticed and unattended to even today. Although examples of the use of foreign policy as an undefined and undifferentiated term are still widespread, a growing interest in the concept and its dimensions can be traced. Blake (1969) has underscored the general need, as have Cohen and Harris (1975) in their recent review of the field. Meehan (1971) has engaged in an extensive analysis of the concept that has been largely absent in the field since Snyder and his associates (1962) discussed state action in 1954. Froman (1968) has produced criteria for evaluating classifications of domestic and foreign policy. Spiro (1966) and C. Hermann (1972a) have conceptualized some dimensions for arraying types of foreign policy, and the same task has been approached by several individuals (e.g., Kegley 1973; Salmore and Munton, 1974; Kegley et al., 1974; McClelland and Hoggard, 1969) using statistical data reduction procedures. Even recent textbooks have demonstrated a greater sensitivity to the task of conceptualizing and categorizing foreign policy (e.g., Coplin, 1974; Lentner, 1974; Holsti, 1972; and Lovell, 1970).

Furthermore, increasing numbers of foreign policy scholars have developed what Rosenau (1968) calls "scientific consciousness," which necessitates a more careful delineation of concepts. With the growing interest in applying the scientific method to the study of foreign policy has come research that involves data collection and statistical analysis of more or less discrete hypotheses about foreign policy. Thus, efforts to identify available data on foreign policy (such as voting records, trade data, and arms expenditures) and to collect new kinds of data (such as policy makers' perceptions of policy and event data) have become increasingly common.

These early efforts at collecting data on foreign policy have been rightly criticized (e.g., Waltz, 1975; Zinnes, 1975) as too frequently undertaken with insufficient specification of the theoretical underpinnings that should indicate what data are required. Yet to the extent that these data-collection efforts have focused attention on how we might identify actions and policies that are to be examined, they have advanced the awareness of the concept of foreign policy.

THE PROBLEM OF GOALS IN THE CONCEPT OF POLICY

Whatever the contribution of empirical research to creating a heightened sensitivity to the concept and dimensions of foreign policy, most analysts do not appear to have dealt with the conceptual issue of purposiveness in policy. Although establishing when any policy is "foreign" requires some conceptual development, the harder issue is probably the more general concept of policy. Consider a brief sample of textbook definitions of policy.

> The foreign policy of the United States refers to the courses of action which official U.S. policy makers determine to take, beyond the territorial jurisdiction of the United States, in order to secure and advance the national interests of the American people, and to enhance the power and prestige of the United States in world affairs. [Irish and Frank, 1975: 1]

> Reduced to its most fundamental ingredients, foreign policy consists of two elements: national objectives to be achieved and the means for achieving them. [Crabb, 1972: 1]

> Policy is a form of action which involves (1) selection of objectives, (2) mobilization of means for achieving those objectives, and (3) implementation, or the actual expenditure of efforts and resources in pursuit of the selected objectives. . . . Foreign policy refers to that portion of a country's life which copes with its environment. . . . Insofar as policies are directed to other countries or have an impact on other countries, they fall within the meaning of foreign. [Lentner, 1974: 3-5]

As the earlier quotation from Cohen and Harris (1975) suggests, the general definitions in the more specialized literature parallel those found in textbooks.[1] One of the recurrent features in these conceptualizations is the idea of purpose, goals, or intent. Rosenau, rightly in our view, has tagged this issue of goals—either elevated to national interests or reduced to policy objectives—as one of the most troublesome in foreign policy. "Few aspects of the field" he observes, "are more resistant to clarifying analysis than the objectives that states pursue in their international relationships" (Rosenau, 1961: 141).

In foreign policy, as in many other areas of analysis of human behavior, interpretation has postulated that nonrandom behavior is purposeful or goal-oriented. Simon (1969) in his pathbreaking essays on the science of the artificial helps us to understand some of the appeal of attributing goals to adaptive (artificial) systems such as governments.

> Thus the first advantage of dividing outer from inner environment in studying an adaptive or artificial system is that we can often predict behavior from knowledge of the system's goals and its outer environment. [Simon, 1969: 8]

In other words, Simon contends that if we know a government's goals and something about the world in which it must operate, we can forecast its actions reasonably well without extensive knowledge about that government, its leaders, or the society they direct.

The attractiveness of postulating goals or purpose is so strong that another thoughtful analyst sees it as the basis for distinguishing two quite different conceptions of humankind.

> The first conception explains man's behaviour as response to his environment; the second explains his behaviour as pursuit of a goal. The first searches for causal processes and determinants of behaviour, and often uses a mechanistic explanation. It has been the implicit basis of much of the best empirical work in sociology, from Durkheim's analysis of the causes of suicide to the present.
>
> The second conception sees man's action as goal-directed, and focuses attention less on present environmental conditions than on future desired states. Man is conceived less as a product of his environment than as the source of preferences which lead to action. This conception has been the basis of much common-sense explanation of behaviour, of some theoretical work in sociology, represented by Weber and Parsons, and of one major theoretical structure: economic theory, based upon a conception of rational economic man. [Coleman, 1973: 1]

To contemporary students of foreign policy, Coleman's reference to "rational economic man" may well bring to mind the parallel of the rational actor paradigm and its variants, which Allison (1971) convincingly argues has dominated Western foreign policy analyses. Central to this conceptualization of foreign policy is the notion that a government acts in foreign policy as a unified rational agent with a coherent set of goals and objectives (see Allison, 1971: 28-36). In his elaboration of this orientation under the designation "analytical paradigm," Steinbruner (1974) makes a compelling case for its pervasiveness in foreign policy study and speaks of its requirement for the integration of value tradeoffs with respect to the actor's set of preferences. In sum, it is not difficult to demonstrate that there is considerable attraction for conceptualizing foreign policy, as well as other types of collective actions, as goal-seeking behavior.[2]

The characterization of policy as goal-seeking behavior, however, immediately poses problems. In what sense is it meaningful to suggest that a complex collective entity such as a government has goals? Certainly it does not seem wise to anthropomorphize a collectivity and treat it as if it were a single human being with a single set of goals and preferences. The investigators of formal organizations have wrestled with this issue and have offered several possible ways in which such collectivities might be regarded as engaging in goal-oriented behavior. In one form, the organization's goals are created by a consensus of the individual members who, upon accepting the goals, seek to behave in ways that promote the shared ends. Another arrangement entails goal-setting by a single individual or small group (e.g., a firm's board of directors), who then arrange to provide all other members of the organization with sidepayments (e.g., salaries, wages, promotions, dividends) if they agree to conduct their organization-related behavior as if they personally sought the stated goals. (In the process of working for an organization, some individuals may internalize these goals as their own and pursue them even if rewards commensurate with their efforts are not forthcoming.) Still another possibility is that the organization actually has no integrated and operationalized set of goals. Thus, the different members and sections of the organization, in pursuit of their own objectives, can interpret goals in conflicting ways with the result that the organization (or its several parts) can engage simultaneously in behaviors supporting conflicting goals. Alternatively, the organization can pursue its goals sequentially and thus not face the implication that what is done at a later time may alter or even cancel the effects of the behavior done previously.

This latter perspective has been emphasized in recent works that have studied foreign policy as a bureaucratic process (e.g., Allison, 1971; Halperin 1974). When foreign policy is viewed as the "resultant" or compromise of the tugging and pulling among various actors and units of government, the likelihood that the final behavior is goal-seeking becomes doubtful. Compromise behavior need not represent the goals of the entire government as stipulated either by the head of state or by other authoritative decision makers. In fact, it might not represent the behavior that would maximize the goals of any subunit of the government; rather, it probably represents some mix of preferences upon which the winning coalition could agree. Of course, it is not necessary to view foreign policy as formulated in this manner, and few would argue that a bureaucratic process operates in any government all the time. It does, however, give one pause in defining foreign policy as the goal-seeking behavior of a government.

Even setting aside for the moment both the challenge raised by a bureaucratic politics interpretation and the assumption that the foreign actions of a government can be viewed as part of a plan of action in pursuit of some goals, the question remains: How does the analyst discern the true nature of a government's goals?

Someone who is not an authoritative policy maker of a government faces several alternatives in attempting to determine that government's foreign policy goals. All of the alternatives are strewn with obstacles. One approach is to take at face value the professed goals and purposes offered by government spokesmen. Although there may be considerable merit in holding government officials accountable for their own expressed statements of the government's goals, it is painfully clear that, in the political environment in which they must operate, policy makers cannot be totally candid about their motives and their goals.

An alternative strategy would be to infer a government's goals from its observed behavior. Unfortunately, it is often possible to attribute the same behavior to several different goals. Moreover, if every behavior is assumed to maximize some goal or set of goals, it leaves no room for the possibility of miscalculation on the part of government officials or for the kind of compromise, logrolling approach to consensus-building envisioned in bureaucratic politics. A variant of the same strategy is to infer goals from the demands imposed on the government by its environment. For example: Japan's standard of living and state of industrialization require far more coal and petroleum than can be produced domestically; therefore the analyst infers that one of Japan's foreign policy goals must be to maintain a secure, affordable, and abundant supply of externally produced energy. Unfortunately, the detectable environmental requirements of foreign policy are seldom that clear and often are contradictory. Moreover, the analyst might perceive these requirements differently from the acting government's officials.

Still another alternative permits the analyst to substitute what he or she judges should be the goals of the government given not only its environment but also its power base relative to other international actors, some set of basic values, and so on. Without a doubt, the evaluation of governmental foreign policy performance against these prescriptive goals can serve a useful purpose. It would be a mistake, however, to assume any necessary correspondence between the analyst's declaration of what he or she believes a government's goals could be or ought to be and what that government's goals actually are.

Let us summarize. Conceiving of policy as goal-seeking behavior is attractive for many reasons. With knowledge of an actor's goals, one can hope to achieve a reasonably parsimonious explanation of behavior. Moreover, a statement of goals provides a means of evaluating an actor's performance. (Was the behavior pursued an effective means for realizing the stipulated goals?) In addition, the specification of a set of goals, preferences, utility functions, or other essentially equivalent terms is necessary to use a variety of analytical tools such as statistical decision theory, game theory, and the various extensions described by Coleman (1973). For reasons such as these it is not surprising that researchers concerned with foreign policy have sought to include the concept of goals as an integral part of the construct of policy. But in so doing they have inherited a number of problems associated with the concept of goals in collective human entities. In addition, they face special problems with the concept of goals that are peculiar to their field of inquiry. As bureaucratic organizations, governments frequently may not have—or may behave as if they did not have—an integrated set of goals. What is more, political organizations, particularly those dealing with multifaceted foreign environments, seldom can be very explicit in stating their goals. Without the assistance of a government in specifying its foreign policy goals, it is extremely difficult for an analyst to detect them reliably. Because we have seldom defined foreign policy, or have done so in only a cursory fashion, these problems with the concept of goals as part of policy have rarely been addressed, and their research implications have been ignored.

THE CREON SHIFT FROM POLICY TO BEHAVIOR

> The behavior of the diplomat or the strategist . . . has neither a goal as determined as that of the soccer player's or even an objective, in certain conditions rationally definable by a maximum, like those of economic subjects. . . . At the outset, let us confine ourselves to stating that diplomatic-strategic behavior does not have an obvious objective, but that the risk of war obliges it to calculate forces or means. [Aron, 1966: 16]

Following Raymond Aron's observation, the CREON Project investigators, whose work this book reports, have opted to conceptualize the external actions of national governments in terms of behaviors rather than goal-seeking policies. This shift has two major consequences. First, we do not require knowledge of the government's goal structure in order to establish a unit of action. Second, we use a limited concept that is more observable. In other words, whereas the concept of policy normally entails not only goals but also a plan or program (i.e., a framework constructed prior to any activity whose realization through a series of actions is expected to promote the selected goals), the CREON investigators confine the focus to discrete actions. One might observe that this shift in focus only sidesteps the problems associated with policy. Perhaps so, but it is a liberating maneuver with some useful implications. Let us consider some of them.

To begin with, notice that it is not necessary to deny that governments may act in accordance with explicated goals. Rather what has been done is to remove the requirement of the presence of goals—and the planning element—as part of the unit of observation and analysis. In fact, the CREON investigators are predisposed to believe that most foreign actions of governments are taken in pursuit of one or more goals. Hence, we normally refer to "foreign policy behaviors" rather than simply to "foreign behaviors," denoting that the behaviors probably are elements of a policy even if the goals and plans of that policy are unknown to the researcher.

A second point to be noted is the researcher's freedom to assemble behaviors in any preferred way. That is, behaviors can be aggregated according to any dimension or property of the behaviors that can be defined. Of course this includes the various approaches to estimating goals previously noted. Indeed, the CREON Project actively classifies behaviors according to several of these strategies, and the remaining behaviors are susceptible to analysis. Thus, we code behaviors according to the professed goals of the governmental actors whenever spokesmen link governmental behavior to some preferred state or condition. Moreover, we attempt *to infer goals from the behaviors themselves* by noting who are the recipients of the behavior, who may benefit, and who may be jeopardized. Additionally, basic values (e.g., respect, security, well-being, wealth) are inferred and coded, which allows the investigator *to analyze a government's behaviors in terms of his or her own goals.* For example, one might ask what proportion of a government's foreign policy behaviors concern the acquisition and dissemination of knowledge. Although we have no special coding procedure to discern a government's *goals through the demands of its environment*, CREON's extensive issue-area classification scheme should lend itself to this approach. Our primary concern here is not to familiarize the reader with the data-collection procedures of one particular project, but rather to illustrate that by separating the unit of observation (behaviors) from the concept of policy it becomes possible either to pursue any of a variety of different strategies for attempting to discover foreign policy goals or to set these strategies aside completely and still remain aware of the behaviors.

A third implication of the focus on behavior is that it makes possible a discrete, definable unit of observation. We believe that a well-defined, disaggregated behavioral unit offers valuable opportunity for advancing our understanding of foreign affairs. The importance of developing a viable basic unit of observation for the comparative study of foreign policy may be underscored by considering another area of scientific inquiry in politics—voting studies. A strong case can be made that voting studies did not advance significantly until researchers adopted the individual voting decision as the basic unit of analysis. The beginning of adequate explanations and reasonably accurate predictions of election outcomes became possible only after the individual voting choice became the focus of analysis. We believe foreign policy behavior is analogous to individual voting behavior with respect to the need for a discrete unit of observation. Concentrating on foreign policy behavior does not prevent one from addressing questions of a more general nature about foreign policy any more than analyzing the individual vote prevents one from asking questions of a more general nature, such as who won the election. The politician, the journalist, the citizen, and the election analyst all share an interest in who wins the election, but the specialist finds it necessary first to study how individuals decide whether or not and how to cast their votes—the basic units of subsequent analysis. We believe a similar situation exists in foreign affairs.

What is a conceptual definition of behavior in the context of governmental foreign policy? It is the discrete purposeful action that results from the political level decision of an individual or group of individuals. Political level decision makers are those whose authority is required to commit or withhold those resources of the nation that are available to those who govern. Thus, a behavior is viewed as the observable artifact of a political level decision. It is not the decision, but a product of the decision. Of course a decision not to act or some failure to decide (i.e., indecision) leads to no new action and regrettably results in no trace for us to record. This limitation is an unfortunate gap, one that is not immediately remedied in cross-national foreign policy analysis.[3] Inaction by one actor, however, often becomes the occasion for inquiry, restatement, probe, or other behavior by one or more other actors and, of course, this then becomes observable and a clue to the inaction of another.

We know that many behaviors of contemporary governments are neither conducted nor announced publicly at the time of their occurrence. In fact, they may be known to only a very few persons in the acting government. It is important to recognize that this is a problem of data sources and reporting rather than of the unobservable nature of human behaviors. Even though such hidden behaviors are not accessible to a contemporary investigator, with the right sources or informants evidence of the behavior could be established if it occurred. This interpretation may not prove very satisfactory in overcoming the very large practical problem of the individual who wishes to study the intelligence activities of various governments. That person's problem is similar to the one of the astronomer who, lacking the proper telescope, may be unable to detect or to determine the composition of certain stars. But in the long run, if we—like the astronomer who believes that all stars emit light or detectable waves—believe that events can be observed, then we are motivated to discover the equivalent of a better telescope. Even with existing public sources, investigators may be able to do far better for some kinds of foreign policy analysis than many would imagine.

To summarize, each separate behavior is the result of some political level decision within the national government. Conceptually, each new political level decision can (but need not) produce new action. Thus, we have a basis for inferring the boundaries of behaviors. In effect, a foreign policy behavior is discrete in that it has a location in time and space; it has a beginning and an end. Thus, foreign policy behavior offers the researcher a basic unit of observation. As defined, behaviors are comparable and they can be operationalized.

One other consequence of shifting from policy to behavior in the examination of foreign affairs is that it becomes possible to utilize a certain type of data that has come into wide use in international relations. We refer to events data.[4] Normally constructed from public sources such as newspapers and chronologies, an event usually consists of an actor, an action, and a recipient. The action component of an event can be a foreign policy behavior. In the CREON Project's events data set, an event is defined as the discrete, purposeful action (the behavior) of an individual or set of individuals (the actor) that is addressed to one or more direct target(s) (the immediate recipient(s) of the action) and one or more indirect object(s) (the subject(s) of the influence attempt). In the CREON Project, actions are assumed to be taken by individual actors, singly or in groups, who are national governmental officials or their representatives acting in an official or governmental capacity. The direct target(s) and indirect object(s), which may be one and the same, can be individuals, groups or collectives of individuals, or entire nations or definable regions. They need not be governments. However, in order to be regarded as a "foreign" event, some direct target(s) or some indirect object(s) must be beyond the political boundaries of the acting nation and be other than citizens of that nation. The purposeful action or behavior is ultimately an attempt to influence some entity (or entities), which is labeled the indirect object. When Khrushchev told Ulbricht and the East German government in public that the Soviet Union would sign a separate peace treaty with Germany if the Western powers did not agree within six months to modify the status of Berlin, the direct target of the Soviet leader's behavior was the East German government. However, the entities that Khrushchev sought to influence by this behavior were the governments of the other occupying powers in Berlin—France, Britain, and the United States—which would become the indirect objects of influence in the CREON event definition.

Although the concept of foreign policy behavior lends itself to exploration through events data such as those defined above as part of the CREON Project, it is important to recognize that the shift from policy to behavior as the basic unit does not require use of a particular kind of data or a given approach. Case studies, historical chronologies, aggregate data (trade, UN votes, and so on), content analyses of public statements, and many other means of analysis can be keyed to this way of conceptualizing the activity of a government's foreign affairs. The basic requirement is not a type of data or a technique of analysis, but rather the limiting of the basic unit to discrete observable actions. The use of sets of goals and plans (which are an integral part of the concept of policy) can then be considered as one of the many possible ways of classifying these behaviors.

ALTERNATIVES FOR CLASSIFYING BEHAVIOR

If one accepts foreign policy behavior as the basic unit of observation, what are the alternative ways in which the observed behaviors can be grouped or scaled? This question becomes one of utmost importance in the study of foreign policy because the answer to it will determine what one seeks to understand and whether or not meaningful insights about foreign affairs can be discovered. Once we do not automatically accept the labels suggested by policy makers for classifying their activities—such as the Truman Doctrine, Alliance for Progress, Wars of National Liberation, or the *force de frappe*—we must search for meaningful alternatives. Someone who aggregates behaviors according to their degree of expressed hostility will construct a profile of behaviors very different from that of another who assembles them according to whether they involve goods, people, information, or some combination thereof. Both will differ from that configuration established by a person who uses substantive issue areas such as arms control, agricultural trade, technical assistance, terrorism, or the like.

This section can only introduce briefly the approaches and possible means of assembling behaviors.[5] In general, two broad approaches can be identified for constructing dimensions of foreign policy behavior. With the first approach, the analyst conceptualizes one or a set of characteristics or types of behavior that he or she regards as intrinsically important for examination. Once the individual has in mind the characteristics to be studied, then some systematic procedure must be established for classifying each observed behavior on the selected characteristics. This arrangement might be called *the a priori specification approach* because the researcher consciously stipulates in advance the dimensions of behavior to be investigated and attaches significance to each separate dimension. In the second approach the individual begins with a relatively large number of seemingly diverse properties of behavior whose individual significance for foreign affairs may be unclear and whose total number may be too great to subject readily to investigation. Of course, the origin of these numerous properties of behavior ultimately is the same as in the first approach, that is, someone must have formed the concept. Unlike the individual in the first approach, however, the second researcher does not intend to use the properties in the form in which they are originally conceived, and he or she will feel less constrained to keep the total number of delineated properties limited. In the second approach, after the diverse properties are established another step is taken to sharply differentiate it from the first approach. Some procedure is employed to consolidate the numerous properties into a smaller number of underlying dimensions. Occasionally the process for reducing the many properties to a few dimensions will be intuitive, but more frequently some statistical routine will be used—such as factor analysis or some clustering algorithm. We might label this second method *the data reduction approach.* Although both approaches are considered in more detail in our volume on foreign policy behaviors (see note 5), we will limit the remainder of this discussion to the introduction of some properties of behavior formed by using the a priori specification approach.

As noted, the a priori specification approach requires the investigator to establish the intrinsic merit of each dimension of foreign policy behavior that is conceptualized. To illustrate some of the ways in which behavior can be classified using this approach, we will introduce the properties of behavior that appear in one or more of the subsequent chapters of this book. Our purposes are to display a wide variety of possible candidates and to suggest that we frequently overlook the richness of possible classifications and thus deny a major potential for discovering vital qualities of foreign activity. At this point each classification should be examined for its own merits.

AUTONOMOUS ACTION

The first group of classifications is autonomous action properties. In other words the value of each variable, whether a point on a continuum or a discrete category, can be determined from knowledge about certain aspects of the actor or, more frequently, its behavior. Later we will consider other properties that require knowledge about the relationship between the actor and the recipient of the behavior; no such relational information, however, need be obtained in order to use any classification in this first set. The brief statement of each classification will present a description of the behavior property and a comment on its potential use.

Coalition Formation. Behavior concerns coalition formation if it is designed to establish collaboration between the actor and one or more other entities to enhance either the possibility of obtaining some value or increasing the amount of it. Notice that knowledge of the recipient and its relation to the actor are not required to establish the actor's desire to form a coalition. Efforts to form or maintain coalitions become important in understanding the relative resources of various actors, the importance they attach to certain values, and the likelihood of success in achieving various outcomes.

Commitment. Behavior scaled according to the amount and irreversibility with which resources are used or transferred to others is defined as commitment. As such this concept provides an indication of the intensity of the government's conviction as expressed in its action. Assuming that a government possesses only a finite amount of resources at any time, the greater the commitment manifested in an action, the more restricted is its freedom of action.

Decision Time. Behavior can be characterized by the time that elapses between recognition of a problem and the initiation of behavior intended to address the problem. Available decision time may be affected by external actors (e.g., an ultimatum), the evaluation of events, or the resources of the actor relative to the demands of the problem. Decision time may affect the quality of the behavior. (If too short, search and innovative treatment are less likely.) It may also indicate the significance the actor attaches to the problem.

Amount of Activity. Behaviors can be totaled or aggregated to indicate the extent of a government's participation in foreign affairs, that is, the total amount of behavior that a government directs toward external entities. Amount of activity can be established for all recipients of an actor's behaviors to indicate the extent of isolation or involvement with affairs beyond its boundaries. Alternatively, amount of activity can be assessed for a particular geographical region or other grouping or for a single entity to determine the extent of an actor's concentration of attention with particular entities. Comparison of reciprocal amount of activity scores for a dyad can suggest the relative equality or inequality of saliency that each partner is for the other. All these variations have value for theories of communication among international actors.

External Consequentiality. Behaviors contain a number of properties that make them more or less likely to be attended to by other members of the international system. This combined estimate of the degree of impact on other actors has been defined as external consequentiality. This concept allows an initial weighting of behaviors in a broad sense according to their likely importance as interpreted by others. Although only a first approximation, it allows a distinction to be drawn between the protocol welcoming of a visiting head of state and a major military invasion.

Goal Enunciation. Behavior that contains some indication of the preferred state of affairs that the actor seeks to promote or maintain is classified in various ways, including whether the goals are short-term and might be realized with a few actions and limited change or whether they are long-range and probably require many actions together with considerable change. Goals that are professed in behaviors may not reveal the government's purposes accurately, but they do provide one indication. Such a classification can be useful for establishing the policies of which the behaviors are a part as well as for exploring various schemes involving the concept of rationality.

Instrumentalities. Behaviors can be classified according to the means or instruments of statecraft that are employed by a government in undertaking action. These human skills and nonhuman resources can be classified into six broad categories of instrumentalities: (1) diplomatic/political, (2) military, (3) economic, (4) scientific/technical, (5) promotive, and (6) natural resources. The distribution of instrumentalities used by a government can reveal considerable information about the balance of institutions and resources on which it can draw and its sensitivity to requirements of its environment.

Position Change. Behavior that represents a different position with respect to the issue addressed than the actor manifested previously is classified as a change of position. The identification of a change in an actor's position on an issue becomes important in attempting to establish when influence has been successfully exercised. It also is important for determining both the possibility of movement in a bargaining or negotiation situation and the continuity or adaptability of the actor.

Specificity. Behavior varies in specificity according to the information provided the recipient about the actor's future expectations. To what extent does the actor convey information about what it intends to do or what it desires some external entity to do? The significance of specificity can be more readily envisioned if it is viewed as that portion of a recipient's uncertainty that is manipulated by the actor's behavior. The nature of the recipient's response, if any—as well as the nature of the actor's own influence attempt—can be revealed by the specificity or ambiguity of the behavior.

Substantive Problem Area. Behavior is classified according to the nature of the problem or issue that the acting government is addressing. Examples of general issue areas might be physical safety, economic wealth, respect/ status, well-being/welfare, and knowledge. Each can be subdivided into more specific types of problems. Problem areas can be considered separately or in comparison to one another. This classical way of conceptualizing the content or substance of behavior needs little justification. It provides a means of determining how a government is allocating its time and resources and indicates to what it is attending.

RELATIONAL ACTION

In each of the ten autonomous action properties presented above, the classification reveals something about the government actor (e.g., its professed goals), about the nature of its behavior (e.g., degree of commitment), or about both the actor and its behavior (e.g., external consequentiality). In other words, the property is defined by examining some dimensions of the behavior alone or with reference to the actor. We now turn to properties of behavior that can be defined only by considering the recipients of the action as well as the actor. These relational action properties often require not just different kinds of information but also more information about the context in which the behavior occurs. In cases where more than one recipient is involved in an event, the value of the behavior dimension may vary from one recipient to another. Consider this simple example: The Soviet Union supplies surface to air missiles (SAMs) to North Vietnam for use against U.S. aircraft operating over Vietnam. There are two recipients of the behavior: North Vietnam (the direct target) and the United States (indirect object). In coding this event for cooperation between actor and recipient, we would obtain quite different values for North Vietnam as compared to the United States. The temptation—indeed, at times the necessity—is to decompose the event into a series of pairs or dyads. (In the example, one pair would be the USSR-North Vietnam and the other would be USSR-USA.) Caution must be exercised in restructuring the event in this manner, however, because there is no justification for assuming there are two actions representing separate political level decisions by the actor. Not all relational characteristics require this kind of discrimination among recipients, but the illustration dramatizes the change in orientation that occurs when behavior is classified according to some relational action property. Below are brief descriptions of the relational characteristics of foreign policy behaviors that will be used in subsequent chapters.

Acceptance/Rejection Ratios. Behavior organized into an acceptance or rejection ratio indicates the nature and amount of feedback that a government receives to various proposals and requests it has made over an interval of time to various external entities. The acceptance ratio focuses on the positive feedback from the environment in the form of agreement or acceptance of proposals advocated by the actor; the rejection ratio focuses on negative feedback from the environment. Such ratios can contribute to understanding the influence a government has with other actors and its need to adjust its behavior depending upon its relative success or failure.

Affect. Behavior scaled according to affect reveals the degree of manifest feeling of the government in terms of hostility (negative affect) or friendliness (positive affect) toward the recipients of its action. Affect bears some similarity to conflict and cooperation, but these concern the actual intent to harm or benefit the recipients, whereas affect indicates the actor's feeling of pleasure or displeasure with the recipient. Sometimes a government may be constrained from assisting or hindering an external entity; therefore, affect provides a more sensitive indication of a government's regard toward recipients of its behavior.

Multilateral/Bilateral Setting. Behavior that involves three or more international entities is multilateral, whereas bilateral behavior involves only two. A multilateral setting introduces the possibility of multiple collaborators with the actor initiating the behavior and/or multiple direct recipients of the actor's behavior in contrast to the "one on one" relation posed by the bilateral setting.

Conflict. Behavior that to some degree harms or hinders something of value to the recipient of the action, or that threatens to do so, is defined as conflict. A major distinction can be made between verbal conflict and that involving physical deeds. Although conflict at this general level can include a wide range of behaviors, awareness of its presence is critical to establishing what entities are deprived by the actor's behavior and, therefore, may have considerable incentive to engage in punitive or corrective responses. Thus, conflict becomes an important element for understanding some of the dynamics of international relations and foreign policy.

Cooperation. Behavior that to some degree benefits or assists something of value to the recipient of the action, or that promises to do so, is defined as cooperation. A major distinction can be made between verbal cooperation and that involving physical deeds. One behavior may have both cooperative and conflictful properties—simultaneously harming some things and benefiting others. As with conflict, knowledge of the presence of cooperation can be important for establishing international dynamics, particularly responsiveness. Repeated recipients of either conflict or cooperation indicate the nature of the actor's enemies and friends, respectively.

Amount of Activity (with specified subset of recipients). Note this is the same classification as listed in the actor-based characteristics except that the frequency of action is determined only for certain designated types of recipients.

Entity Identification. Behaviors classified according to entity identification concern the nature of the human collectivities (e.g., internal groups, other governments, alliances) that are involved in the problem confronting the acting nation. Specifically, entity identification characterizes the source of the problem, the location of the problem, and the beneficiary if the problem is solved. Such a classification allows one to explore not only with what other entities the government deals but also the nature of the relationship.

Face-to-Face. Behavior that involves direct encounters between actor and recipient representatives is classified as face-to-face. The substitution or augmentation of indirect means of communication with this kind of exchange can be significant for various reasons. It affords more opportunity for individual personal characteristics to affect the message content; it permits much more rapid feedback (both verbal and nonverbal signals); and, if private, it may allow communication to be directed at a very particular recipient without other communication to other audiences.

Independent/Interdependent. Behaviors are independent when the government initiates unelicited action and acts alone; behaviors are interdependent when the government responds to the initiatives of others and acts in concert with others. The two dimensions of this behavioral concept (alone versus collaboration and initiative versus response) can be combined or analyzed separately. Taken together they provide an indicator of the government's coordination of its behavior with others.

Inertia. Behavior is stipulated as inertial when its essential characteristics repeat prior behavior manifested by the present actor to the same or comparable recipients. In other words, the present behavior repeats previously initiated activity with respect to the target or object. As with reciprocity, the recurrence of this type of behavior provides insights into the sources and dynamics of foreign policy. It may indicate the durability of foreign policy. It may indicate the durability or inflexibility (depending on the stability of the relative environments) of the actor's coping procedures.

Reciprocity. Behavior involves reciprocity when its essential characteristics are shaped by the prior behavior the actor has received from the recipients of the present action. This stimulus-response quality of behavior is important for understanding the dynamics of a government's foreign policy and the factors that determine its behavior. Problems such as escalation and responsiveness can be examined through this characterization of behavior.

Scope of Action. Behavior that is aggregated according to the dispersion among recipients (nations or other international actors) is defined as scope of action. It includes how many recipients are addressed and the distribution of recipients according to some criteria such as geographical region or type of recipient (e.g., national government, international organization). Scope of action involves aggregation of behavior by the number of recipients, whereas degree of activity involves aggregation by the number of behaviors. Scope of action offers an indication of the range and diversity of the acting government's interest in and attention to other entities.

Before concluding the initial survey of some alternative classifications of foreign policy behaviors, reference should be made to several procedures for combining and assembling separately classified properties. One simple way of assembling properties is to aggregate repeated occurrences of the same property across time to form a distribution, proportion, measure of variability, or central tendency. Some of the twenty-one behavioral properties described above are by definition meaningful only in this aggregated form—for example, degree of activity, acceptance/rejection ratios, and scope of action. Most classifications, however, need not be considered only in the aggregated form, and in those cases it is possible to analyze an individual occurrence of behavior with respect to a given property. Thus one can, for example, consider the degree of commitments or the identified entities found in a particular instance of foreign policy behavior. All those properties that can be examined for individual behaviors also can be aggregated for a period of time to form patterns of behavior. The distinction between discrete behavior properties and aggregated behavior properties will be used as a major distinction in models presented in the final chapter. Aggregating variables through time also can take the form of rates of change in a given property. For example, one might explore the annual rates of change in the average expressions of commitment by each member government in the European Economic Community toward all the other members.

Another procedure is to combine several properties to form new ones. Examples of these "second-order" behavior properties might be continuity, innovation, responsiveness, consistency, heterogeneity, complexity, or flexibility. Of course, the exact construction will depend on the meaning that is assigned to such terms. As an illustration, consider the often discussed concept of continuity in foreign policy. (Is there continuity in a country's foreign policy across different regimes? Do parliamentary systems display more continuity in foreign policy than presidential ones?) One might define foreign policy continuity as a government's attention through time to the same problems with the same or equivalent strategies and means. To specify this concept in terms of the behavior properties described above, we might look at the extent to which, in a given *substantive problem area*, the *same goals were enumerated* with reference to the *same entities (entity identification)* using approximately the *same mix of instrumentalities.*

Still another alternative for aggregating discrete behavior properties involves their combination to form indicators. The distinction between forming new second-order concepts in the manner just described and combining properties to form indicators is subtle but significant. In the former, the researcher strives to fully represent the new concept by the combination of separate components. In the latter, the investigator recognizes that the concept is not captured by the combination of properties but that they can be used to indicate the presence of a phenomenon because of their assumed high incidence of co-occurrence with it. For example, we might construct a set of indicators to identify events that had a high probability of precipitating a crisis for the recipients of those events. (Possible relevant properties for such an indicator might be negative affect, high external consequentiality, and short decision time.) In the same fashion one could combine properties to form indicators of a government's propensity to take risks or to initiate negotiations. All these procedures—statistical aggregation over time, second-order concepts, and indicators—provide means of using the behavior measures in collective as well as individual ways.

USING THEORETICAL PERSPECTIVES
TO ACCOUNT FOR FOREIGN POLICY BEHAVIORS

This chapter suggests that, as a result of the neglect of the composite nature of the phenomena labeled foreign policy, the definitional implications of the concept of foreign policy have seldom been considered. We also have argued that the means for classifying foreign policy have been inadequate both from a theoretical and from an empirical point of view. Because of the difficulty posed by the idea of national goals that is embedded in the concept of policy, we have proposed to concentrate upon discrete, observable actions, which will be referred to as foreign policy behaviors. It has been shown that these behaviors can be classified in a number of potentially meaningful ways.

In the remainder of this book we will concentrate on the theoretical perspectives that we believe can be used to explain the various classifications of foreign policy behavior introduced in this chapter. Each theoretical perspective will consider only a few of the properties of foreign policy behavior described here and the particular classifications used will vary from chapter to chapter. Elsewhere the CREON investigators are exploring the empirical relationships between the theoretical perspectives and a common set of behavior measures (see note 5). To levy that requirement on the present undertaking, however, would dissipate the primary purpose of this book, which is to have each perspective focus on those foreign policy behaviors it appears best suited to explain.

It may be helpful to know that each of the chapters dealing with an individual theoretical perspective will follow a common format consisting of five major sections. The first section, "Overview of the Perspective," provides an introduction to the nature of the perspective as it will be advanced in the chapter. It is followed by "Relation to Previous Studies" that, as the title implies, connects the present perspective to some of the most important previous work done on that perspective and indicates how the present effort builds on, or departs from, prior inquiries. The third section, entitled "Development of the Perspective," stands at the core of each chapter. Here the author(s) identifies the key variables in the perspective and sets forth the explanatory logic that relates these variables to foreign policy behavior. The fourth section, "Selected Assumptions," usually is no more than a numbered set of sentences recounting the primary assumptions underlying the perspective.

By assumptions we mean certain givens that identify the necessary conditions for the explanatory logic and the descriptive hypotheses. In some instances (but not all) the assumptions could be empirically investigated, but within the context of a particular theoretical perspective they are being asserted as valid without empirical inquiry. No claim is made that the listed assumptions comprise an exhaustive set for any of the perspectives, but we anticipate that they are among the primary necessary conditions. Because the list of assumptions is incomplete, it is not possible to show how testable hypotheses logically follow from the assumptions. Despite this shortcoming, we believe that the statement of key assumptions can serve useful purposes. Even an incomplete statement of assumptions (a) reminds us that the propositions are not claimed as valid for all time and under all conditions, (b) identifies possible conflicts between the foundations of different perspectives, (c) aids in the search for other unstated assumptions, and (d) provides one means of moving toward the integration of the separate perspectives.

After the presentation of assumptions, every chapter concludes with a section on "Illustrative Propositions" that provides examples of direct relationships between key variables in the perspective and certain kinds of foreign policy behaviors. These propositions provide the linkage between a given perspective and foreign policy behavior as presented in the chapter.

Several reasonable alternatives existed for ordering the remaining chapters within this volume. We have elected to arrange them so that the reader moves outward from consideration of those perspectives whose units of analysis are most immediately proximate to the formation of foreign policy behavior toward those that are more distant. Thus, the book begins with an examination of the personal characteristics of leaders (chapter 3), followed in order by discussions of decision structures and processes (chapter 4), political regimes (chapter 5), national attributes (chapter 6), and international political systems (chapter 7). The two perspectives that do not fit neatly into this organizing scheme concern the forces that influence specific types of response. These perspectives focus on prior foreign behavior (chapter 8) and transitory qualities of the situation (chapter 9). After reading all the perspectives, the reader may discover other ways of ordering them to fit different problems, as we have done in the concluding chapter (chapter 10).

In closing, let us note once again that our intent in this volume is to present the reader with a set of theoretical perspectives for studying foreign policy behavior. These perspectives focus on many of the types of variables that are most frequently mentioned as influencing foreign policy. The perspectives go further, however, than has usually been the case to date by developing the underlying explanatory logic that links key variables to foreign policy behavior. We hope that, as a result of having examined these perspectives, both the reader and the authors can move more rapidly toward the formation of a set of multicausal models for explaining foreign policy behavior.

NOTES

1. For a survey of some of the definitions of foreign policy in the research literature, see C. Hermann (1972a: 70-71).

2. Some individuals have found it instructive to classify the purposes of foreign policy using a series of concepts that can be arranged from the most general to the most specific (e.g., see Bloomfield, 1968). The most general characterization of national purposes is represented in the concept of national interests, which refer to the broad, durable goals of a nation. Use of the term national interests escapes none of the problems to be discussed here and adds several additional ones. Moreover, if national interests are the extremely broad and enduring purposes, we still have to identify the more specific ones designed to support these larger interests. Hence in this discussion we will use the more generic term of goals to cover all the related concepts including national interests, objectives, and programs.

3. We are grateful to Vincent Davis who effectively reminded us of this inevitable limitation in the early stages of the CREON Project.

4. A survey of the nature of events data, the major data sets, and some illustrative applications appear in the following materials: Azar and Ben-Dak (1975), Azar,

Brody and McClelland (1972), Burgess and Lawton (1972), Gamson and Modigliani (1971), Hermann et al. (1973), Kegley et al. (1975), McClelland and Hoggard (1969), Sigler, Field and Adelman (1972), and Rummel (1972).

5. This entire chapter, but particularly the present section, introduces issues that are examined in much greater detail in a CREON book on foreign policy behaviors under the editorship of Linda P. Brady that is now in preparation. The issues touched upon here are more thoroughly explored in that volume. At a panel during the 1975 American Political Science Association meetings, papers were presented on four of the theoretical perspectives; the effects of explanatory variables from these perspectives were used to account for a common set of six foreign policy behaviors—see Brady (1975); East (1975); M. G. Hermann (1975); and Salmore and Salmore (1975). More work on the exploration of a common set of foreign policy behaviors using all the theoretical perspectives is now underway.

3

EFFECTS OF PERSONAL CHARACTERISTICS OF POLITICAL LEADERS ON FOREIGN POLICY

Margaret G. Hermann

How do the idiosyncratic characteristics of political leaders affect their governments' foreign policy behavior? This question has fascinated scholars down through the ages (e.g., Plato, 363 B.C.; Machiavelli, 1640; Pareto, 1916). In this chapter we will argue that personal characteristics of political leaders can affect what governments do in their relations with other nations. This relationship, however, is not straightforward. Personal characteristics of political leaders will have more of an impact on national foreign policy behavior if the political leaders are high level policy makers such as heads of state. Moreover, the chances of finding a relationship between a head of state's personal characteristics and his government's foreign policy behavior are enhanced if the situation facing the government is taken into account. Focusing on the head of state himself, several of his characteristics are proposed as influencing when, in general, his personal characteristics will affect his government's foreign policy behavior. These are his interest in foreign affairs, his training in foreign affairs, and his general sensitivity to the environment. Having set the stage for when a head of state's personal characteristics will influence national foreign policy behavior, we will discuss which types of characteristics are expected to affect foreign policy behavior and how. The chapter will conclude with a list of assumptions underlying this perspective and some illustrative propositions.

OVERVIEW OF THE PERSPECTIVE

The extent of the influence of a political leader's personal characteristics on public policy has generated much controversy (see, e.g.,
Bronfenbrenner, 1960; Greenstein, 1969; Hook, 1943; Leontief, 1963).
Discussions of foreign policy are not unaffected by this controversy.
Statements have appeared that personal characteristics of foreign policy
decision makers are only of minor importance in determining foreign
policy (e.g., Rosenau, 1972) and also that they are more important than
any other single factor in determining foreign policy (e.g., Shapiro and
Bonham, 1973). Moreover, analyses of the same data indicate for one
researcher the relative unimportance of personal characteristics in explaining foreign policy (Rosenau, 1968) and for another researcher the importance of such characteristics in shaping foreign policy (Stassen, 1972).

What are some of the reasons for this debate? Three criticisms underlie
the arguments against the importance of a political leader's personal
characteristics in the formation of foreign policy. First, individual actors
are limited by social forces in the impact they can have on events. As
Singer (1961) argues, the international system so shapes and constrains
policy that individual decision makers can have little impact. Second, the
critics state that in the foreign policy arena leaders who have different
personal characteristics behave similarly when placed in common situations. "Names and faces may change, interests and policies do not"
(Holsti, 1973: 8). Third, the critics argue that because foreign policy
decisions are made in complex bureaucracies, organizational constraints
limit the effect of individual characteristics (e.g., see Verba, 1969; chapter
4 in this volume).

Such criticisms are fairly devastating. But as Holsti (1973: 9) notes,
"these arguments are often the initial premises that guide, rather than the
considered conclusions that emerge from systematic research." Let us
examine each of these criticisms in more detail to see where the researcher
who is interested in exploring how a political leader's personal characteristics affect foreign policy should begin.

The first criticism forms the basis for the centuries old "great man"
versus "zeitgeist" debate. Must the times be right for the man or will the
man be a great leader regardless of the times? For example, would Lincoln
have been as effective if he had been president in the 1920s instead of the
1860s? After carefully analyzing both sides of this debate, Searing (1972)
suggests that the advocates of each side approach the study of leaders with
different models of man and society. Advocates of the "zeitgeist" or
situation operate from an organismic model, while "great man" advocates
operate from a mechanistic model. Moreover, Searing argues that these

positions form two extremes along a continuum, with most cases falling somewhere between the two extremes, and he urges an examination of the interrelationship between the situation and the man.

Research on leadership also indicates that neither position seems tenable by itself (see Gibb, 1969; Stogdill, 1974). Although most leaders do appear to have certain characteristics (they are self-confident, extroverted, and exhibit interpersonal sensitivity or empathy), a leader in one situation is not necessarily a leader in a different situation. Moreover, leadership is bestowed by a group on the basis of the values and needs of that group, all of which can change. Students of leadership propose that it is the interaction between the characteristics of the individual and the characteristics of the situation that determines both who will become a leader and the kind of behavior that the leader will exhibit (see, e.g., Fiedler, 1967; Hollander and Julian, 1970). Therefore, the researcher who is interested in examining the effect of a leader's personal characteristics on his nation's foreign policy would probably be wise to take into account the total situation in which the decision maker is acting, as well as the traits of the decision maker. Based on such a consideration, Paige (1972b: 69) defines political leadership as "the interaction of personality, role, organization, task, values, and setting as expressed in the behavior of salient individuals" who can have an effect on policy.

The second criticism concerns the "agent" or "representative" nature of political leadership. Here the critics argue that political leaders merely reflect the views, beliefs, and ideologies of the constituencies they lead and, as a result, react to common situations in a similar manner. Thus, as some Kremlinologists would have us believe, all Soviet foreign policy follows from the dictates of Marxism-Leninism. In order to become a political leader, an individual must have internalized the goals and norms of the elite that grants him power (see, e.g., Kolko and Kolko, 1972). His personal characteristics become subservient to these group characteristics.

Interestingly, however, even advocates of this "agent" position (e.g., Shils, 1954; Verba, 1969) grant that in certain situations the effects of personal characteristics on political behavior are probably enhanced rather than reduced. Greenstein (1969: 47) has rephrased this criticism in a manner appropriate to this discussion: "Under what circumstances do different actors (placed in common situations) vary in their behavior and under what circumstances is their behavior uniform?" Propositions (e.g., see Greenstein, 1969; Hermann, 1976B; Holsti, 1973; Verba, 1969) concerning the circumstances under which political leaders' personal characteristics will influence foreign policy focus on three types of conditions. Personal characteristics will have more impact on policy (1) in situations that force the political leader to define or interpret them (e.g., ambiguous situations), (2) in situations in which the political leader is likely to participate in the decision-making process (e.g., crises), and (3) in situations in which the political leader has wide decision latitude (e.g., the "honeymoon" period following a landslide election). The researcher interested in examining the effects of personal characteristics on foreign policy may well want to focus on circumstances fitting into one of these three categories.

The third criticism focuses on the organizational constraints that limit the expression of a leader's personal characteristics in policy. In effect, the critics argue that one of the ways in which organizations maintain their effectiveness is by the "complete elimination of personalized relationships and of nonrational considerations (hostility, anxiety, affectual involvements, etc.)" (Merton, 1940: 561). This criticism may be more true of decision makers in the lower levels of an organization. Some evidence suggests that personal characteristics of decision makers at higher levels in an organization may influence policy.

Snyder and Robinson (1961: 158) have observed from research on organizations "that when asked if personality plays as great (or greater) a part in behavior as organizational factors such as communication, officials who are at lower echelons tend to say no, while those at high echelons tend to say yes." Roles are less likely to be well defined the higher in an organization one is located; the role occupant has more responsibility for delimiting and/or expanding his functions. Furthermore, there are fewer, if any, people above one to change or modify the decision. Recall the famous sign on Truman's desk saying, "The buck stops here." Studies by Palumbo (1969) and Welling (1969) indicate that as a person moves higher in the organizational hierarchy there are fewer organizational and role constraints placed on him. Moreover, the less specific the individual's role, the greater his power is. As Stassen (1972: 118) notes with regard to foreign policy:

> Top-level executives are not under tight hierarchical constraint. . . .
> They must be persuaded and bargained with rather than simply
> commanded. . . . Therefore, preferences and belief-sets are likely to
> be important for top-level executive decision-makers. . . .

Based on this information, the researcher interested in investigating the effect of a leader's personal characteristics on foreign policy will probably want to focus on high level policy makers such as foreign ministers and heads of government.

Our discussion thus far sets boundaries on when one might expect the personal characteristics of political leaders to affect foreign policy and implies that there are circumstances when the leader's characteristics will have little or no impact. In effect, both of the contradictory statements at the beginning of this section are tenable—but for different policy makers and under different circumstances. The chances of finding a relationship between a political leader's personal characteristics and his nation's foreign policy are enhanced if the researcher examines the characteristics of high level policy makers and takes into account the situation—specifically, circumstances in which the leader has wide decision latitude, in which the leader is forced to define or give interpretation to the situation he faces, and in which the leader is likely to be involved in the decision-making process. Figure 3.1 summarizes the discussion thus far, indicating when the personal characteristics of political leaders will affect their government's foreign policy. The rest of the discussion of this theoretical perspective works within the framework just described, focusing on those political leaders and those conditions that are most likely to show a relationship between personal characteristics and foreign policy.

RELATION TO PREVIOUS STUDIES

Most of the research to date relating political leaders' traits to foreign policy has resulted in political biographies (e.g., George and George, 1964; Rogow, 1963; Wolfenstein, 1967, 1969) that rely heavily on psycho-analytic theory. As a consequence, the writers attempt to show how the early childhood experiences of the leader influence his later political behavior and decision making. Often because extensive material about the leader's early life is not available, these writers are forced to speculate about his childhood. An interesting exception to this pattern is Erikson (1962, 1969), who has linked developmental crises in the adulthoods of both Luther and Gandhi to their political behavior. Erikson (1950) also has extended the development stages in psychoanalytic theory into adult-hood, indicating that people do not cease to develop psychologically at puberty but continue psychological development throughout their lifetimes.

In the last decade several groups of researchers have tried to explore more systematically how the personal characteristics of higher level policy makers affect foreign policy. One group of researchers has focused on political leaders' operational codes, based on George's (1969) reformula-tion of the operational code construct developed by Leites (1951, 1953). George (1969: 197) describes the operational code of a political leader as: "A political leader's beliefs about the nature of politics and political conflict, his views regarding the extent to which historical developments can be shaped, and his notions of correct strategy and tactics." An

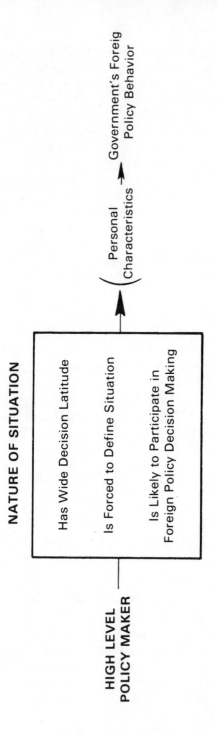

Figure 3.1. The conditions under which the personal characteristics of political leaders are expected to affect their government's foreign policy behavior.

operational code is composed of two types of beliefs—the policy maker's philosophical and instrumental beliefs about political reality. Philosophical beliefs refer to a political leader's "fundamental assumptions" about the nature of politics (e.g., his orientation toward opponents, his beliefs about the role of chance in political events); instrumental beliefs represent the political leader's beliefs about styles and strategies appropriate to acting in a political world defined by the philosophical beliefs (e.g., preferences for planning versus acting, risk-taking preferences). The operational code is viewed as setting the boundaries within which the leader will act.

Studies of the operational codes of Acheson (McLellan, 1971), Brandt (Ashby, 1969), Dulles (Holsti, 1970), Mao (White, 1969), Rusk (Gutierrez, 1973), and Trudeau (Thordarson, 1972) follow the George framework. Most of these studies have used qualitative content analysis (see George, 1959). Therefore, although able to move faster and cover more material than is possible with more time-consuming quantitative content analysis, these researchers have not had to worry about operationalizing their concepts and, as a result, it is hard to compare or generalize from their research. Moreover, their tendency to focus on one case limits the generality of the findings. To date most research on operational codes has been descriptive—what is X's operational code?—rather than dealing with the linkage between operational code and foreign policy.

A second group of studies stems from psychological research on personality. Making content analyses of speeches and interviews with high level policy makers or focusing on the verbal output of simulated leaders, these researchers have examined the relationship of a particular personality trait to a specific foreign policy activity. The usual research query concerns what the political consequences are for a nation of having a leader who has more or less of the trait under consideration. The hypotheses guiding the research represent extrapolations from small group and individual experiments. Some results that have received support in at least two studies include: (a) the more cognitively complex the high level policy maker, the more cooperative his government's foreign policy (Driver, 1976; Hermann, 1976A); (b) the more nationalistic the high level policy maker, the less external commitment of its resources his government will make (M.G. Hermann, 1974, 1976A); (c) the greater the high level policy maker's need for power, the more aggressive his government's foreign policy will be (Terhune and Firestone, 1967; Winter 1973).

A central issue with this last type of study is validity. With regard to the simulation studies, one might question the similarity between college students and professional politicians. How generalizable to the world of the politician is information about college students in a simulated international environment? A second validity question focuses on how the researcher gathers information about the personal characteristics of high level policy makers who are virtually inaccessible for the usual techniques of interview and questionnaire. Generally, the investigator's only option is content analysis of material either spoken or written by the decision maker. Personal traits are inferred from the content by counting certain words, sentences, or themes. But what about material planned by the speaker to convey some point of view or ghost-written for him by another? Can personal characteristics legitimately be inferred from such material? Moreover, are such word, sentence, and theme counts measuring similar characteristics as those supposedly assessed by questionnaire? Several writers have discussed these issues in some detail (see Hermann, 1967; Hermann and Hermann, 1967; M. G. Hermann, 1974; Holsti, 1973).

All three types of research that we have briefly reviewed lack an explicit conceptual framework stating what personal characteristics might be expected to influence what foreign policy behaviors and why. As Holsti (1973: 26) notes:

> The student of foreign policy is interested in beliefs and cognitive processes [of the policy maker] because these are assumed to be among the independent or intervening variables that are systematically related to the substance and quality of decision outputs. But linkages to . . . the dependent variable are not always satisfactory. . . . It is not uncommon to find in the conclusion a statement to the effect that, "the preceding analysis of X's belief system establishes its utility for understanding X's political behavior." It is less common to find an explicit and convincing demonstration of why this is the case.

We now turn our attention toward the task of explicating a conceptual scheme for linking the personal characteristics of political leaders to their nations' foreign policy.

DEVELOPMENT OF THE PERSPECTIVE

Assume that we have high level policy makers such as heads of state and situations that require interpretation, that present the leader at the moment with wide decision latitude, or that are likely to force participation in the policy-making process. Given such individuals and situations, how do we expect the policy makers' personal characteristics to affect foreign policy? Political leaders' personal characteristics probably will have little effect unless the policy maker has some general interest in foreign affairs. Interest acts as a motivating force. One consequence of interest in foreign policy will be increased attention to the foreign policy-making process. The head of state will want to be consulted on decisions and will want to be kept informed about what is happening in foreign affairs. Moreover, the reasons behind the head of state's interest in foreign affairs may predetermine the course of action he will implement. Such reasons can include placing value on good external relations, fearing an enemy takeover, and seeing foreign affairs as a way of gaining reelection. With little interest in foreign affairs, the head of state is likely to delegate authority to other people, negating any effect of his personality on the resultant policy except, perhaps, as his spokesman's personality is similar to his own.

If the policy maker has an interest in foreign affairs, a second personal characteristic of importance is his training or expertise in foreign affairs. By training in foreign affairs we mean that before becoming head of state, the policy maker was a foreign minister, an ambassador, a member of a ministry dealing with foreign affairs, or held a nongovernmental position in the general community dealing with the foreign relations of the nation. The head of state with little or no training in foreign affairs has no personal expertise to draw upon. He has no previous experience to suggest possible alternatives or plans of action. As a result, his natural problem-solving predispositions come into play. The head of state with training, on the other hand, has some knowledge about what will succeed and fail in the international arena. As a consequence of his experience he has learned to match a strategy to a specific issue and target nation. In effect, the head of state with training has a wider repertoire of possible foreign policy behaviors to consider than the head of state with little or no training. Thus, we expect that it will be more difficult to predict the foreign policy behavior that a head of state with training will urge his government to use from knowledge of his personal characteristics.

A third personal characteristic, general sensitivity to one's environment, affects the consistency of the relationship between other characteristics and foreign policy. Sensitivity to one's environment indicates the extent to which an individual is responsive to incoming stimuli from objects in the milieu in which he operates. How important are incoming stimuli from the environment to the political leader in determining what he will try to influence his government to do? The less sensitive the political leader is to his environment, the more fixed the impact of his traits on foreign policy—the less likely the leader is to have cause to change, for example, his goals and attitudes or the foreign policy strategy he has always used. The more sensitive the leader is to his environment, the more likely he is to accommodate himself to new information and to the necessity for change suggested by the environment. In a sense, the less sensitive policy

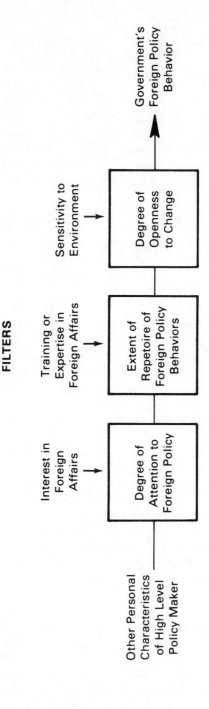

Figure 3.2. The effect of the filter variables on the relationship between the personal characteristics of political leaders and their government's foreign policy behavior.

maker adjusts incoming stimuli to fit a certain set or viewpoint while the more sensitive policy maker attempts to deal with his environment, changing his views if incoming stimuli warrant such adjustment.

Interest, training, and sensitivity to the environment act as filters on the relationship between a leader's personal characteristics and his nation's foreign policy. These three variables indicate how much attention the policy maker will pay to foreign policy problems, how large a repertoire of possible foreign policy behaviors the policy maker is likely to have, and how consistent the trait/foreign policy relationship will be. Figure 3.2 diagrams the effect of these three personal characteristics. Once we know the degree of interest a head of state has in foreign policy, we know whether or not he will take advantage of the situation in which he finds himself to have an impact on foreign policy. Once we know his expertise in foreign affairs, we know the extent of his repertoire of plausible foreign policy behaviors. Once we know how sensitive he is to his environment, we know the consistency of his impact on foreign policy—how open he will be to change.

These filters influence the relationships between four other kinds of personal characteristics and foreign policy. The four types of personal characteristics that seem most relevant to foreign policy making are a political leader's beliefs, motives, decision style, and interpersonal style. By relevant here we mean that variables from these clusters of traits have often been described as important, idiosyncratic determinants of political behavior.

Beliefs refer to the philosophical beliefs of the operational code described earlier. In other words, beliefs represent the leader's fundamental assumptions about the world. Such beliefs can be very general, as, for example, a political leader's notions about his ability to control events in his life, or they can be more specific, as, for example, a political leader's notions about his ability to shape political events for his nation. The effect of a person's beliefs on his interpretation of his environment has received much research attention. Psychologists and political scientists (e.g., DeRivera, 1968; Frank, 1968; Holsti, 1967; Jervis, 1969; Osgood, 1962; Verba, 1969) alike have found this an interesting research question. As Holsti (1962: 244) notes, "a decision maker acts upon his 'image' of the situation rather than upon 'objective' reality."

Motives of political leaders refer to the reasons why they do what they do—the desires that activate them. One motive, need for power, has long been discussed as a potent force driving the politician. For example, Lasswell (1930, 1948) proposes that the primary motivation for political activity is emotional insecurity or low self-esteem, and these are compensated for by a drive for power. Recently Winter (1973) has reported that the higher a president's need for power, the more forceful and aggressive his government's foreign policy is. Other motives may be relevant to policy making. Some that come to mind are need to achieve, need for support or approval of one's ideas, need to be independent, and need for structure.

By decision style is meant preferred methods of making decisions. Can we discern certain ways of approaching a decision-making task that characterize the political leader? Snyder and Robinson (1961: 164) suggest the following five elements comprise decision style: "a) confidence, b) openness to new information, c) preference for certain levels of risk and sizes of stake, d) capacity for postponing decision without anxiety, and e) rules for adjusting to uncertainty." Other possible components of decision style include preference for compromise, preference for an optimizing as opposed to satisficing mode of decision making, and preference for planning as opposed to activity. In a sense, decision style is quite similar to what George refers to in the operational code as instrumental beliefs. Moreover, much of Barber's (1972) discussion of presidential character deals with decision style. His four basic character patterns carry with them distinctive decision styles of flexibility, compulsivity, compliance, and withdrawal.

The last trait—interpersonal style—is concerned with characteristic ways in which a policy maker deals with other policy makers. Paranoia or suspiciousness is one way of dealing with others that has often been attributed to politicians (see Rutherford, 1966). Machiavellianism is another interpersonal style often attributed to political leaders. Tucker (1965) has suggested that these two characteristics are interrelated in a type of political leader who has a warfare personality, e.g., Stalin and Hitler. The warfare personality is characterized as being highly suspicious, as defining all but his favored associates as enemies, and as thriving on manipulating others. Alternative ways of dealing with others that might be interesting to investigate are the leader's means of persuading (threats or praise), his sensitivity to others, his sense of political timing, and whether or not he is a task-oriented or person-oriented leader.

The discussion to this point has focused on personal characteristics. What about the dependent variable, foreign policy—how do these personal characteristics influence foreign policy? Two aspects of foreign policy seem to be affected by a political leader's personal characteristics: the strategies that the government employs in its foreign policy and the styles in which the foreign policy is made and executed. Foreign policy strategies are a government's basic plans for action, such as adopting a generally cooperative or competitive stance toward other nations, acting alone or in concert with other nations, deciding to commit or not to commit resources to other nations, engaging in bilateral rather than multilateral agreements, and emphasizing certain self interests over others. Styles of foreign policy are the methods a government chooses to use in making and executing its foreign policy—for example, the channels used for announcing policy, the particular skills and resources used in implementing policy, the tendency to use words instead of deeds, the use of personal diplomacy, and the relative involvement of the bureaucracy in foreign policy. In effect, strategies focus on the content or substance of foreign policy, whereas styles focus on the means of making and executing foreign policy.

Why do we expect a political leader's personal characteristics to affect the strategy and style of his government's foreign policy making? Let us consider beliefs and motives first. Because beliefs and motives suggest ways of interpreting the environment, the political leader is likely to urge his government to act in ways consistent with such images. Specifically, the political leader's beliefs and motives provide him with a map for charting his course. As George (1969: 197) notes:

> (1) The political actor's information about situations with which he must deal is usually incomplete; (2) his knowledge of ends-means relationships is generally inadequate to predict realiably the consequences of choosing one or another course of action; and (3) it is often difficult for him to formulate a single criterion by means of which to choose which alternative course of action is "best."

Some kind of map is needed. The political leader's cognitive map provides ways to overcome the conditions that George describes and suggests the appropriate steps to one's goal—so strategies of foreign policy making evolve. For example, Dulles (see Holsti, 1962, 1967) believed the Russian leadership was incapable of any good will toward the United States—its goals were to thwart rather than to assist the United States. As a result, even when the Soviet Union made some conciliatory moves (e.g., the Austrian peace treaty, troop reductions), these were interpreted as indicating bad faith on the part of the Communists. The Soviet Union was defined as the enemy, and the United States' resources were used to counter its influence in the international arena. One additional point: the high level policy maker is likely, when possible, to appoint to policy-making positions persons with beliefs and motives similar to his own, helping to insure that his interpretation of political reality permeates the bureaucracy (see Bennis, 1973).

In relating the other two types of personal characteristics—decision style and interpersonal style—to foreign policy behavior we make an assumption that the political leader will generally engage in similar stylistic behavior regardless of arena. Thus, the political leader's preferred methods of making personal decisions and personally interacting with others will carry over to his political behavior. Style is probably one of the first differences noted when heads of state change. Each new leader tries to make himself comfortable in his role. For example, one head of state may focus foreign policy making within his own office, while his predecessor may have been willing to let the bureaucracy handle all problems except those of crisis proportions. One head of state may have been given to rhetoric in the foreign policy arena; his predecessor may have wanted action.

Robinson (1972: 168) has written an interesting description of the styles of Chou En-Lai and Lin Piao:

> Chou is verbal; Lin was not. Chou revels in public appearances; Lin was at his worst under such circumstances. . . . [Moreover] there is a difference in the timing of their political involvement. Lin followed his military tendency to attack suddenly only after preparation, thereby seeming to be only sporadically involved. Hence, he disappeared from the scene for long periods and then suddenly exploded into view again. Chou, on the other hand, is more or less constantly involved. There is also an obvious difference in attitudes toward planning in politics. Lin planned to the extreme; Chou seems to adopt a posture of muddling through. Furthermore, Lin liked to simplify problems, whereas Chou tries to make them more complex. Finally, Lin and Chou differ fundamentally in their attitudes toward others. Lin appeared to treat others as enemies, at least initially. Chou does not seem to make this initial assumption. Thus, to Lin, politics was zero-sum; to Chou it is not.

If we assume that the personal styles of high level policy makers will influence the styles of their political behavior and, in turn, the style their government's foreign policy takes, then we would expect—based on Robinson's account—foreign policy under Chou to be more word-oriented, to involve more public than private diplomacy, to be less planned, and to be more open to compromise than foreign policy under Lin Piao.

Figure 3.3 summarizes our discussion of when and how the personal characteristics of political leaders will affect their government's foreign policy behavior. Based on this discussion, it seems appropriate to propose that beliefs and motives form the basis for a political leader's views of the world that, in turn, affect his choice of strategy. If the political leader is a head of state and the situation is one in which he is in a position to influence other foreign policy makers in his government, his views of the world will shape his government's foreign policy strategies. Similarly, the political leader's decision style and interpersonal style form the basis for his personal political style, which influences the way he behaves in his

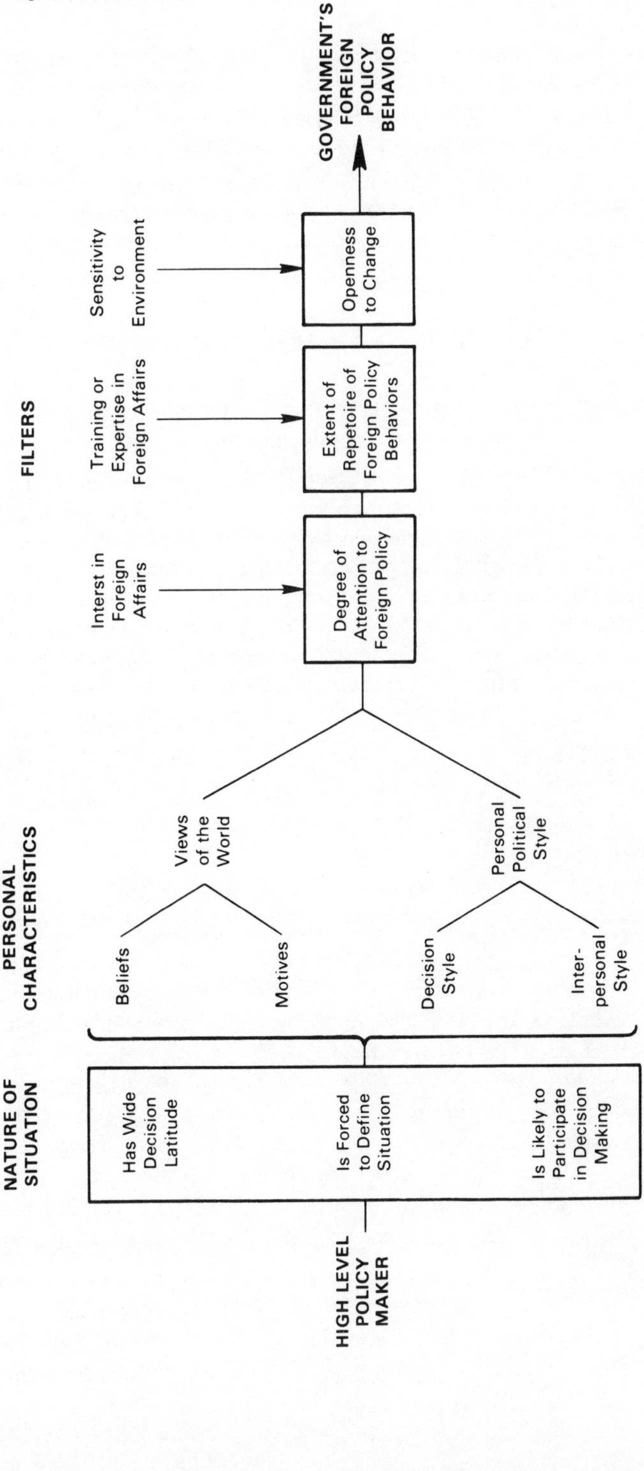

Figure 3.3. Summary of proposed relationships between personal characteristics of political leaders and their government's foreign policy behavior.

attempt to make foreign policy. Here again, if the political leader is a head of state and the situation is one in which he is in a position to influence other foreign policy makers in his government, his personal political style will affect his government's foreign policy style. Thus, we have the high level political leader's views of the world affecting his government's foreign policy strategies, his personal political style affecting the style of foreign policy making.

SELECTED ASSUMPTIONS

At the heart of the previous discussion relating personal characteristics and foreign policy are some key assumptions or "givens" which help to provide the conditions necessary for the generation of testable hypotheses. The following list of assumptions is meant not to be exhaustive but suggestive of the foundation on which hypotheses and research in this perspective build. Although in some cases the assumptions could be tested empirically, we will state them as givens for the present.

Before listing the assumptions, a more specific definition of personal characteristics is pertinent. Personal characteristics refer to an individual's biographical statistics, training, work experiences, personality traits, beliefs and attitudes, and values. In other words, personal characteristics are all aspects of an individual *qua* individual. Moreover, when we talk about a political leader's personal characteristics we are interested in his characteristics at both general (across situations and roles) and specific (for political situations and roles) levels.

The following are some key assumptions for this perspective:

ASSUMPTION 3.1: *Individuals have certain stable personal characteristics that are measurable.*

ASSUMPTION 3.2: *Certain personal characteristics of political leaders influence their views of the world and personal political style.*

ASSUMPTION 3.3: *Political leaders' views of the world and personal political style can influence their governments' foreign policy behavior.*

ASSUMPTION 3.4: *The impact of political leaders' personal characteristics on foreign policy behavior will be greatest under certain situational conditions,* specifically when the political leaders have wide decision latitude, when the political leaders are forced to define the situation, or when the political leaders are likely to participate in foreign policy making.

ASSUMPTION 3.5: *Three personal characteristics of political leaders—interest in foreign affairs, training in foreign affairs, and sensitivity to the environment—serve as filters or mediating variables that increase or decrease the influence of all other personal characteristics on foreign policy.*

ASSUMPTION 3.6: *Political leaders' interest in foreign affairs will influence the degree of attention that they pay to foreign policy.*

ASSUMPTION 3.7: *Political leaders' training or expertise in foreign affairs will affect the extent of their repertoire of plausible foreign policy behaviors.*

ASSUMPTION 3.8: *Political leaders' sensitivity to their environments will affect their openness to change.*

ASSUMPTION 3.9: *Of all other possible personal characteristics (excluding the three filter variables), four clusters of traits are most relevant to foreign policy making—beliefs, motives, decision style, and interpersonal style.*

ASSUMPTION 3.10: *Beliefs and motives form the basis for political leaders' views of the world and, as established in Assumptions 3.2 and 3.3, views of the world influence foreign policy behavior.*

ASSUMPTION 3.11: *Decision style and interpersonal style form the basis for political leaders' personal political style and, as established in Assumptions 3.2 and 3.3, personal political style influences foreign policy behavior.*

ASSUMPTION 3.12: *Those political leaders of a government whose personal characteristics are most likely to influence foreign policy behavior are heads of state and foreign ministers, and between these two the personal characteristics of heads of state will have more influence than will the personal characteristics of foreign ministers.*

ILLUSTRATIVE PROPOSITIONS

Based on these assumptions, let us propose some propositions linking a political leader's personal characteristics with his government's foreign policy behavior. This list, like that for the assumptions, is meant not to be exhaustive but suggestive. After stating each proposition we will discuss its rationale and show how it relates to the assumptions just described. One proposition is discussed for each cluster of personal characteristics in Figure 3.3. Then three other propositions are presented to indicate how the filter variables function.

VIEWS OF THE WORLD

PROPOSITION 3.1

The more nationalistic the head of state, the more conflictful his government's foreign policy will be.

Nationalism is a belief in one's own nation in which one's nation is viewed
as superior to other nations. As a belief, nationalism represents one view of
the world. Believing as the nationalist does that his nation is good and that
other nations cause the world's problems, his cognitive map becomes
figured with his nation and outsiders. The outsiders are considered enemies
and one is conflictful with enemies. As Rosenblatt (1964: 141) notes,
nationalism increases one's ability "to cheat, to fight, or to kill" the
outsider. Thus, nationalism leads to a certain foreign policy strategy. As a
result of Assumption 3.12, this proposition and the others that follow
focus on heads of state.

PROPOSITION 3.2

*The greater the head of state's need for achievement, the more
cooperative behavior his government will initiate.*

Need for achievement refers to an individual's desire to be successful in
competition with some standard of excellence. As such, need for achievement is a motive and, thus, a generator of a view of the world. Terhune
(1968) has observed that achievement-oriented persons in international
relations games are cooperative *first* in hopes that their opponents will be
cooperative, leading to the development of a trusting relationship that can
be mutually rewarding. Once a mutually rewarding relationship is established in one area, rewarding relationships in other areas become more
realistic. Here a motive produces a foreign policy strategy.

PERSONAL POLITICAL STYLE

PROPOSITION 3.3

*The more dogmatic the head of state, the less likely his government
is to change its position on a well-established policy.*

Dogmatism indicates a fairly rigid and inflexible set of ideas or thought
patterns that represent, with a high degree of certainty, only one side of a
problem. Dogmatism is a decision style variable and, as such, will probably
affect a political leader's personal political style. Research on dogmatism
indicates the importance of tradition, rules, and principles to the dogmatic
individual. As Vacchiano et al. (1968: 84-85) state, the dogmatic person is
"conservative and respecting of established ideas." The dogmatic political
leader will be loath to change any policy or position that he views as a
traditional part of his nation's repertoire of activities. Such desires are
probably quickly noted and adhered to by assistants. In this way a
personal decision style becomes a part of the government's style of foreign
policy.

PROPOSITION 3.4

The more Machiavellian the head of state, the more face-to-face foreign policy interactions his government will have.

Machiavellianism refers to having a manipulative way with other people. The Machiavellian can easily become emotionally detached from others since he is unlikely to become personally involved with others (see Christie and Geis, 1970; Guterman, 1970). The Machiavellian's motto is "a sucker is born every minute." Machiavellianism is an interpersonal style and, as such, contributes to a political leader's personal political style. Research (see Christie and Geis, 1970) shows that the Machiavellian is less successful in using his manipulative tactics when he is not in direct communication with the other party. One way to have direct communication in the foreign policy arena is to have face-to-face meetings with other heads of state or to engage in personal diplomacy or "summitry." Thus, the more Machiavellian head of state's preference for direct manipulation is translated into a foreign policy style for his nation.

EFFECT OF INTEREST

PROPOSITION 3.5

The more interest the head of state has in foreign affairs, the more likely Propositions 3.1 through 3.4 are to be supported.

The more interested the head of state is in foreign affairs, the more attention he will pay to foreign policy making. As a consequence of his increased attention, his views of the world and personal political style will have more of an opportunity to make an impact on the foreign policy styles and strategies of his government.

EFFECT OF TRAINING OR EXPERTISE

PROPOSITION 3.6

The less training or expertise the head of state has in foreign affairs the more likely Propositions 3.1 through 3.4 are to be supported.

The head of state with little training has a small repertoire of foreign policy behaviors. He has little but his predispositions—his views of the world and personal political style—on which to rely when faced with a foreign policy decision. His influence on his government's foreign policy behavior will probably bear the stamp of his views of the world and personal political style.

EFFECT OF SENSITIVITY TO THE ENVIRONMENT

PROPOSITION 3.7

The less sensitive the head of state is to his environment, the more likely Propositions 3.1 through 3.4 are to hold across substantive problem areas and situations.

Sensitivity to the environment affects the consistency of the relationship between a head of state's personal characteristics and his government's foreign policy behavior by influencing a head of state's openness to change. The less sensitive head of state tends not to differentiate between types of situations and substantive problems but tends to group stimuli and to react in a basically similar manner to a wide variety of stimuli. The more sensitive head of state differentiates between types of situations and problems and reacts in ways appropriate to each stimulus. Thus, the views of the world and personal political style of the less sensitive head of state are probably more consistently related to styles and strategies of foreign policy than are those of the more sensitive head of state.

SUMMARY

In this discussion we have attempted to suggest how and under what conditions the personal characteristics of political leaders can affect their government's foreign policy. We have proposed that the personal characteristics of only a few high level policy makers affect foreign policy and, even then, only under certain conditions. Granting these constraints, we have argued that a political leader's views of the world and his personal political style can influence his government's strategies and styles of foreign policy behavior. The magnitude of the relationships between these personal characteristics and foreign policy behavior, however, is affected by the political leader's interest in foreign affairs, his training in foreign affairs, and his sensitivity to his environment.

This discussion sets the stage for a more realistic appraisal of the effect of the political leader qua political leader on foreign policy behavior. Moreover, it begins to suggest possible linkages to the other perspectives in this book. Several examples are pertinent: (1) regime change is thought to accentuate the effect of a new leader's personal political style on the style of his government's foreign policy; (2) situations that are ambiguous promote interpretation by the political leader and are posited as a condition for his personal characteristics to influence foreign policy; (3) political leaders in nations that are small are likely out of necessity to participate in foreign policy and, thus, their personal characteristics can impact on the government's foreign policy. These illustrations suggest the dependence of the leader's functioning on regime, situation, and national attribute variables.

4

DECISION STRUCTURE AND PROCESS
INFLUENCES ON FOREIGN POLICY

Charles F. Hermann

The Politburo of the Communist Party of the USSR, President Jomo Kenyatta of Kenya, the General Political Department of the Chinese Peoples Republic, the National Security Council of the United States, the House of Commons of Great Britain, and the Foreign Ministry of Indonesia all have one thing in common. At one time or another each of these entities has been responsible for making decisions and initiating the foreign policy behaviors of its national government. The diversity of this extremely small sample of national foreign policy decision units or structures is striking, not only for their cultural diversity, but also for their varied composition (individuals, small groups, bureaucratic ministries, national assemblies, political party leaders), their styles, and their rules of operation.

The role of entities such as those mentioned above are the concern of the theoretical perspective developed in this chapter. Simply put, the

AUTHOR'S NOTE: All the contributors to this volume offered many useful comments on an earlier draft. I am particularly grateful to Linda Brady, Margaret Hermann, and Barbara Salmore for their written comments. I also wish to acknowledge the generous assistance of Roger Coate and Bill Dixon. In an important respect some of the insights upon which this chapter is based result from my year on the National Security Council staff as an International Fellow of the Council on Foreign Relations. I am indebted to the Council for that extraordinary opportunity.

perspective contends that various decision structures and their procedures exert a powerful influence on the substance and form of foreign policy behavior. If different decision structures or processes are employed, then frequently the nature of the resulting foreign policy can be expected to change.

OVERVIEW OF THE PERSPECTIVE

Why should decision structures and processes affect foreign policy? The answer will be developed throughout the ensuing pages, but the basic orientation that underlies this perspective can be advanced immediately. For every national government, foreign policy can be viewed as a series of problem-solving tasks. The appropriateness of a particular means of coping with a foreign policy problem is seldom certain. In fact, many foreign policy problems require policy makers to reach a series of decisions under conditions of substantial uncertainty. The uncertainty is multifaceted. The intentions of other international actors may be uncertain; the tradeoff between values and goals to be protected or advanced may be uncertain; and the first and second order effects of various options, tactics, and strategies almost assuredly will be uncertain. In the face of these uncertainties, reasonable individuals often can be expected to disagree on the appropriate course of action for coping with a foreign policy problem. The nature of the decision unit will influence how uncertainties are perceived. It also will determine the customary methods used to handle disagreements among individuals who may differ as to the preferred course of action given the uncertainties. A group that is dominated by one individual whose preferences are tantamount to the group decision may regard the uncertainties associated with a problem quite differently from a group that decides by majority votes. Faced with an ambiguous problem, three people from the same bureau may interpret the problem and means of dealing with it more similarly than three people from different agencies having different missions (e.g., finance, military, foreign affairs). In the example of the group consisting of three individuals from different agencies, their ability to reach an agreement may depend on their status within their respective agencies. Departmental heads may have greater latitude to alter their position than would subordinates. Such varying decision structures and their associated processes for handling problems influence the actions that we observe as foreign policy behaviors if, and only if, the decision is for action rather than inaction and the action becomes public.

In brief, this chapter advances a perspective that seeks to explain foreign policy in terms of variations in the immediate human settings in which policy makers reach foreign policy decisions. The theoretical perspective develops from three basic points. The first major point is that foreign policy decisions are taken by individuals who normally are located in some kind of decision structure or decision unit. These decision structures can vary as a result of numerous factors, including culture and tradition, type of problem, change in regime, and stage of the decision process. Despite their many forms, all decision structures are configurations of roles and support facilities that comprise the unit responsible for one or more phases of the problem-solving task. Normally, they are embedded in the bureaucratic organizations that governments establish to cope with the complex and varied demands generated by foreign affairs.

A second point in this perspective is that variation in the decision structure frequently alters the likely decision process. Of course, many other factors besides the decision structure affect decision processes, but structural characteristics are important influences. By decision process is meant the procedures—norms, decision rules, techniques, and so on—employed by the participants in a decision structure to attempt to make the choices that always are at the core of any decision situation. (At minimum, there is a choice to be made between a possible course of action and doing nothing.) The simplest decision process (and it it not really simple at all) occurs within the mind of a single individual. Because the personal characteristics of individual leaders appear in a separate theoretical perspective, this chapter concentrates on decision processes involving two or more people.

The third basic point is that changes in decision processes result in variation in the resulting behavior. This linkage makes the perspective salient to persons who desire to understand foreign policy. The form and substance of foreign policy behaviors will vary depending on the processes used by the authorities charged with the conduct of foreign relations. Together the three basic points suggest an explanation of foreign policy based on a simple, two-step, linear relationship:

decision structure ⟶ decision process ⟶ foreign behavior.[1]

For many reasons the actual relationships are vastly more complex than the diagram implies. Only one complication will be noted in this introduction. It will be used as an illustration because it highlights a misunderstanding that often arises whenever decision making is considered. Frequently, decision making is defined exclusively as the act of choice between two or more alternatives. In contrast to this restricted conceptualization, most serious efforts to apply the term to political phenomena have referenced a broader span of activity ranging from initial recognition of a problem necessitating decision to any resulting implementation. To illustrate one possible elaboration of the initial two-step explanation of foreign policy behavior noted above, assume that a decision can be organized into the following stages: (1) information collection and interpretation, (2) option formation, (3) choice making, and (4) implementation.[2] In dealing with foreign policy problems, a number of governments will assign one or more different decision structures to the different aspects of the decision. Thus, information collection will be handled by one structure, which will then turn the problem over to other groups for option formation, and so on. As a result, the relationship between decision structures, processes, and behavior could more accurately be represented as shown in Figure 4.1. Even this diagram is inadequate because decision making seldom moves in neat cycles from one stage of the process to another but instead may double back to a prior process. For example, when the Foreign Ministry of Australia presents a set of foreign policy options to the Prime Minister for a choice, he may refer the issue back to the Ministry for more information before deciding. In addition, at each step of the decision there may be not one decision structure, but a series of them with the problem being passed from one to the other.

The purpose of introducing the decision stages was to note the multiplicity of decision units and processes and the possibility of movement back and forth among them within and between stages of a foreign policy decision. In this chapter we will concentrate on processes associated with the choice stage of a decision.[3] This focus is not as restrictive as it might seem because each stage involves some aspects of the choice process. (For example, in the information collection and interpretation step, choices must be made as to what information to collect, how it should be interpreted, and to whom it should be transmitted.) The basic orientation of this perspective, however, should not be lost in these qualifications. Provided we understand that what we are doing is a shorthand for a more complex set of relationships, this theoretical perspective can be summarized by stating that decision structures result in changes in decision processes that in turn produce variations in foreign policy.

After reviewing the works of others who have influenced the present formation of this theoretical perspective, the balance of this chapter will address the following questions:

1. What are some of the common types of decision structures or units in foreign policy?

2. What processes frequently occur with each type of structure?

3. What effects do the processes have on foreign policy behaviors?

4. What do observable indicators reveal when given structures are being employed?

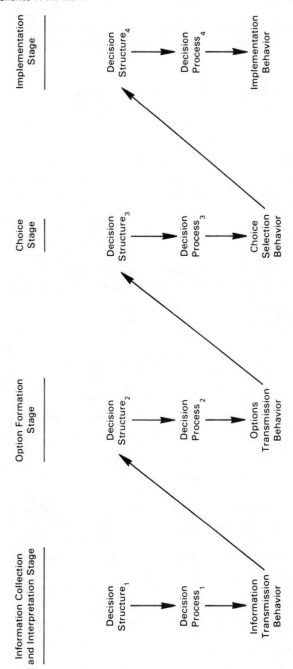

Figure 4.1. An initial elaboration of the relationship between decision structures, decision processes, and behaviors to indicate that distinctive structures and processes can be operative at different stages of a decision.

5. What illustrative propositions indicate how foreign policy behavior is affected by changes in decision structures and processes?

RELATION TO PREVIOUS STUDIES

One of the subjects given substantial attention in contemporary English-language writing on foreign policy appears under the heading of bureaucratic politics—the struggle among individuals within a government to advance the position of their bureau, agency, or department and enhance their personal position. A partial listing of the contributors would include Allison (1969, 1971), Allison and Halperin (1972), Brady (1975), Chayes (1972), D. H. Davis (1972), Destler (1972), George (1972, 1974), Halperin (1972, 1974), Halperin and Kanter (1973), Hammond (1965), Hilsman (1967), Hoffman (1968), Huntington (1960), Kanter (1972), Kissinger (1966), Neustadt (1970), Steinbruner (1974), and Yarmolinsky (1970-1971). Despite a number of variations, the individuals committed to such analysis seem agreed that when the participants from multiple, large bureaucracies engage in the formation and execution of foreign policy, certain characteristics of the bureaucratic process will significantly affect the nature of the resulting policies. Indeed, many of these analysts would contend that some foreign policy actions can best be understood in terms of bureaucratic politics within a government (e.g., Neustadt, 1970; Halperin, 1972). Some (e.g., Allison, 1971) would argue that foreign policy often is the unintended "resultant" of the internal bureaucratic process rather than the consequence of deliberate strategy or external factors. For the present theoretical perspective, the most significant assertion made in this collection of literature is the bold, unequivocal declaration that how foreign policy is made influences the substance of foreign policy.

Yet with some notable exceptions, the work on bureaucratic politics has some important limitations. Little effort has been devoted to establishing the limiting conditions under which the effects of bureaucratic politics occur. Assuming that bureaucratic politics does not operate with equal force on all issues for all countries, what are the circumstances under which it becomes an important source of explanation? This question remains largely unexamined. Moreover, from the perspective of comparative foreign policy, it is noteworthy that almost all the work concerns postwar American decisions. Another weakness is that the exact effects on foreign policy behavior have tended to be stated in either the idiographic terms of a single case or in vague and general statements. (For some other critiques, see Art, 1973; Destler, 1972; Krasner, 1972.)

Although the subject of bureaucratic politics attracts much current interest, concern with the effects of foreign policy decision making has a longer history and engages a broader literature. Young professionals reading Snyder et al. (1962) in the context of contemporary scholarship sometimes have difficulty grasping the revolutionary nature of their ideas when first advanced in 1954 because much of what they said has now been absorbed into our basic understanding of foreign policy processes. Nevertheless, that effort and other work on decision making in an organizational context (e.g., Braybrooke and Lindblom, 1963; Blau, 1974; Cyert and March, 1963; March 1965; March and Simon, 1958; Simon, 1957; Thompson, 1967) represent an important foundation, parts of which still have not been fully utilized in studying foreign policy despite the basic recognition of the centrality of human choice processes taken in the context of collective entities.

Complementing the study of organizational behavior has been the effort to examine decision making in small groups. This extensive field of scientific research has been well reviewed by Collins and Guetzkow (1964), Collins and Raven (1969), and Kelley and Thibaut (1954, 1969). However, relatively few efforts have been made to link small group and organizational settings for decision. (Golembiewski, 1965, provides a useful beginning to this task.) Nor has a continuing effort been made to follow Ulmer (1960), Verba (1961), and Barber's (1966) lead in applying the knowledge of small group decision making to politics in general or to foreign policy as proposed by DeRivera (1968). The most important exceptions to the last observation are George (1974) and Janis (1972). In his analysis, George (1974) highlights the fundamental contribution of group process when he explores the effects of stress on political decision-making in the small group as well as the individual and organizational context. Janis's (1972) effort to delineate the effects of excessive concurrence-seeking in small, foreign policy groups is of particular significance to the present theoretical perspective because he explicitly links group processes to foreign policy behavior.

The topic of foreign policy issue areas provides another avenue of inquiry relevant to any study of the effects of decision-making structures and processes. Not all the efforts on issue areas are applicable because some are concerned primarily with classifying broad substantive problem areas in foreign policy, such as international fiscal policies, arms transfers, or the cross-national movement of laborers. Important in its own right, this concern with substantive problem areas can be distinguished from procedural issue areas. The latter studies rest on the assumption that the participants and decision processes may vary from one type to another. Thus, they contribute to this perspective by highlighting the need to examine various decision processes. Following the pioneering use of the issue area concept in Dahl's (1963) study of New Haven, a number of others including Huntington (1960), Lowi (1967), Rosenau (1967) and Zimmerman (1973) have developed procedural issue area schemes for foreign policy. Yet with the exception of Lowi, few other investigators have been sufficiently attracted to any proposed typology to either elaborate it or apply it systematically to empirical materials.

All these types of studies—those concerned with bureaucratic politics, organizational decision making, small group behavior, and procedural issue areas—represent vital parts of the foundation on which this theoretical perspective attempts to build. This chapter draws upon and extends all these sources to address the questions: What are the characteristics of the primary foreign policy decision structures found in contemporary governments? What decision processes are associated with each type of structure? How do structure and process influence the nature of foreign policy?

DEVELOPMENT OF THE PERSPECTIVE

DECISION STRUCTURE

Reference already has been made to George's (1974: 179) use of small groups along with individuals and organizations as "three contexts, or subsystems, in which the task of achieving rational determination of complex policy matters may be, and frequently is pursued." C. F. Hermann and Brady (1972) also propose similar units of analysis. At first glance one might propose that these three categories—the isolated individual acting alone, small groups, and large organizations—serve as the logical set of decision structures for detecting the major variations in foreign policy decision processes. Further reflection, however, indicates that such a classification may not be a very satisfactory set of units for explaining variation in foreign policy choices in most contemporary governments. Occasionally, an ambassador pressed for a quick decision on a matter of seemingly limited consequence for his government may act by himself or a head of state—perhaps alone in bilateral talks or forced to respond to a press conference question—may decide an issue without consulting anyone. Even for small states, however, the number of nontrivial matters handled by a single individual is probably quite small. Some interpersonal discussion seems likely. Consultation can range from a systematic governmental review to the most haphazard interaction with trusted confidants or individuals who happen to be in the proximity of the individual assuming the task of decision (e.g., immediate family members, bodyguards, personal secretaries or aides, or subordinate staff members).

The burden of foreign policy decision-making is seldom undertaken by one individual completely alone.

At the other extreme, large complex organizations as a totality seldom serve as a decision unit. (The image of an American Secretary of State calling all foreign service officers into the Department of State auditorium and convening the assemblage as a decision unit does not bear correspondence to reality.) In fact, one of the major purposes of organizations is to permit a division of labor and specialization. One part of an organization or representatives from multiple organizations can address a particular problem while most of the members of that bureaucracy or set of bureaucracies attend to other matters. It is likely that in most foreign policy organizations throughout the world the structural units of choice are small groups embedded in large organizations. In the course of handling a problem, it may move from one small group to another located at a different horizontal or vertical point in the same or different governmental organizations. Occasional exceptions to organizational decision making by small groups are found in parliaments and national legislatures. But even in many of these assemblies, small groups predominate. In summary, we need a more complex typology than individual, group, and organization. A classification is required that more nearly accounts for the diversity of small groups that seem to be the prevalent type of twentieth-century foreign policy decision structure.

In constructing a typology of decision structures that attempts to represent variation in decision processes and to account for most of the units that make foreign policy choices in contemporary national governments, this theoretical perspective distinguishes structures along three dimensions. These dimensions or structural properties are physical size, power distribution, and member role. The size of the decision structure refers to the number of participants. For the purposes of the typology, we wish to distinguish between large and small groups. Following J. H. Davis (1969: 4), a human group will be defined "as a set of persons . . . among whom there exists a definable or observable set of relations." Considerable literature exists on the boundaries of a small group as, for example, has been summarized by Thomas and Fink (1963). Although the exact breakpoint between large and small units must necessarily be arbitrary, the position taken here is that a significant division point may frequently occur when the number of participants reaches between twenty and thirty individuals. More important than the precise number are changes in group choice processes that occur when (a) subgroups within the larger collective begin to dominate decision tasks, (b) individual participation begins to be sharply inhibited by group size, or (c) rules of procedure proliferate to govern group interaction. The term "group" will be the abbreviation for small group and "assembly" will be used to denote a large group.

The typology also involves the distribution of power within the decision unit. Social power or influence is another concept that has been extensively explored in decision making. (See the review in Collins and Raven, 1969). In this chapter, the distribution of power will be represented by the presence or absence of an authoritative leader. By authoritative leader we mean an individual who can commit the decision unit even against the opposition of every other member. This ability represents one extreme in the distribution of power within the decision unit. We will refer to those structures in which no individual exercises such power as having distributed power even though the power of individual members may vary substantially.

The final property, member role, refers to whether the individual participants in a decision unit have the latitude to take any position they wish or whether they represent a governmental bureau or agency whose approval they must maintain. Druckman (1976) provides a valuable review of the influence that the role of representative has on negotiations. Members who represent an outside constituency are designated "delegates" and those who do not are referred to as "autonomous" participants. Individuals who are autonomous tend either to be the highest authority in a governmental agency and, hence, may have the latitude to adopt any position they wish, or they represent only themselves. Groups frequently contain a mixture of autonomous and delegate roles. If the number of participants assuming the role of delegate approaches a simple majority, their requirements will force the group to behave similarly to one consisting exclusively of delegates. If the proportion of delegates is small enough that their needs can be largely ignored, the group will approximate one with a membership of only autonomous members. Before leaving this structural property, note that it explicitly introduces one type of influence of large organizations on smaller decision structures. If a member of a group assumes a role as the representative of an outside organization, then features of that organization (e.g., its goals and resources) may enter into the choice process.

When these three structural properties—size, power distribution, and member role—are dichotomized as described above, eight types of decision structures result as depicted in Figure 4.2. This chapter will use this system for identifying decision structures for which distinctive decision processes will be associated. In the cells of Table 4.1 names have been given to each type of decision structure. Close inspection reveals that two different types have been designated in the same cell located in the upper left corner of Table 4.1. We will begin our descriptions of the decision structures with this anomaly that results in there being a total of nine types of structures.

FIGURE 4.2

Decision structures resulting from three dichotomized properties

SIZE

	Small Group			Assembly	
	Member Role			*Member Role*	
Power Distribution	Autonomous Members	Delegates		Autonomous Members	Delegates
Leader	1. Leader-Staff Group	3. Leader-Delegate Group		8. Consultative Autonomous Assembly	9. Consultative Delegate Assembly
	2. Leader-Autonomous Group				
Distributed	4. Autonomous Group	5. Delegate Group		6. Autonomous Assembly	7. Delegate Assembly

1. **Leader-Staff Group.** This category includes those instances in which an authoritative decision maker actually acts alone or with no consultation other than a small number of subordinate personnel on his own staff. Subordinate advisors or aides are persons who are entirely dependent upon the decision maker for continuance of their present position, have no independent power base, and have no role that permits them to regularly obtain information or perspective on foreign affairs different from the decision maker they serve. Macridis (1972: 101) provides an example of leader-staff groups when he states that under President De Gaulle

> decisions [are] made by the president and his immediate advisers. . . . He negotiates directly with foreign representatives, prime ministers, and heads of state; he outlines the goals of the government—at times taking even the cabinet and the prime minister by surprise.

East (1973b: 497) has suggested that the same kind of decision-making may frequently occur in Uganda under Amin.

With respect to Table 4.1 the leader-staff category seems to be misclassified. In what sense are personal staff participants "autonomous"? The point is that they represent no one other than the principal decision maker and hence are not delegates. This decision unit is a close approximation of a decision maker acting alone as a single independent entity.

2. **Leader-Autonomous Group.** As in the previous category the decision structure includes one authoritative decision maker (the leader), but the membership also includes individuals who have some independence from the leader. He may still be able to remove them from office, but not without significant political costs. Moreover, they have a position in government or outside of it which not only gives them a political base, but also a perspective for viewing foreign affairs which is different from that of the authoritative decision maker. They may be heads of major departments of government, legislators, or political party chieftains. Each associate has the ability to take a position or offer advice without clearing it with some outside body. In short, they are not delegates. The cabinets of some European parliamentary systems may illustrate leader-autonomous groups when presided over by a strong prime minister with the other participants having ministerial posts but whose primary affiliation is as members of parliament. The leadership of the Standing Committee of the Chinese Communist Party's Politburo, at least until recently, also serves as an example. As Scalapino (1963: 560) notes, there were seven men, dominated by Mao Tse-tung, "who have long led the Party and who hold such state offices as they determine."

3. **Leader-Delegate Group.** In this type of decision structure the small group consists of an authoritative decision maker and other individuals,

most of whom are representatives of some group or bureau. By definition, delegates are spokesmen for their organization or other entity, and the advice they give the leader is not necessarily their personal view. Instead, they provide the official position of those they represent. Often, they cannot alter their advocated position without consulting with their home unit or, if they do take an independent initiative, it may adversely affect their future career in that organization. Such delegates frequently enter into participation in a decision structure with a perspective valued by the unit they represent. Their task is to protect and further that perspective. The British Defense and Overseas Policy Committee, whose membership might average fifteen, is presided over by the Prime Minister. Vital (1968: 60) relates an episode that suggests it may occasionally be a leader-delegate structure. He characterizes that Committee's examination of the question of selling arms to South Africa in late 1967 as "a classic case of interdepartmental conflict overshadowed, complicated and intensified by inter- and intra-party strife."

4. **Autonomous Group.** In the first three types of decision groups power was unequally distributed among the participants. The authoritative leader had the ability to commit the government to a course of action even if all other members opposed it. In the autonomous group no individual has that ability and power is equally distributed among the members, although there is seldom an exact equality of power and a leader in the form of a convener and moderator exists. All or most of the participants act for themselves and have the ability to change their position or compromise on an issue without consulting groups outside the decision structure. In other words, the participants either speak for no one but themselves or have sufficient authority in the organization they represent so that no consultation is required. An example of an autonomous group exists in the collective leadership of the USSR Communist Party's Presidium immediately following Stalin's death.

> The removal of Beria and the dismantling of his secret police apparatus introduced an uneasy equilibrium among the various factions in the Presidium, none of which was powerful enough to overwhelm the others. [Aspaturian, 1972: 196]

Similarly, military juntas that lack one dominate figure often take the form of autonomous decision structures.

5. **Delegate Group.** This decision structure consists of a small number of members of roughly equivalent power all or most of whom act as instructed representatives for some entity with which they are associated that exists outside the decision unit. To indicate that a participant is instructed does not mean that he cannot make minor shifts in position

or even participate in the creation of major compromises or alternative positions. They cannot, however, commit the organization they represent to such a change without seeking approval. In recent years, the United States has used Interdepartmental Groups (IGs) for conducting some foreign policy activities. These groups, which illustrate the delegate decision structure, normally are chaired by an Assistant Secretary of State and include representatives from all the other governmental agencies concerned with a given geographical area or functional problem. It is a classical coordination and decision device for complex organizations and, as such, finds many counterparts at various levels within and between bureaucracies. In the Executive Branch of the United States and many other governments that conduct much of their foreign policy through large organizations, foreign policy problems pass through a series of delegate groups at various decision stages.

6. **Autonomous Assembly.** With the introduction of this type of decision structure, we move from small groups to large ones. The number of participants is so great that they cannot have an exchange of views in which every participant can (or is willing to) express himself or herself within a reasonable period of time without an elaborate set of rules that tend to formalize debate. Also subunits begin to emerge within the assembly. In addition to the large size, autonomous assemblies are characterized by a rough equality of power among the members who have the authority to act without obtaining the approval of any outside reference group. This classic form of Greek democracy, in which all individuals represent themselves, is hard to find in an era of very large membership groups (who normally select delegates to represent them) and large hierarchically organized bureaucracies. The tribunal at the 1975 World Conference of the International Women's Year permitted any of the large number of people attending the sessions in Mexico City to participate without representing anyone but themselves. The Council of Europe offers another example in its body appropriately called the Consultative Assembly. The over 100 participants are invited to attend by the governments of member nations, but the participants "are representatives of themselves only in their speeches and votes" (Curtis, 1965: 30).

7. **Delegate Assembly.** This type of decision structure also consists of a large group of members who are approximately equal in power, although it deserves repeating that there can be substantial variations in power in such decision units as long as one individual cannot override all the others. In the delegate assembly, participants are representatives for groups outside the decision structure. As the example indicates, and as Edmund Burke elegantly asserted, in delegate assemblies those represented may not exercise much control over the positions taken by their representatives—

certainly less so than in either the leader-delegate groups or delegate groups. This increase in the delegate's decision latitude is a function of both the size of his constituency and the constituents' lack of organization into a single, coordinated body. Examples of delegate assemblies can be found in Norway among the many boards and committees, appointed by the government, that include representatives of both ministries and non-governmental interest groups; among such decision structures, two in foreign affairs are the Advisory Committee on Disarmament and Arms Control and the Norwegian Export Council; see Orvik (1972: 64-75) for details.

8. and 9. **Consultative Autonomous Assembly and Consultative Delegate Assembly.** These last two decision structures are included for completeness even though they are not very effective decision structures for foreign policy. Both are large bodies acting as a whole with a leader who has the authority to ignore the recommendations of that assembly. In effect, they are advisory or consultative mechanisms at best, and at worse they are "rubber stamp" organs designed to legitimate or publicize decisions made elsewhere. The consultative autonomous assembly consists of members who have the ability to act without formal review by some outside constituency, whereas the members of a consultative delegate assembly are responsible to some external entities whom they represent. It may be that the Chinese Friendship Associations described by Scalapino (1963: 561) as designed "to serve some of these [unofficial] aspects of Chinese diplomacy" illustrate consultative autonomous assemblies. In a number of countries, national legislatures appear to have the status of consultative delegate assemblies, at least with respect to foreign policy. For example, the Congress Party of India, which has controlled the Parliament since India's independence, "is not inclined, substantively and for good political reasons, to deny the prime minister's conclusions if a positive stand is taken and support is requested" (Park, 1972: 377). Furthermore, the Central Committee of the Communist Party of the Soviet Union as well as the Party Congress would appear to be consultative delegate assemblies.

DECISION PROCESSES AND BEHAVIORS

Given decision structures having the characteristics described above, what are the related decision processes and how do they influence behavior? In reality the three decision unit properties used in this perspective are very unlikely to be sufficient in and of themselves to determine decision processes. There are other decision structure properties, such as the permanency of the unit and its status in relation to other structures, that have not been considered. Elements other than decision structures, such as personality characteristics of the participants, also influence decision processes. We will maintain, however, that the three properties of decision structures developed above increase the probability that certain processes are likely to occur with a given structure. In this section the processes that have an increased probability of being used with each type of decision structure will be examined. Immediately after each typical process has been described, we will identify some behavioral properties that are hypothesized to be more likely given the noted decision process. It bears repeating that neither the specified decision process nor the behaviors is hypothesized as always occurring given the designated decision structure. Rather the expectation is that these processes and behaviors become more likely. We leave to the future the critical task of identifying the other elements that interact with these variables to determine a given behavior.

1.1 **Positive Reinforcement.**[4] In considering decision processes two central questions are: (a) does assessment of the appropriate action vary among the participants? (b) if participants advocate different positions, how are these differences resolved? In the leader-staff decision structure the process is strongly affected by the close association between the leader and his staff. The staff members empathize with the needs and skills of the leader and the pressures upon that person. They share much of their chief's perspective on the world and are largely dependent upon the same sources of information. Hence staff assessment of the appropriate behavior often is similar to the leader's. It is not necessary for staff to be conscious "yes men" in order for them to filter out contrary views that will add to the difficulties of their overburdened boss and to emphasize information that will please or simplify the authoritative decision maker's tasks. Therefore, staff tend to reinforce the leader's preferences for action (or what they believe are the leader's preferences) and, thus, they provide positive feedback for his or her predispositions. To the extent that they disagree with the leader, staff will attempt informal persuasion. But if the leader expresses displeasure with their arguments, they are likely to desist or to become extremely subtle and indirect in expressing their opinions—procedures that make it easy for the leader to ignore or miss them entirely.

1.2 **Quick/Nonconservative Behaviors**. The decision process just described results in quick decisions. Staff are in close physical proximity and are motivated to react promptly when the superior asks for advice. Furthermore, by confirming the leader's interpretation of the action requirements (and sharing in some limited sense the responsibility for the decision), leader-staff groups tend to encourage the leader to a less cautious, less conservative response than might have resulted if the leader did not consult with aides. The staff has reinforced the leader's view of the world and given added confidence. This procedure appears to create the conditions for what social psychologists have called the "risky-shift" (Kogan and Wallach, 1964). The process is not likely to add much diversity in perspective, information, or options beyond that already recognized by the leader.

2.1 **Advocacy.** In leader-autonomous member groups the process is likely to be somewhat analogous to a judge hearing and deciding among advocates for various points of view. Because the group members in this structure have some autonomy from the leader and because their own judgment and expertise (not that of some outside organization) are engaged, the incentive for careful argumentation is high. As with a trial lawyer, each autonomous member of the group can argue his position with strong conviction, taking care only to avoid tactics that he believes to be displeasing to the leader. The decision structure itself does not create pressure for consensus; however, the participants can alter their positions to reach agreement more readily than if they were delegates. Because the members speak for themselves, value statements and statements of preferred goals are likely to be common. Advocacy processes result in the introduction of evidence and expert assessment, but not necessarily in a balanced manner (see George, 1972: 759).

2.2 **Innovative Behavior.** The advocacy process can produce behavior that involves a reevaluation of goals and values because of the prominence of value assertions in the deliberations. This potential for reevaluation is part of a larger tendency toward innovative behavior that results from the possibilities for members' open expression of diverse perspectives and the relatively greater ability of members to shift their positions and acknowledge the merits of new ideas. The argument for and against various actions also increases the likelihood that the behavior will be couched in qualified terms and contain greater recognition of the weaknesses as well as the strengths of whatever course of action is pursued. This outcome is in sharp contrast to the positive reinforcement process that tends to push toward a less cautious, more extreme action.

3.1 **Persuasion.** When the decision structure consists of a leader-delegate group, the prominent action of most group members is to advance the preferred position of their constituency. To do this a delegate must persuade the leader that the position of his agency is in the best interest of the government. Minimally, this means protecting against undesirable decisions by the authoritative decision maker. Two tactics seem possible and both processes may be operative in a single decision structure. One means of protecting against an unwanted choice by the leader involves the formation of a coalition among all or most of the members before the leader enters into the group process. If such a coalition can be formed, the leader may be faced with only the one agreed course of action or with that option plus several "extreme" alternatives characterized so as to minimize their attractiveness. If a coalition cannot be achieved or if one or several delegates find their organization's interests not well served by the position advocated by the dominant coalition, then the dissatisfied delegates have an incentive to maximize the differences between their viewpoint and that of the others. This tactic requires the competing spokesmen to engage in exaggeration of the strengths in their own position and the weaknesses in that of their opponents. The process resembles the advocacy procedure in leader-autonomous groups, but because the participants are delegates there is less mobility for maneuver and concession. Positions tend to be rigid and the incentive for innovation is reduced. The inflexibility of viewpoints tends to be a quality of the procedure, whether or not a total coalition or a difference maximization process occurs. The possibility of distortion of information also increases. Thus, a leader will tend to find the group either united in the view that only one course of action is reasonable or sharply divided with each side magnifying the consequences of failing to adopt its position.

3.2 **Unconditional Status Quo.** If the leader is persuaded to accept the unified group position or one of the competing positions (if they emerge), then the resulting behavior is more likely to be stated in unconditional or unqualified terms. This characteristic results from having generated the alternatives in an atmosphere that discourages the acknowledgment of limitations and promotes the overstatement of merits. Because the process encourages each delegate to protect what his or her agency has, the outcome behavior is unlikely to shift dramatically from reiteration of past actions—that is, the reaffirmation of the status quo. If a consensus has been reached by the delegates on a preferred course of action different from past policies, the behavior is likely to be stated in broad, vague terms to cover disagreements that might otherwise exist.

4.1 **Group Maintenance.** The three decision processes described above share certain characteristics as a result of the dominant position of the leader in the decision structure. The next set of decision processes, however, are most likely when no one in the decision unit has the power (or elects to exercise it) to override group preferences. In the autonomous member group, for example, the responsibility for the unit's performance is more likely to be shared by the entire group. In groups that attend to a variety of problems over an extended period of time, this decision responsibility combines with the knowledge that respect from other group members will be needed for support on future issues and, as a result, concern about group welfare is more probable. Creating personal antagonisms or taking advantage of members who express a minority position reduces the attacked individual's sense of responsibility for the present decision and fosters a spirit of revenge for the future. To avoid these undesirable consequences, autonomous groups tend to adopt decision processes that foster group cohesion and avoid putting any member in the position of "loser" in the resulting decision.[5] Considerable effort is devoted to creating a consensus through discussion and appeals to maintain group cohesion. Impersonal decision rules are employed when appeals to group solidarity fail to resolve differences. Such decision rules might be "to split the difference" or to let external developments dictate the choice (i.e., "if X happens we'll follow your plan, but if Y happens we'll go with mine"). To make these decision rules appropriate it is often necessary to ignore the actual situation or to distort information about it.

4.2 **Assertive/High Commitment Behavior.** Janis (1972) has suggested that when group concurrence-seeking becomes excessive the quality of decision performance deteriorates markedly. Among the eight symptoms he mentions are group illusions of invulnerability, collective discounting of conflicting information, stereotyped views of enemy leaders as evil, and illusions of unanimity concerning judgments. Even if not all these deficiencies are manifested, problems arise when the well-being of the group is put ahead of effective problem solving. In the efforts to persuade others, information distortion can occur through discounting liabilities of the proposed response and the problem can be simplified to make it conform to the emerging group preference and the appropriateness of applying the decision rules. The simplification and stereotyping make possible zero-sum interpretations of the situation and characterization of the group's position as good while those opposing the group are viewed as bad. The result is highly assertive behavior accompanied by strong commitments—in short, an expression of the actions of a decision unit that has convinced itself of the necessity and correctness of its course of action.

5.1 **Bargaining.** In delegate groups, the participants are likely to feel cross-pressured between loyalty to the decision structure (for the same reasons as are autonomous member groups) and to the organizations they represent. Ordinarily, the primary commitment is to the constituent organization. As with the autonomous member group, the delegate group has no authoritative leader for making actual choices, so its decision processes must include group means of selecting between alternatives. Instead of appeals to group loyalty and alterations of reality, the primary process becomes incremental bargaining among group members. It is incremental because of the need of most participants to confer with their home agencies before offering or agreeing to a new position. Each delegate is likely to make concessions or revisions in fairly small steps to maintain the support of his or her constituency and to determine that other members also are making concessions. The slowness of the process increases the likelihood that new information and evidence will find their way into the deliberations. Trade-offs, logrolling, and compromises tend to be prominent means of bargaining. Because the loyalty of delegates to their organizations is likely to be greater than to the decision group, appeals to concur with the majority for the well-being of the group are unlikely to be successful on major issues about which a delegate and his or her constituent organization feel strongly.

5.2 **Slow/Compromises.** Behaviors resulting from a decision structure using the processes just described tend to emerge gradually. Quick responses to problems are unlikely, as are extreme actions or ones that involve significant reversals of existing policies. Compromise behavior that occurs when bargains can be struck often contains parts of the initial positions of several of the delegates. Not only will the composite action avoid extremes, but it may appear to be lacking a consistent logic. Specification of important qualifications or limiting conditions—necessary to obtain the agreement of some delegates and protect their agencies' interests—is likely to be evident in the behavior. On issues that cannot be resolved through bargaining, the basic result becomes either to postpone decisions or to refer the unresolved aspects of the problem to another decision structure. Instances of no action in response to some problems, therefore, increases.

6.1 **Coalition Voting.** We now turn from decision processes for groups to assemblies. The large size of these latter units increases the likelihood that all such decision structures will use formal voting as the basic decision process. Voting will be accompanied by established rules governing various aspects of the voting procedure, e.g., when a vote will be taken, what weight to assign votes, who may vote, what determines a successful vote, and so on. The particular nature of these voting rules will determine to a considerable degree what other decision processes tend to be followed. Brief comments can be made, however, about the probable effects of the other decision structure properties (e.g., power distribution and member role) on the process. In the autonomous member assembly, participants are likely to form coalitions to increase the chances of their preferred outcome being adopted. Because the members represent themselves or have considerable decision latitude from outside organizations to which they belong, the coalitions tend to be problem specific and the coalitions tend to be reconstituted after a particular issue has been resolved.

6.2 **Moderate Transitory Behaviors.** Such coalitions encourage compromises that in turn tend to increase the moderation of positions. The resulting behaviors can be expected to reflect this tendency. Because the participants in autonomous assemblies have fewer constraints on changing their positions (than do delegates) and less pressure to maintain a consistent stand from problem to problem, reversals in behavior or inconsistencies in behavior from one issue to another frequently occur.

7.1 **Bloc Voting.** The members of delegate assemblies are more likely than members of an autonomous member assembly to have clusters of relatively stable interests cutting across a variety of problems. The reason for this stability of interests is each member's affiliation with some outside entity that he or she represents. More than independent individuals, such entities are likely to have relatively inflexible commitments to a range of concerns. As a result, the coalitions formed by members of delegate assemblies tend to have more permanence than the issue-specific coalitions formed in autonomous member assemblies. The delegate assembly coalitions take on the form of more or less continuous voting blocs or parties.

7.2 **Ideological Behaviors.** The behaviors generated by such bloc voting are less subject to the changes and reversals noted previously. Furthermore, if one bloc or coalition controls the assembly, compromise together with its moderation of behavior is less likely. Regardless of whether one coalition controls a delegate assembly, the more or less permanent blocs will develop an ideology that will unify their members and characterize the behaviors they succeed in getting the assembly to adopt. By ideology is meant a series of beliefs about relevant aspects of the environment together with pertinent goals and programs of action. These goals and programs tend to change only gradually, if at all, and the behaviors designed to achieve them may also show resistance to change.

8.1 **Resolution Formation.** Neither the consultative autonomous member assembly nor the consultative delegate assembly has the power to require that the leader adopt its decisions. Therefore, their decision processes are designed to persuade the authoritative decision maker to accept their position. In summary, the consultative assemblies are advisory bodies. If the assembly is divided, the leader can use the split to indicate a lack of agreement among reasonable people and thus be freed of their influence attempt. Accordingly, the primary process of both types of assemblies is the attempt to pass unanimous (or nearly so) resolutions voted on by their entire membership. They may also direct speeches and statements supporting their position to the authoritative decision maker. Frequently these public statements will be either of a moral tone or will stipulate that their willingness to support the leader in other arenas (such as reelection to office) depends upon the acceptance of their position on the present issue. The latter tactic is more effective in consultative delegate assemblies in which the delegates' organizations have a membership that can presumably be mobilized to back up the statements concerning future support.

8.2 Unanimous Resolutions. As we have seen both consultative autonomous member and consultative delegate assemblies tend to persuade an
authoritative leader through formulating unanimous resolutions. The
effort to make resolutions unanimous is likely to give these behaviors two
other characteristics. First, they will be stated as broad generalizations or
principles without reference to details that could be sources of division.
Because the assembly as a body does not have the authority to implement
its recommendations, it need not concern itself with the details or even the
feasibility of its general resolutions. Second, unanimous resolutions will
often represent a negative position or state opposition to some specific
type of action. Thus, participants in the assembly can join in supporting
the resolution even if their opposition is based on such different positions
that they could not agree on an alternative positive action.

Summary. We have identified one type of decision process and associated
behavior for the last two decision structures—consultative autonomous
member assemblies and consultative delegate assemblies. In this entire
section, therefore, we have described a total of eight decision processes
and behaviors for the nine original types of decision structures. Table 4.1
summarizes the presentation. The thoughtful reader already will have
noticed that the paragraphs describing behaviors contained somewhat
more diverse characterizations of the expected behaviors than are captured
in the single phrase descriptions used as headings in the section and
reproduced in Table 4.1. Moreover, the behavior characteristics have not
been stated in a way that facilitates comparisons among them. Some effort
will be made to do this in the section on propositions.

OBSERVING GOVERNMENTAL STRUCTURES AND PROCESSES

As with the other perspectives in this book, the present one is designed
to establish the basis for empirical research. More specifically, the perspective in this chapter seems to invite systematic cross-national investigations
to determine if the hypothesized relationships among structure, process,
and behavior can be confirmed. It should be clear, however, that even the
most open governments seldom reveal the decision structures and the
procedures they use in dealing with particular problems. The few occasions
when such information is provided tend to involve problems of great
national importance and of an unusual nature. Even this very nonrandom
sample of reporting is limited to a few Western democracies, primarily the
United States. The problems of detecting the structures and processes used
in decision making have undoubtedly been a major obstacle to the use of
internal decision making as an explanation of foreign policy on a comparative basis.

TABLE 4.1

Decision Processes and Behavioral Tendencies Associated with Types of Decision Structures

Decision Structure		Decision Process		Behavioral Tendency	
1.0	Leader-Staff Group	1.1	Positive Reinforcement	1.2	Quick/Non-Conservative
2.0	Leader-Autonomous Group	2.1	Advocacy	2.2	Innovative
3.0	Leader-Delegate Group	3.1	Persuasion	3.2	Unconditional Status Quo
4.0	Autonomous Group	4.1	Group Maintenance	4.2	Assertive/High Commitment
5.0	Delegate Group	5.1	Bargaining	5.2	Slow/Compromises
6.0	Autonomous Assembly	6.1	Coalition Voting	6.2	Transitory Position
7.0	Delegate Assembly	7.1	Bloc Voting	7.2	Ideological Position
8.0	Consultative Autonomous Assembly	8.1	Resolution Formation	8.2	Unanimous Resolution
8.0	Consultative Delegate Assembly				

Note: Numbers refer to numbers used in the text. The first number indicates the type of decision structure (see Figure 4.2); the second number denotes a process if 1 and a behavioral tendency if 2.

$$H = \sum_{i=i}^{N} - P_i \log_2 P_i$$

Is the problem insurmountable? Three methods of studying the relationships among structure, process, and behavior in foreign policy seem possible. All have significant limitations, but when used in combination they can provide an adequate means of checking the utility of a theoretical perspective such as this one. The three methods are case studies, laboratory exercises and simulations, and what we shall call research through indirect, observable indicators. Most of our present knowledge about foreign policy decision making comes from case studies. As Paige (1968) and Russett (1970) have argued, there is a need for more good case studies, particularly ones that (a) use a common framework, (b) explore a range of nations and time periods, and (c) proceed in conjunction with aggregate techniques of analysis addressed to comparable questions. Most of our systematic knowledge about decision making in small groups comes from laboratory studies by social psychologists and sociologists, most of whom have not been particularly concerned with relating different types of group decision making to the resulting collective behavior. To date, few investigators have followed Barber's (1966) initiative in using laboratory studies to explore such linkages particularly in foreign policy, although some limited work with games and simulations (e.g., Kirk, 1974; C. F. Hermann, 1969a) has been undertaken. In addition to games and simulations, any major research strategy on decision making should include the quasi-experimental study of natural decision units rather than depend exclusively on those contrived in a laboratory setting. Natural, on-going decision-making units that are not part of a government's foreign policy machinery may be more accessible than those that are, and the former may prove to be a valuable source of evidence and insight.

In addition to these methods, research should focus on the availability of public information on governmental foreign policy that would allow one to construct a chain of inferences indicating the likely presence of certain structures and processes. The procedure is not unlike that used by the detective who builds his case from a series of clues or the historian and archeologist who reconstruct the past by fitting together documents and artifacts that allow them to infer what may have transpired. To study governmental structures and processes we must become attentive to the indirect but observable indicators associated with certain governmental procedures.

The fundamental question is: What observable and regularly reported phenomena serve as either indicators or causal conditions for various structures and processes? For this theoretical perspective, we could concentrate on indirect indicators of the three structural properties—physical size, power distribution, and member role. Two kinds of indirect indicators of these structural properties seem promising. One class of observ-

TABLE 4.2
Governmental and Situational Indicators of Selected Decision Structure Properties

Governmental Conditions (characteristics of particular national governments that may co-occur with decision structure properties)	Situational Conditions (characteristics of specific types of problems that may increase the likelihood of certain decision structure properties)
(1) *National Legislature Active in Foreign Policy* — By definition such assemblies are almost certain to be large and if they participate regularly in foreign policy, larger decision units can occasionally be expected.	(1) *Complexity of Problem* — The more complex a problem, the more likely it is to involve the skills of more people.
(2) *Style of Head of State and Foreign Ministers* — Tendencies to convene large bodies for other policy activities, and the degree of consultation with the legislature or other assembly, are indications of a style suggesting large decision structures, whereas personal diplomacy may indicate small decision structures.	(2) *Resource Allocation* — More agencies will feel they have a stake in the outcome if substantial resources are involved; agencies seeking participation will increase the unit size.
	(3) *Threat* — The more widely recognized the threat posed by a problem, the more individuals will be involved.
	(4) *Decision Time* — The longer the decision time, the more people can be involved.
	(5) *Away from Capital* — Occasions for decision that occur away from governmental offices—particularly with a short decision time—reduce the probable size of the decision unit.
(1) *Head of State with Strong Personal Interest in Foreign Affairs* — The more concerned the head of state is with foreign affairs, the	(1) *Ceremonial/Protocol Situation* — The presence of an authoritative leader may be required for symbolic reasons in such situations.

SIZE

POWER DISTRIBUTION

more likely is his or her participation (assuming the head of state is an authoritative leader).

(2) *Existence of Powerful, Independent Foreign Minister or Deputy Overseeing External Affairs* — If a minister or ranking authority charged with foreign affairs has wide-ranging authority and the confidence of the head of state, the likelihood of an authoritative leader in decision structure increases.

(3) *Number of Known Agencies Dealing Regularly with Foreign Affairs* — The frequency of interagency conflicts will likely increase as this number expands, thus creating more situations requiring resolution by the head of state or an authoritative decision maker.

(2) *Threat* — Situations that threaten national goals or a leader's continuation in office likely will involve him or her.

(3) *Nonroutine* — Unusual or surprise situations can less readily be handled by established routines; hence, an authoritative decision maker may be required.

(4) *Issue of Personal Interest* — If a problem deals with a topic of particular interest to the authoritative decision maker, he or she is more likely to be involved.

ROLE

(1) *Number of Known Agencies Dealing Regularly with Foreign Policy* — The more agencies, the greater the coordination and the more likely will delegates be needed to achieve integrative tasks.

2) *Large Number of Political Appointees* — When individuals hold office at will of an authoritative decision maker, they are more likely to be loyal to him than to represent some other organization.

(3) *Level of Governmental Participants* — Higher level officials participating in a decision structure are more likely than lower officials to represent themselves.

(1) *Threat* — The greater the threat, the more likely it is that high level officials who represent themselves will participate.

(2) *Decision Time* — The shorter the decision time, the less opportunity there is for obtaining clearances and, therefore, the less likely it is that delegates will be used.

(3) *Complexity of Problem* — As complexity increases, multiple agencies are likely to be involved, requiring coordination that can initially be assigned to delegates.

able indicators concerns the general operations of a government and, thus, varies from country to country. The other indicators tap particular problem situations that make certain structures and processes more likely in specific kinds of situations. Table 4.2 lists both governmental and situational variables that might be used to infer each of the three structural properties. This list is by no means exhaustive. The requirements for such variables are (a) that they be capable of reliable estimation for governments or situations of virtually all contemporary nations and (b) that they be highly correlated with a relevant decision structure or process. Assuming that procedural issue areas (as discussed in the section on previous studies) meet these criteria and can be identified independently of the resulting governmental behavior, they could be very promising indirect indicators of decision structure and process.

We have devoted more attention to the problem of operationalizing structure and process than will be done for the other perspectives in this book for an important reason. For this theoretical perspective, one of the major issues is whether or not we can accurately ascertain for most governments what structures and processes were actually used in their foreign policy decisions. In addition to case studies and experimental work, we have proposed that the nature of these variables might be inferred from the presence of other observable indicators.

SELECTED ASSUMPTIONS

Many of the assumptions upon which this theoretical perspective rests already have been advanced. As a means of summarizing the essential aspects of the presentation to this point, and to prepare the way for the propositions in the next section, we will enumerate some of the necessary conditions. It should be emphasized that although these statements are necessary for this perspective, we do not claim that they are a sufficient set from which all the propositions could be derived.

ASSUMPTION 4.1: *All contemporary national governments face a more or less continuous stream of foreign policy problems that are frequently characterized by uncertainty and complexity.*

ASSUMPTION 4.2: *A number of these foreign policy problems, if inappropriately handled, could lead to deprivation for those who dealt with them, the entire government, and/or other people within and outside the acting nation; conversely, if properly handled, the results promote values desired by all or some of the same individuals and groups.*

ASSUMPTION 4.3: *Although some government officials have the authority to decide upon certain responses by themselves, uncertainty, complexity, and decision consequences normally lead them to create and use decision structures involving other people to facilitate a response.*

ASSUMPTION 4.4: *When multiple people are introduced as participants in a decision structure dealing with complex problems under conditions of uncertainty, the possibility of different interpretations of the situation and alternative assessments of the appropriate response increases.*

ASSUMPTION 4.5: *The choice of decision structure is not uniform but can vary with a number of factors, including preferences of the governmental leadership, regime, governmental and national traditions, and types of situations faced by the government.*

ASSUMPTION 4.6: *Variations in decision structure strongly influence the processes used by participants, including those affecting (a) the recognition and expression of different perspectives on the problem, (b) the nature and forcefulness with which alternatives are expressed, and (c) the means of choosing among any proposed alternatives.*

ASSUMPTION 4.7: *Size of the decision unit, distribution of power, and role of group members are among properties found in all decision structures that strongly increase the probability that certain processes are more likely to be used than others.*

ASSUMPTION 4.8: *Variations in the decision processes used by decision units influence the foreign policy behaviors that are selected.*

Several observations about these assumptions are in order. First, the particular decision processes (i.e., persuasion, positive reinforcement, bargaining, and so on) that result from various combinations of the three structural characteristics are treated as assumptions. However, they can be treated as testable hypotheses. Although we have not listed the assumed relationship between each combination of structural properties and a given process, the reader should include them for a more comprehensive enumeration. Second, the relationship between certain decision processes and foreign policy behaviors have not been included in the list of assumptions because these are the empirically testable hypotheses that the theoretical perspective seeks to explore and that will be illustrated in the next section.[6]

ILLUSTRATIVE PROPOSITIONS

PROPOSITION 4.1

Leader-staff groups using positive reinforcement will tend to require less time for decision than will the other decision structures, whereas autonomous member assemblies using coalition voting and delegate groups using bargaining will tend to require the most time.

In responding to foreign policy problems, the time needed to make a response can be a crucial factor because delay occasionally can result in the deterioration of the situation through the actions of external forces. In other cases, allowing time for the situation to unfold may be beneficial to the government faced with a problem. When quick responses are required, however, a positive reinforcement process is likely to be the fastest, primarily because of the absence of strong challenges to the leader's views on the appropriate action and the normally easy accessibility of personal staff members for consultation. At the other extreme, delegate groups must engage in incremental bargaining in which one member after another makes modest concessions until either an agreement or an impasse is reached. Similarly, autonomous member assemblies are slow—particularly if the problem faced is new—because coalitions have to be formed and reformed until a winning coalition in terms of voting strength emerges. It bears repeating that we have been concentrating throughout the chapter on the choice stage of decision making and, therefore, the total amount of time depends not only on the process used in this phase of the decision but in all the other stages as well.

PROPOSITION 4.2

Leader-staff groups using positive reinforcement and autonomous member groups using group maintenance processes tend to produce more high commitment behaviors than do the other decision structures, whereas delegate groups using bargaining and autonomous member assemblies using coalition voting tend to engage in more low commitment behaviors than do the other decision structures.

Commitment involves binding the future of a government and its country to a course of action that usually associates it in some way with other entities. As such, commitment behaviors represent some of the most revealing acts of governments because they usually, but not always, involve the present or future use of resources and establish the areas in international affairs where the values are most vital to the nation. A number of the decision structure and process combinations occasionally produce behaviors involving high commitment. Leader-staff groups and autonomous member groups are hypothesized to initiate more high commitment behaviors than do others because they employ processes that dampen the collection of information and the expression of views that would tend to argue against strong commitments. The positive reinforcement process frequently found in leader-staff decision structures not only inhibits such challenges, but by providing positive feedback to the leader may increase that individual's confidence in the correctness of his or her judgment so that the commitment may be greater than if the leader acted entirely alone and consulted no one. Autonomous member groups that tend to treat group well-being as the primary value not only deal harshly with competing information that would tend to question their intended choice and reduce their commitment, but they also tend to reinforce one another as to the correctness of the proposed action, thus moving the decision toward less cautious behavior as in leader-staff groups.

At the other extreme, the internal negotiating that figures prominently in the processes of both delegate groups and autonomous member assemblies often serves as a brake on strong commitments even when many observers might regard such behavior as appropriate. If one organization represented by a delegate insists on avoiding such binding action, the delegate's group's eventual choice must take that position into account to some degree or lose the support of the delegate's organization. Similarly, to build a winning coalition among the independent individuals in an autonomous member assembly, concessions frequently have to be made to the needed members wanting lesser commitment.

PROPOSITION 4.3

Leader-autonomous member groups using advocacy processes will tend more frequently to select behaviors involving change from the government's previous position than the other decision structures, whereas delegate groups using persuasion and delegate assemblies using bloc voting will tend to select behaviors involving change less frequently than will other decision structures.

Change or innovative behavior and continuity or status quo behavior have frequently been viewed as significant characteristics of a government's foreign policy (see Waltz, 1967). A government that continuously alters its foreign actions can be a source of difficulty for those that must deal with it. Such a government may gain a reputation for inconsistency and poor reliability. At the other extreme, a government that fails to change in response to a changing environment or a failing policy also can reap disaster. The advocacy process in leader-autonomous member groups encourages the introduction of new ideas and their evaluation. Furthermore, the involvement of an authoritative leader provides the capability to set aside or revise previous government positions if they are no longer judged to be appropriate. Both delegate decision structures—which involve representatives of organizations that exist outside the unit making the choice—discourage change by their processes. Most organizations that delegates represent are likely, as a minimal strategy, to be interested in preserving the programs and arrangements that they currently have. Collectively their representatives will find it difficult in time, effort, and creativity to find a new option from which everyone benefits; hence, a bias against change develops in the process. In the delegate assembly the bloc voting process leads to the formation of ideological positions. To change the ideology endangers breaking up the coalition or party; thus, this process also tends to retard changes in behavior.

PROPOSITION 4.4

Autonomous member groups using group maintenance and consultative assemblies (both delegate and autonomous member) using resolution formation will tend to express stronger affect in their behaviors than will appear in the behaviors of other decision structures, whereas delegate groups using bargaining and autonomous member assemblies using coalition voting will tend to express more moderate or neutral affect in their behavior than will the other decision structures.

Affect is the expression of support or hostility toward some entity and is an indicator of the pleasure or displeasure that a government has toward certain objects or their activities. As such it marks the areas in foreign policy where conflicts arise. Sometimes a government's expression of affect in words and deeds is muted and tends to be neutral. At other times, it is intense and reveals strong friendship or hostility. As was noted earlier, both types of consultative assemblies not only tend toward expressions of affect, but also specifically tend toward negative affect. The unanimity necessary for such advisory bodies to adopt resolutions having some force is more readily achieved with a general statement of opposition than with a specific affirmative proposal. Autonomous member groups can generate behaviors having either strong negative or positive affect. The intensity results from the stereotyped evaluation of objects as either good or bad (supportive or opposed). Strong affect also is promoted by the tendency to screen out information that might qualify the group position and its judgment of others, thereby threatening group cohesion. As has been mentioned previously, both delegate groups and autonomous member assemblies must negotiate among the participants in order to reach a consensus concerning the appropriate decision. Assuming that any group involving delegates involves some diversity of interests, then for every representative who advocates strong condemnation or praise of an entity, there is likely to be another representative whose agency sees reasons for caution or moderation toward that entity. Of course, this balancing of interests will not occur all the time, but it is more likely in structures involving delegates or large numbers of autonomous members. In autonomous member assemblies, even though the participants are not delegates the large number increases the likelihood of diverse interests that must be considered because some needed individuals cannot be persuaded to change their views. Furthermore, because there is no authoritative leader in either decision structure, there is a tendency to compromise on a behavior that is bland or moderate with respect to affect.

PROPOSITION 4.5

Leader-autonomous member groups using advocacy tend to initiate behaviors having greater specificity than other decision structures, whereas delegate groups using bargaining and consultative delegate assemblies or consultative autonomous member assemblies using resolution formation processes tend to initiate behaviors having less specificity than other decision structures.

The specificity of an actor's behavior provides a means of influencing the degree of uncertainty experienced by the recipients of the behavior. Of course, the amount of uncertainty that a behavior creates for a recipient results from a number of sources, but that portion which the initiator of the behavior can control is specificity. The degree of specificity is the amount of information—particularly about the actor's intent and expectations—that is contained in the action. A behavior having low specificity can be called ambiguous. It leaves the recipient uncertain as to exactly what was done, why, and what is expected in return. Leader-autonomous member groups tend toward more specific behaviors for several reasons. Advocacy introduces more information into the deliberative process than normally occurs in some other procedures. Moreover, it can be evaluated somewhat more dispassionately. Thus, the capability for specificity is higher. Furthermore, the existence of an authoritative leader means that a choice can be made without introducing ambiguity to cover over points where disagreement might exist. It is exactly this latter problem that confronts both delegate groups and consultative assemblies. They tend to employ processes for choice in which the absence of specificity and the use of broad generalizations are means for building the necessary consensus.

SUMMARY

In 1965, Robinson and Snyder (1965: 456) concluded an essay as follows:

The main purpose of inquiries about decision making processes is to determine whether and how decision processes affect the content of decision outcomes. Does the process of making a decision make any difference for the substance of the decision? Do different kinds of processes reach different results?

This theoretical perspective has suggested one way in which an affirmative answer might be given to these inquiries. More recently the authors of a review of problem-solving groups (Hackman and Morris, 1975: 46) noted a puzzle with respect to the structure of such groups. At one extreme, for example, group members may work together so badly that members do not share with one another uniquely held information that is critical to the problem at hand; in this case, the quality of the group outcome surely will suffer. On the other hand, group members may operate in great harmony, with the comments of one member prompting quick and sometimes innovative responses in another, which then leads a third to see a synthesis between the ideas of the first two, and so on; in this case, a genuinely creative outcome may result.

The proposed theoretical perspective suggests that such differences may be due in part to variations in decision structures (i.e., physical size, power distribution, member role), which in turn influence decision processes in such a way as to affect behavior. We have concentrated on one phase of the decision process—the selection or choice of a course of action (or inaction). Detecting the presence of one of the nine proposed types of decision structures and determining if the hypothesized processes and behaviors result will be difficult, particularly on a cross-national basis, but we have argued that it is possible.

One issue that this chapter has not fully addressed is the relative quality of decision unit performance. Simply put, which combination of structure and process will produce the "best" results? Overall assessment of performance quality is indeed a task that can be approached through this perspective. However, such a judgment seems unwarranted based on the limited speculation undertaken in this chapter. Before one can begin to draw such conclusions several lines of development must be pursued. These include empirical investigation, examination of the other stages of the decision process together with the manner in which they may influence the structures and processes in the choice stage, and finally, examination of the possible impact of variables from other theoretical perspectives. It is to the latter task that the other chapters in this volume can contribute.

NOTES

1. The general paradigm identified here also has been used in the study of small, problem-solving groups. According to Hackman and Morris (1975: 50) in their review of this literature, "the fundamental assumption underlying the paradigm . . . is that input factors affect performance outcomes through the interaction process." Group structure is explicitly identified in the review as one type of input factor.

2. A fuller discussion of the suggested stages of the decision process appears in C. F. Hermann (1971). A more elaborate conceptualization of the phases of the decision process appears in Lasswell (1963).

3. In concentrating on the smaller decision structures frequently involved in the choice stage of decision-making, it is important to recognize that the larger organization remains an influence on the decision in several ways. First, the organizational variables may impinge upon the small group in ways that significantly affect the group's behavior. Certainly, studies of bureaucratic politics are emphasizing the impact of organizational factors on those individuals making the choice when they call attention to the influence of organizational membership and loyalty on a person's policy position—or, as Halperin (1974: 17) suggests, "where an individual sits in the process determines... the stand that he takes." Second, the large organization in its entirety may be more dominant in other stages of a decision. For example, to explain the effectiveness of the implementation stage of a decision involving a large military action, one might need to examine the command, control, and other capabilities of the entire military organization. Finally, organizational variables may be necessary to account for the effects of the movement of a problem in some governments through a succession of smaller groups. Even in the choice phase, some problems in governments like that of the United States are transferred sequentially among several decision groups. A problem moves up through the organizational hierarchy for validation of the choice made by lower groups or for resolution of their disputes; it moves laterally among decision groups in the organization for consultation and coordination. For illustrations in the U.S. Department of State, see Pruitt (1964-1965: 31ff).

4. The two-digit numbers preceding these paragraphs relate the different types of decision processes and behaviors to the appropriate decision structures. The first digit denotes the type of decision structure (see Table 4.1). The second digit indicates whether the paragraph discusses processes or behaviors. Processes are denoted by a 1 and behaviors by a 2.

5. Initially, a group member who fails to adopt an emerging group position will be the focus of much attention and communication. However, if an individual persistently refuses to go along with the group across a series of issues, then others in the group will tend to reduce their communication and isolate that member if he or she cannot be expelled from the group completely (see Schachter, 1951).

6. None of the mentioned assumptions deals with the methodology for exploring the effects of structure and process empirically. Any methodology involves its own set of assumptions, including the indirect indicator system advocated in this chapter. One basic assumption concerning that procedure might be stated as follows: Given the presence of an observable indicator of selected qualities of situations, governmental organizations, or procedural issue areas that are known to generally co-occur with selected properties of decision structures or processes, one can infer the presence of the unobserved decision structure or process from the indicators with which it is associated.

5

POLITICAL REGIMES AND FOREIGN POLICY

Barbara G. Salmore and Stephen A. Salmore

In this chapter, we argue that the internal political structure of a country is a major determinant of its foreign policy. The specific aspect of internal politics on which we will concentrate is the structure and environment of the regime. Regime is defined as that role or set or roles in a national political system in which inheres the power to make authoritative policy decisions.[1]

In examining the role that regime structure plays in influencing foreign policy, we adopt a model of rational decision making. We argue that a regime's primary goal is to maximize its political support and, hence, power. Regime members advocate policies in order to attract and retain support. The leaders of nations opt for war or peace, trade relations, détente, and other actions not so much because of their intrinsic worth, but largely in terms of how they will affect the regime's political fortunes.

OVERVIEW OF THE PERSPECTIVE

The instruments of foreign policy are probably concentrated more exclusively in the hands of the executive than are those of any other

AUTHORS' NOTE: We wish to thank the other contributors to this volume and the members of the Rutgers foreign policy seminar (Fred Butler, Leonard Champney, David Rosen, Scott Taylor, and Naomi Wish) for their many useful comments on this chapter.

policy domain. It has often been observed that the importance of foreign policy to the national defense and basic sovereignty of the state makes it a process where it is desirable for the nation to speak with one voice. Thus, given the relative independence of the regime in the domain of foreign policy, the tendency to use this domain for the expansion and consolidation of support is very strong.

It is clear, however, that some limits operate on all regimes as they determine and implement foreign policy decisions. The nature of these limits varies with the type of regime and the larger environment in which it is set. Regimes are limited both by their own internal structure and by the general system of domestic politics within which they operate. Three broad sets of variables may be identified that will affect the foreign policy outputs of regimes. These are the amount of political resources that the regime has at its disposal for implementing foreign policy, limits on such resources imposed by political constraints, and the regime's disposition to use the resources that are at its disposal.

The political resources available to a regime are conditioned by the syndrome of factors that Huntington (1968) has called institutionalization and scope of government. A regime that is well established, autonomous from other sectors of society, and in control of the disposition of many societal resources will be freer to act and will have a larger number of policy options than will a regime that does not have these characteristics. Another more diffuse, but no less real, resource is the extent to which the regime enjoys general societal support. Public opinion, willingness to sacrifice, and other sorts of indications of generalized support for the regime and acceptance of its legitimacy are all important in determining a regime's freedom of action.

Regardless of the resources that a regime possesses, there are other factors that may constrain governmental action. One set of such constraints that limits the use of resources has to do with the unity or fragmentation of the regime, both internally and within the larger environment in which it is set. If the actors who comprise the regime—that is, those who make authoritative policy decisions—are in general accord and exercise clear lines of authority, the regime will be less constrained than where this is not the case. For example, a unified one-party regime will be freer to act than will a coalition; a unified military junta will be less constrained than one rent by interservice rivalries or significant policy disagreements. Such factors relate to internal regime coherence or fragmentation. Beyond these internal constraints is another set of factors tapping the degree of support external to the regime itself. Regimes differ in their degree of accountability to wider publics—an accountability that may be measured by the levels of participation and public contestation present in the polity and by the general rules of the political game. Participation and contestation result in different levels and kinds of accountability both to members of the government outside the regime, such as legislators and bureaucrats, and to the wider public. Another element of interest is the representativeness of support for the regime by identifiably different publics and their degree of inclusion in the regime. In a society that is highly fragmented, the nature of the support base among such publics may be crucial in determining a regime's freedom to act.

In addition to the amount of political resources and fragmentation of political support that are present, a third broad class of variables deals with the disposition of the regime to exert its power or to use the resources at its disposal. Such a set of factors may be called leadership orientation. It infuses all political behavior of a regime, in both domestic and foreign arenas. Two regimes may have similar resources at their disposal and similar kinds of constraints, but they may have different dispositions to use those resources. The intensity and direction of such a disposition may be conditioned by such factors as ideological predispositions, socialization experiences, or other characteristics of the regime leaders. Thus, in pursuing the goals of survival and success, the alternatives for action that are open to the regime are conditioned by the political realities both within the regime and within the political system of which it is a subset.

Looking at foreign policy outputs from the perspective of the regime is of course only one way to approach the explanation of the external behavior of nations. Other approaches that also focus on internal characteristics of nations—such as the effect of national attributes, leadership personality, and bureaucratic structure—are closely related to a regime perspective. For example, actions attributable to variations in leadership personality and decision structures and processes may be significantly affected by the nature of the regime in which individuals find themselves operating. Similarly, certain national attributes (slow-changing features of the society) may significantly affect both the amount of physical resources available to the regime and the scope of government. The shape of the international system may also be thought of as a less proximate type of constraint on the behavior of regimes. Furthermore, a situational perspective can specify those conditions under which regime differences will be most salient.

RELATION TO PREVIOUS STUDIES

As we will demonstrate in this section, much research on foreign policy and international relations discounts or ignores the impact of regime differences on external behavior.

Many discussions of national attributes and foregin policy concentrate less on explicitly political factors than they do on other internal attributes such as size, economic development, power, capabilities, and the like (e.g., Morgenthau, 1967; Wilkinson, 1969). In addition, writers have studied, with varying degrees of comprehensiveness, the effects of internal political arrangements on external behavior. A recent survey of this literature concluded: "The conventional wisdom of academic interpretation, it would be fair to say, remains that foreign policy is an elite process, dominated by the executive" (W. Wallace, 1971: 40). That is to say, it is argued that in the arena of foreign policy as opposed to domestic policy executive decision makers act more freely, respond less to other political institutions and mass publics, and suffer fewer consequences as a result of unsuccessful or "wrong" decisions.

In the opinion of many, this executive dominance of foreign policy is present regardless of variations in other internal factors such as the accountability of the particular regime to the mass public or the internal coherence of the regime. Epstein (1964: 93) writes of British policy during the Suez crisis, for example, that "it is plain that the Suez commitment was an executive decision made without the prior approval, formal or informal, of Parliament. It may even have been a personal decision of Eden rather than the cabinet as a whole." Scalapino (1967: 300) observes that the ruling Japanese party is "well aware of the fact that elections are not won primarily on the basis of issues, particularly issues of foreign policy." Frankel (1963: 20) summarizes this viewpoint by arguing: "Even in well-established democracies the idea of open politics (where appeal is open to representative assemblies and in the last resort to the electorate) does not fully govern foreign policy."

If this argument is advanced in terms of open regimes, it is made even more forcibly in the case of closed ones. Klein (1962: 121) asserts that foreign policy in China "rests with the inner core of the Politburo," and that the Chinese foreign ministry and Party Congress are completely subservient to party dictates on the highest level. Aspaturian (1972: 191) states flatly that institutions in the USSR "have been subordinated to relatively permanent personalities, the institutional aspects of the decision-making process are little more than ceremonial. Decision making is essentially personal."

How did this situation of executive dominance come about even in the most open systems? In general, two arguments are advanced. The first is that mass publics generally show less interest in, and knowledge of, foreign affairs than domestic problems, and that public opinion intervenes only rarely, usually in a "negative" way. Many students of democratic politics and foreign policy have been concerned about the presumed effect of public opinion. For example, de Tocqueville (1944: 234-235) wrote that "a democracy can only with great difficulty regulate the details of an important undertaking, persevere in a fixed design and work out its execution in spite of serious obstacles. It cannot combine its measures with secrecy or await their consequences with patience." Similarly, Lippmann (1965: 20) has argued that mass opinion

> compelled the governments which usually knew what would have been wiser or was necessary or more expedient to be too late with too little, or too long with too much, too pacifist in peace and too bellicose in war; too neutralist or appeasing in negotiation or too intransigent. Mass Opinion . . . has shown itself to be a dangerous master of decision when the stakes are life and death.

Later, more empirical studies of the effect of public opinion on foreign policy in open systems have to some extent supported these arguments. Their determination is that foreign affairs, in periods of noncrisis, are not the issues that move mass publics, except perhaps when a costly policy fails to bring the desired results after a long period of time (Rosenau, 1964: 36). However, it appears that although foreign policy issues may eventually breach the public consciousness, even widely held negative views have little effect on governmental conduct. For example, writing of the domestic upheaval in the United States over the Vietnam war in the mid-sixties, Waltz (1967: 291) asserted: "Obviously President Johnson has been keenly aware of the domestic political risks he was running. To have changed policies because of electoral fears would not have been honorable." Similarly, consistently negative public opinion polls in Britain did not deter the Conservative Party from pushing ahead with plans for entry into the Common Market, nor did they deter the West German negotiations on *Ostpolitik*. When the American, British, and German mass publics had some opportunity, through national or subnational elections, to pronounce judgment on these decisions, in no case was their electoral punishment very decisive. Judgments on other issues such as race relations and the economy were probably equally or more important.

The second argument for executive dominance of foreign policy deals not with the effect of mass publics, but rather with the strategy of organized opposition within the governing institutions of the system. W. Wallace (1971: 10), among many others, observes:

> In almost all democratic governments there is a widely-held belief that foreign policy ought to be insulated from the rough and tumble of domestic debate, that bipartisan politics should be sought by both government and opposition, that politics should stop at the water's edge; that continuity in foreign policy, wherever possible, should be ensured even when governments change.

Added to these rather idealistic reasons, it is argued that foreign policy issues are not the ones on which political power is gained or lost. Waltz (1967: 287) writes of the United States: "Numerous surveys have indicated that both parties are looked upon as competent to manage foreign policy. . . . International affairs have gone badly when Presidents of both parties were in power. Neither party has suffered any very deep political damage as a result." Vital (1968: 72) offers a British perspective:

> The first business of a government is to ensure its own survival. Except where a government is subject to subversion by a foreign power, the political survival of the group or party in power is almost exclusively dependent upon internal factors.

> The fact is that there can be little doubt that foreign affairs play only a very limited role in British domestic politics—these being conceived as the organized quest for formal power and the conflicts that are consequent upon it.

If these observations are in fact the case, one may well argue that organized opposition, or even the "outs" who are nominal members of the governing coalition, will make a stand for control on issues other than foreign policy. The picture that thus emerges is of quite firm executive control, with little influence on foreign policy by variations in the internal political structure. The result of this stance is to encourage foreign policy research into those domestic factors that are either internal to the executive branch, such as patterns of bureaucratic decision making or leadership personality, or internal to the national political system but external to the government, such as power capabilities.[2]

We are convinced that the exclusion of regime factors from the study of foreign policy is unwise. It may well be that domestic considerations loom larger when a democratic electorate goes to the polls or when the groups that support a less accountable regime assess whether or not their interests have been served. But there seems to be evidence that foreign policy is perceived both by governing regimes and by their internal support groups as part of the activity upon which their staying in power is judged and that internal differences in regimes affect the type of foreign policy that is pursued. This evidence should be considered.

Part of the difficulty in studying this problem is a tendency in the literature to confound the ideas of *system* and *regime*. In referring to the national political *system*, what is generally meant is a pattern of interaction that extends far beyond the roles and role occupants that comprise the regime. Types of political culture, the kind and scope of demand and support groups, and many other components comprise the political system. The regime, or authoritative political leadership, is obviously a subset of the political system. Many writers who have pursued the question of the relationship between internal political variables and external acts have conceptualized the internal variables as systemic rather than regime-based. For example, Rummel (1963) and Tanter (1966) sought to examine the possible connection between levels of internal and external conflict. Conceptually, this linkage involves the responses of regimes to discontent on the part of mass publics, but Rummel and Tanter make no attempt in their studies to distinguish the responses of different types of regimes to internal conflict. They find no relationship between the two types of conflict, whereas Wilkenfeld (1968, 1969), who divides nations into what might be termed regime types, investigates the same question and does find that internal conflict can predict external conflict behavior for *certain types of regimes.* Some evidence of this can also be found in Burrowes and Spector's (1973: 316n) longitudinal study of internal and external conflict in Syria.

Also confounding regime and system, Rosenau (1970: 1-2) writes of "the interdependence of national and international life" and defines adaptation as: "Any external behavior undertaken by the *government* of any national society . . . when it copes with, or stimulates, changes in the external environment that contribute to keeping its *essential structures* within acceptable limits." Thus, Rosenau does not appear to view foreign policy activities as behaviors that serve to keep a *regime* in power, but rather as behaviors that serve to keep an entire society, or political system, from collapsing into its environment—a concept related to systems-oriented functionalist writers such as Levy and Almond. Indeed, Rosenau (1970: 22) states that "from an adaptive perspective the form of the policy-making process is not regarded as an essential dimension of the political structure," which he defines as one of four essential structures. It is clear, therefore, that much of the research into the effect of internal political factors on external behavior relates more closely to the national political system in general than to the regime in particular. By far the greatest amount of research deals with the shape and impact of public opinion on democratic policy making. Mass public opinion, however, affects regime structure only at long intervals and rarely offers a clear mandate for a particular policy. It is much less relevant for that considerable number of nations that have regimes only marginally (or not at all) affected by public opinion.

Another area that is fairly well researched deals with what are often called "democratic" and "totalitarian," or "open" and "closed," systems. These terms are usually vaguely defined, and many different types of regimes seem to fall under one rubric. For example, one might regard both a one-party mobilization regime and a narrowly based semifeudal one as "closed," although there are obviously important differences between them. Similarly, an unstable multiparty coalition and a "dominant one-party system" could both be considered "democratic" if both nations have electoral competition. These are the sorts of questions to which we will address ourselves in the next section. However, accepting the "open-closed" categorization for the moment, a review of the literature reveals that hypotheses about such systems tend to revolve around their effect on two issues: the adaptability of foreign policy in such nations and its stability or continuity (see, e.g., Brady, 1971; Butler and Taylor, 1975). Tests of these hypotheses, to the limited extent that they exist, are generally only by example and are rarely cross-national. Further, the hypotheses are often contradictory. One multinational and empirical test (Brady, 1971) of the presumed effect of accountability on stability of policy finds no significant differences. On the basis of the data presently available, one may conclude with the Sprouts (1962: 212): "There remains a hard core of disagreement as to what forms of government are best, or least, adapted to cope with the ever more complicated problems which confront government everywhere these days."

DEVELOPMENT OF THE PERSPECTIVE

Examination of the literature convinces us that a more careful delineation of the regime factors that influence foreign policy is essential. To restate the basic definitional stance, regime is that set of roles in which inheres the power to make authoritative policy decisions. A regime change occurs when the role incumbents change—or when the roles themselves change even when role incumbents do not. This latter case is unusual, but can occur, as in the case of the transition from the Fourth to the Fifth Republic in France. Differences in regimes among nations and changes in regimes within nations are hypothesized to be important in explaining patterns of foreign policy outputs. Further, changes in the internal structure of the regime, such as shifts in support, can notably affect foreign policy. It would therefore follow that policy is most likely to be stable and unchanging when there is no change in regime, other things being equal. Change in foreign policy is directly related to the amount of change involved in the coming to power of a new regime. If a new regime consists of the same support groups as the one it follows, and perhaps even some of the same personnel, change is likely to be small. The less the old and new regimes have in common, the more likely there is to be change in policy. *Ceteris paribus*, the more similar two regimes in different states are, the more similar their foreign policy. A further development of the discussion of the constraints on regimes begun in the first section should serve to clarify the argument. Regime constraints result from (1) differences in available resources, (2) limits on resource use, and (3) the disposition to use resources.

RESOURCE AVAILABILITY

Differences in available resources result from the scope of societal activity under the control of the regime, its degree of political institutionalization, and its level of public support or acceptance. Scope of societal activity refers to the extent to which a regime can control societal resources that may be relevant to the conduct of foreign policy. These include areas such as control over natural resources, public opinion, manpower, the size and direction of industrial output, and other facets of the economy. Regimes with wide governmental scope will be freer to act and to take actions involving high levels of commitment because they have the resources to do so. It is important to distinguish between the size of the resource base and the regime's ability to manipulate such resources. A regime operating with a relatively small resource base that it controls absolutely will have more freedom of action than a regime in a resource-rich society that cannot as easily command the deployment of such resources.

Similarly, high levels of political institutionalization give a regime freedom of action. A political regime that is highly institutionalized—that is, autonomous from other centers of power in society, operating within the context of a complex and efficacious bureaucracy, and having structural arrangements and decision-making processes that are well established—is in a better position to act than one that does not enjoy these advantages.

Finally, the resources a regime is free to utilize may well depend ultimately upon the level of societal support it is able to engender. High levels of governmental scope and political institutionalization must be accompanied by such support if the regime is to have real freedom of action. A complex bureaucracy can mire decisions in red tape if it wishes. Production managers can falsify quotas. Mass publics whose quiescence stems more from coercion or apathy than genuine approbation of the regime can easily find ways to do less than is required of them. In short, the extent to which a regime is genuinely free to act may have in the end much to do with levels of public trust and support.

POLITICAL CONSTRAINTS

Once it is determined what sorts of resources are at the disposal of the regime, it is important to know the possible political constraints that may be placed on the use of these resources. Three such constraints appear to be critical: the degree of coherence or unity within the regime itself and between the regime and other governmental institutions, the nature and extent of regime accountability, and the degree to which the regime represents the wider society.

Any given regime may have few or many internal constraints—that is, restraints on leadership action coming from within the regime itself. A ruling group consisting of a cabinet in a parliamentary system, where one party is strong enough to form the entire government, is less internally constrained than a coalition government, in which debates that could cause the government to fall apart are avoided in an effort to stay in power. Military governments or regimes of one party in a one-party state may or may not be split by doctrinal or other differences. The extent to which a regime is constrained by these kinds of fragmentation or disunity is important in determining limits on its ability to use available resources.

Another type of constraint, that of accountability, is external to the regime itself but internal to the larger domestic political process. Accountability refers to the political "rules of the game," especially those relating to the de facto and de jure procedures for implementing policy and attaining and retaining political office. Rules of the game have at least three dimensions: the extent of political contestation, the extent of political participation, and the methods of affirming or replacing the political leadership or regime. Regime members who operate in an atmosphere where significant political competition is present are constrained in a variety of ways that need not trouble those operating where public contestation is absent. Contestation means that regime members can stand or fall as a result of legislative votes or electoral results, and foreign policy actions must be taken with these facts in mind. Indeed, approval of bodies external to the regime may be needed before some actions are taken. The scope of political participation will also affect a regime's freedom of action. The narrower the participation base, the fewer number of interests a regime must serve, and the greater is its freedom of action. The last accountability variable, which deals with the affirmation or replacement of regime members, is to some extent related to participation and contestation. The hereditary monarch who could count on lifelong tenure in office had few worries that policy actions would end his career. A president and cabinet at the beginning of a fixed term may act with the knowledge that only the most egregious or unsuccessful decisions will remain long in the public mind. Somewhat more vulnerable is the parliamentary-based regime that may be subject to special elections or votes of confidence; also more vulnerable may be the leaders of a factionalized majority party or unstable military juntas without long accepted and formalized leadership selection procedures.

Finally, under certain conditions, the extent to which a regime represents diverse societal interests may serve as a constraint on its behavior. In a polity that is relatively homogeneous—ethnically, religiously, ideologically, and so on—this question of representativeness may not arise. However, when there are powerful single or plural groups with strong interests, these interests may inhibit freedom of action. A single powerful group may force a regime to espouse or eliminate a number of theoretically possible policy options. At the other extreme, diverse groups with opposing interests can entirely paralyze policy making.

DISPOSITION TO USE RESOURCES

We have already observed that regimes differ as to the extent of resources they can deploy and the possible objective constraints on their deployment. A final set of variables that is related to the foreign policy actions of leaders deals with their disposition to actually use such resources. Such a disposition is generally part of a policy stance or style of leadership that can have domestic as well as external ramifications. Two dimensions comprise this policy stance: rule change orientation and resource change orientation.

Rule change orientation deals with the extent to which a regime is willing to change the political rules of the game in order to achieve power and to implement policy. *Minimalist* regimes are those that sought office according to the prevailing norms and that seek to implement policy according to the prevailing norms. They are defenders of the political status quo. *Moderate* regimes are those that sought office and attempt to implement changes in prevailing norms through established processes. Acceptable strategies for a moderate regime would include such devices as the legal expansion of the franchise in an accountable polity or seeking acceptance of changes in the delegation of authority from the senior military or party central committee in a less accountable polity. *Maximalist* regimes are those that are willing to subvert or ignore established processes in order to gain office or implement policy. Such strategies might include coups or the encouragement of civil war, the bypassing of constitutional bodies or legal requirements, and the like.

Resource change orientation deals with the extent to which a regime seeks to expand either the resource base of a society or its control over these resources. A regime may or may not choose to expand such governmental activities as natural resources discovery and exploitation, public education, industrial production, scientific research, or the communication and informational apparatus. Likewise, it may or may not seek to expand its own control of these resources through devices such as taxation policy, regulation policy, censorship, domestic budget allocations, or nationalization.

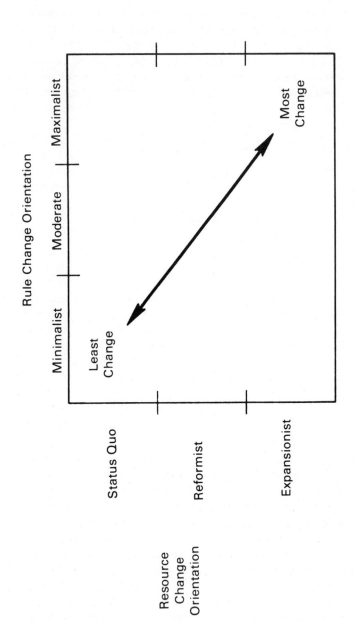

Figure 5.1. Types of regime change orientations.

A leadership style that is expansionist in resource change orientation might not be maximalist in rule change orientation, but empirically these orientations are likely to vary together, since expansion of regime control over resources is likely to run headlong into institutional opposition of various kinds. The possible relationships between rule change and resource change orientation are shown in Figure 5.1. Regimes located toward the upper left portion of the figure seek few changes either in the political rules of the game or in the resource base of the society and its control by the regime. Regimes at the lower right portion of the figure seek great changes in these arenas. We hypothesize that such leadership styles are reflected in a regime's conduct of foreign policy. Minimalist, status quo regimes are likely to pursue foreign policies similar to those of their predecessors and their own past behavior. Maximalist, expansionist regimes are likely to attempt to significantly alter their external environments.

EFFECTS ON FOREIGN POLICY

To empirically demonstrate the utility of a regime approach for explaining foreign policy, two strategies can be utilized. The first is to show in what ways the constraints under which varying regimes operate make for differences in foreign policy behavior. The second is to show in what ways regime leaders can manipulate foreign policy in order to advance the desired goal of staying in office. We may consider these briefly in turn.

One method of studying the effects of constraint might be to contrast the successes of regimes in initiating, or bringing to a successful conclusion, major changes in foreign policy. In terms of the perspective presented here, major successful initiatives would likely be taken by unified regimes; failures would be higher for initiatives undertaken by fragmented regimes, when taken at all. Empirical examples abound. A good case in point is the French experience in Algeria. The Fourth Republic finally disintegrated in its failure to deal with this issue, clearly in large measure due to the "negative majority" on the left and right whose views of French policy in Algeria were sharply divergent. It was only when the Fifth Republic instituted a strong executive with majority backing of one party that France could successfully disentangle itself from the Algerian crisis and escape the vacillation that characterized the weak coalition governments of the Fourth Republic. The policy orientation of the Fifth Republic under De Gaulle was also more maximalist than that of its predecessor, and accountability was somewhat reduced by the move from a parliamentary to a presidential regime.

Another example is a comparison of the important foreign policy moves of Presidents Johnson, Nixon, and Ford. By the end of Johnson's term, widespread national disaffection for his policies in Southeast Asia had arisen. However, from beginning to end, he commanded a significant partisan majority in the Congress and was able to implement all his policies regarding Indochina. When public opinion could make itself felt in the form of electoral judgment, he was compelled to withdraw from the race. On the other hand, Nixon, despite high levels of public approbation for his handling of foreign affairs at the start of his second term, was forced to end American involvement in Asia in a different way than might have been the case had he commanded a legislative majority. At the start of a term without demonstrated electoral support, with a falling position in the polls, and having only a legislative minority, Ford was further constrained in such areas as policies toward the Middle East, Southeast Asia, and the Soviet Union. In addition, Ford had a significantly more minimalist policy orientation than that of his predecessors. Another example is that of the maximalist regime of Salvador Allende. His election brought diplomatic recognition of nations in the Communist bloc and a visit from Fidel Castro, but Chile's moves "eastward" were certainly limited by a vocal center and right opposition that dominated the legislative branch and military thinking and that was eventually responsible for his overthrow.

Even in cases where divided regimes have implemented important foreign policy measures without a united regime, the process has been touch-and-go. Willy Brandt's *Ostpolitik* was a radical departure in West German foreign policy, but its success depended heavily on the acquiescence of the Social Democrats' coalition partner, the Free Democrats, whose wavering at times could easily have spelled doom for the policy.

Changes in regimes and their internal support structure have also been evident in less "open" or nonelectorally-based regimes. Brzezinski and Huntington (1964) have noted that the fortunes of regime leaders in the Soviet Union have risen and fallen with the issue positions that they took, including foreign policy issues. Indeed, these authors observe that changes in regime have brought significant changes in Soviet foreign policy. Khrushchev's tenure in office brought a great "thaw" in east-west relations. However, failure on his part to pay heed to "the counsel of such articulate and relatively cohesive interest groups as the army, the secret police and technocracy contributed to their rise in political awareness, and undermined his own power in the process" (Stern, 1968: 93). Changes in policy resulting from changes in leadership in Rumania, Poland, and Czechoslovakia at various times over the past twenty years are also well known. Recent moves from Western to neutralist or anti-Western attitudes in such non-Communist "closed" states as Iraq, Libya, and Yemen have co-occurred with regime change.

In addition to the limits placed on foreign policy behavior by constraints on regimes, we have noted that leaders self-consciously use foreign policy as a means of perpetuating themselves in office. One prime method of doing so is to select policy alternatives that will appeal to some of the constituencies that are strong supporters of the regime. Frequently, for example, important ethnic groups in a society have a stake in a conflict that is going on elsewhere. A relatively "cheap" method of gaining favor with such groups is for a regime to voice support for the party to the conflict that internal constituencies support. Similarly, important business, labor, and issue-oriented groups may have an interest in seeing that the foreign policy of their nation favors a certain set of arrangements with another nation. American policy in the Middle East and toward the International Labor Organization, for example, and the differing positions of the two major British parties toward South Africa and Rhodesia may well be rooted in such considerations.

Leaders may also use foreign policy initiatives to enhance their own prestige. It has been widely noted that it is rare for concrete accomplishments to emerge from exercises in summitry, but the gain in prestige for the leader may be great. In recent years, such well-publicized events as Nixon's trip to China, Tanaka's visit to the USSR, and the Adenauer-De Gaulle meetings stand as important examples of the use of foreign policy for the purpose of consolidating internal support. A variant of such a technique is that of the regime leader who attempts, through rhetorical statements and low resource-use actions, to become a spokesman for a regional or other pan-national constituency. In recent times, both Nasser and Khadaffi have sought, through anti-Israeli behaviors, to become chief spokesmen for the Arab world and thus to consolidate their positions at home through their stature as world leaders. Fidel Castro and other members of his regime sought a similar position in the Third World generally and in Latin America in particular. Nkrumah, Amin, Senghor, and Selaissie have all striven to become the chief spokesmen for Black Africans and, indeed, Blacks around the world.

Another common example of the use of foreign policy for the consolidation of a regime's domestic position is the creation of, or attention directed to, a purported external threat in order to divert the populace from internal problems that might threaten the regime's solidarity. Although this is a particularly common device among regime leaders seeking to mobilize a populace after a revolution or divisive coup, it is also used in other settings. A case in point is Nixon's frequent and pointed appeals to Americans to direct their attention to matters of international security and national defense rather than to domestic economic problems and Watergate revelations.

RELATION TO OTHER VARIABLES

Let us summarize the regime perspective presented in this section. Any regime acts to retain power and support. In doing so, it is limited by the resources at its disposal, the constraints on those resources, and its disposition to use the resources available to it. Different combinations of these characteristics will produce various kinds of limitations on a regime's freedom of action. The regime with the most freedom of action probably has great scope of governmental action, high institutionalization, strong public support, internal unity, low accountability, and an expansionist and maximalist leadership style. It should be immediately noted, however, that these aspects of a regime and its relationship to the larger national political system do not function in a vacuum. Other variables, relating to the system itself and to its place in the international system, may be seen to mediate between regime structure and external behavior. Two sets of variables that are particularly important are invariant or quasi-invariant national attribute variables and environmental constraints.

The first set of factors relates to the amount of physical resources at the disposal of the system, such as its size and level of economic development, two factors that have received very prominent attention in the literature of international relations and foreign policy (Rosenau, 1975; S. A. Salmore, 1972). In combination, these variables are often regarded as an index of the power or capabilities of the system. These interact with the political constraints placed on a regime. Physical resources give a nation the capacity to act; the type of regime determines its freedom to act.

Another set of factors external to the regime that may affect regime behavior includes the past policies and previous commitments that earlier regimes may have enacted toward external entities. Research into some domestic policy arenas has revealed that prior actions are the best predictors of future behavior. Put more colloquially, this may be called the "weather" theory—the same tomorrow as it was today. In addition, a type of environmental constraint that may influence regime behavior involves conditions external to the national system, such as a nation's place in the international system and its membership in multinational organizations.

SELECTED ASSUMPTIONS

The perspective that has been developed in the preceding sections makes some important assumptions about the behavior of those who lead governing regimes. It assumes that leaders perceive the kinds of constraints that have been described and act in accordance with them. This set of assumptions has much in common with the "rationality" assumptions developed by Downs (1957) in his discussion of rational behavior for aspirants to political office.

ASSUMPTION 5.1: *Political leaders are rational in that they use their resources efficiently to achieve desired ends.* The desired end of a political leader is to obtain and consolidate power and support. The failure to act rationally means that this end will not be obtained.

ASSUMPTION 5.2: *The leaders of a governing regime, or groups that can speak for and commit the nation to foreign policy behaviors, act to preserve themselves in power by the use of resources that they can control.* The resources that are available to them are limited to those available to the national system. Depending on the system, many important resources—such as authority over wealth, morality, and other values—may be partially or entirely distributed to sectors or persons outside the governing regime.

ASSUMPTION 5.3: *One of the most critical resources that is available entirely or partially to the regime is the making of public policy, defined as the ability to commit the government to action.* Foreign policy is one such policy; indeed, it is the one most likely to be in the exclusive control of the governing regime.

ASSUMPTION 5.4: *Leaders of a regime are expected to conduct foreign policy so that it maximizes their likelihood of retaining power.* It is at this point that the constraints we have discussed in the last section come into operation.

ASSUMPTION 5.5: *If a regime is free from constraints internal to the regime and free from domestic constraints external to the regime, it may act without consideration of the internal effect foreign policy decisions will have on the regime's tenure in office; conversely, when constraints are high a regime will select those foreign policy options (which are far fewer) that will not tend to cause discord either within the fragmented regime or in the larger society.*

ILLUSTRATIVE PROPOSITIONS

A number of simple bivariate propositions can be drawn from this discussion of the assumptions underlying the regime perspective. It should be clear that we consider it possible that the mediating variables we have previously noted may add explanatory power to these propositions. The further testing of hypotheses derived from all the perspectives discussed in this volume should lead to a more complete and satisfying explanation of foreign policy behavior. However, the propositions presented below are intuitively satisfying and, in some cases, are already supported by preliminary analysis of foreign policy events data (Salmore and Salmore, 1970, 1972).

PROPOSITION 5.1

Highly constrained regimes will have a lower amount of foreign policy activity than will less constrained regimes.

This proposition may be tested by recourse to a simple count of the amount of behavior among high and low constraint regimes. In accord with the perspective we have presented, highly constrained regimes with more freedom to act should, in fact, act more often.

PROPOSITION 5.2

The foreign policy of highly constrained regimes will evidence lower levels of commitment than that of less constrained regimes.

It would be expected that highly constrained regimes, in an attempt to preserve the fragile bases of support among the mass public and competing governmental factions that keep such a regime in power, would act in a manner that was as "unexceptional" as possible. Therefore, we would anticipate that highly constrained regimes would engage most often in behavior that was low in resource commitment.

PROPOSITION 5.3

The foreign policy behavior of highly constrained regimes will be more interdependent and less independent than that of less constrained regimes.

We would expect that highly constrained regimes would take fewer independent actions and more interdependent ones than would less constrained regimes. Independent actions, as defined in Chapter 2, involve both taking initiatives and acting separately from other entities, whereas interdependent actions are collaborative responses (i.e., include multiple actors) made in reaction to initiatives of others. Acting with other nations serves as a kind of guarantee that actions will not be laid at the doorstep of the regime alone. It is possible to compare behaviors that involve actions taken alone or in concert with other nations and to compare behaviors that occur within the context of international, regional, and functional organizations. Furthermore, highly constrained regimes will largely confine their external behaviors to reacting to the behaviors of other states rather than formulating new initiatives or following a concerted policy of their own, again due to the problems of a factional base. It is anticipated that, in comparison with less constrained regimes, the behavior of highly constrained regimes will have a higher proportion of actions elicited by another entity rather than actions indicating a coherent policy toward such an entity.

PROPOSITION 5.4

Highly constrained regimes will express less intense affect in their foreign policy behaviors and they will be less likely to express negative affect than less constrained regimes.

It is likely that the extent to which a regime is constrained will be related to the direction of affect (positive, neutral, or negative) and the intensity of affect (mild or strong expression). Given the characteristics of constrained regimes, they ought to tend toward neutrality and mild expressions of hostility and friendship in order not to provoke any internal or external antagonism which could destabilize them. In other words, high constraint should be negatively related to intensity. Furthermore, high constraint regimes are less likely to engage in hostile acts (negative affect) than they are to participate in friendly and neutral acts. Less constrained regimes should manifest sharper affect intensity scores and also should express more negative affect than highly constrained regimes.

PROPOSITION 5.5

Highly constrained regimes will engage in less goal enunciation than will less constrained regimes.

In accord with the perspective presented, highly constrained regimes will be unwilling to take actions that have specific goals that might be a matter of dispute among the parties comprising and supporting the regime. Highly constrained regimes should thus enunciate fewer goals than less constrained regimes.

SUMMARY

We have argued that the study of the effect of regime type and regime change both within and between nations will add significantly to the explanatory power of any perspective purporting to explain variations in foreign policy behavior. The uses made of foreign policy by the leaders of regimes, the constraints placed on foreign policy behaviors by the nature of the regime, and the internal political system in which the regime is embedded promise to be important concepts for explaining foreign policy behavior. Throughout this essay, we have cited, for this perspective, evidence drawn primarily from a large number of case studies. Attempts to test such a perspective in a cross-national context are much scarcer, but already enough evidence exists to encourage further investigation. We have previously mentioned the important work by Wilkenfeld (1968, 1969) that indicates that the relationship between one type of foreign policy behavior, external conflict, and internal conflict varies across regime types. In our own earlier work (Salmore and Salmore, 1970), we found that accountable regimes are significantly more cooperative and generally less active in the external arena than are nonaccountable regimes. Through the use of a different data set, this hypothesis was again confirmed (Salmore and Salmore, 1972). A preliminary analysis of the same data also revealed that unified and fragmented regimes have distinct behavioral profiles. Unified regimes, as we would predict, are significantly more conflictful and active in the international system than are fragmented regimes. Change of regime also consistently explains 50% to 60% of the variation in total volume of behaviors, conflictful and cooperative behaviors, and "word" and "deed" behaviors. By contrast, differences in size and development only explain 18% to 28% of the variation for these same variables. The salience of political leaders' freedom of action is also the focus of a recent attempt to explain domestic and external policy outputs in a cross-national context (Russett and Monsen, 1975). The ability to construct more complex indicators of foreign policy behavior and regime structure should permit us to extend and broaden analyses in the future. We would expect that regime will continue to play an important role as we develop and refine multivariate explanations of foreign policy behavior.

NOTES

1. The reader should note that our definitions of regime and government are diametrically opposed to those of some other writers who use the terms, most notably Rose (1969, 1971). Rose (1971: 26) defines regime in terms of permanent institutions within the state and government as the group of people occupying the important positions in the "regime." As described in the text, our definitions of these two terms are precisely the reverse. We have elected this stance because in common language regimes are generally associated with persons (e.g., "the Trujillo regime"). Often, this use of the term regime is associated with authoritarian leaders. In our use of the term "regime," we have not confined it to authoritarian leaders, but by parallelism of construction we have extended it to the national leadership in all types of political systems.

2. See chapters 3, 4, and 6 in this book.

6

NATIONAL ATTRIBUTES AND FOREIGN POLICY

Maurice A. East

The study of national attributes and their relationship to foreign policy is a respected tradition in foreign policy analysis. Academicians and practitioners alike have long assumed that such variables as population, geography, military capabilities, and technology levels have an impact on foreign policy.

This chapter presents a perspective that focuses on national attributes as major explanatory factors accounting for foreign policy behavior. In the course of our discussion, we shall attempt to delineate clearly our area of concern by specifying what constitutes that rather broad and poorly defined set of variables called national attributes. Then we shall present a theoretical framework that includes the concept of "capacity to act" as the construct integrating most, if not all, national attributes when related to foreign policy. Capacity to act refers to the amount of resources a nation has and its ability to utilize these resources. Size and level of social organization are proposed as two dimensions of capacity to act. The theoretical relationship between these two dimensions and foreign policy

AUTHOR'S NOTE: This chapter has benefited greatly from the comments and contributions made by members of the University of Kentucky comparative foreign policy group. In particular, I would like to acknowledge the contributions of Barbara Winters and Joe Hagan. As is the case with the other chapters, this one has been considerably improved as a result of discussions with my colleagues on the CREON Project.

behavior is discussed. In brief, we shall argue that differences in the capacity to act levels of nations relate to differences in nations' foreign policy behavior. Finally, we point out some of the basic assumptions underlying this perspective and offer several selected propositions as examples of the type of research that can be carried out using this perspective.

OVERVIEW OF THE PERSPECTIVE

The national attributes perspective, as it will be developed in this chapter, is based on the central notion that differences in the national attributes of nations will be related to differences in the foreign policy behavior patterns of these nations. National attributes operate so as to affect the amount of resources a nation has and its ability to utilize these resources in various ways. The latter two concepts comprise a nation's capacity to act. Insofar as national attributes differ across nations, we will find differences in the capacity to act levels of nations that will be related to differences in their foreign policy behaviors.

With this brief synopsis, we can turn to a closer examination of some of the elements in the national attributes perspective. Almost as soon as one begins to think about this, it is evident that a large variety of factors has been referred to as "national attributes." The broad scope of the concept is perhaps best illustrated by Rummel (1965: 131), who defines a national attribute as "any empirical concept that is applicable to a nation as a whole and on which nations can be compared." This definition is too all-encompassing to be of much use since it excludes virtually nothing. However, it can be used as the starting point for a discussion of the distinguishing characteristics of national attributes as the concept will be used in this perspective. In the course of this discussion, we will draw several distinctions between national attributes and various other types of factors that have also been offered as explanations of foreign policy.

National attributes can be said to have three general distinguishing characteristics:

1. They refer to characteristics of the national unit as a whole and not to characteristics of sub-units within the nation.

2. They are characteristics that can be conceptualized and measured without reference to entities outside of the nation itself.

3. They are characteristics that are relatively stable over time.

The first characteristic is explicitly referred to in Rummel's definition—a concept "applicable to a nation as a whole." By requiring this characteristic, it is possible to distinguish between national attributes and other attribute concepts that describe various components or sub-national units such as the ideological orientations of individual political parties, the strength of different interest groups, the size of various government agencies, and the like. When making this distinction, we do not mean to imply that sub-national units have no effect on foreign policy, but by definition they are not national attributes. However, it is possible to have national attributes that do in fact make reference to sub-national units. For example, a variable measuring the *total number* of political parties in a nation can be considered a national attribute.

The second characteristic—to be able to conceptualize and measure the variable without reference to external entities—allows us to distinguish between national attributes and what have been referred to as external variables (Harf et al., 1974). Both have the nation as the unit of analysis, but external variables are those that tap characteristics of a nation in relation to some external entity or referent, i.e., referents physically located outside the boundaries of the nation that is the unit of analysis. Examples of external variables include:

1. number of alliances to which a nation belongs,
2. number of intergovernmental organizations (IGOs) of which it is a member.
3. distance in air miles from the Soviet Union,
4. number of votes supporting the United States in the United Nations.

All of these are variables that can plausibly be assumed to affect foreign policy behavior, and all have the nation as a whole as the unit of analysis, but they are excluded from our conceptualization of national attributes because of their reference to external entities. To use a simple distinction, national attributes are considered to be *internal* rather than external variables.

The third distinguishing characteristic is that national attributes have relatively stable values over time. Our assumption is that they are descriptive of a nation's on-going pattern of characteristics, not of its day-to-day fluctuations. The time over which national attributes are expected to change is years or decades rather than days or weeks. Of course, we should note that it is quite possible for national attributes to change rather drastically over the short run. For example, a nation's territorial size or population can be radically altered as a result of a peace treaty. It is assumed, however, that such changes do not take place frequently.

National attributes can also be considered as parameters within which other types of variables operate. For instance, changes in the regime of a nation can occur without necessarily having a change in national attributes. Looking at it from a different viewpoint, regimes can work to change the parameters of the nation—attempting to raise its level of economic development, for example—but this is a slow and difficult task.

Having delineated the theoretical boundaries of the concept of national attributes, we can now specify the three ways in which national attributes are thought to affect a nation's foreign policy behavior:

1. as factors affecting the amount of resources that can be used in the execution of national actions;
2. as factors affecting the nation's ability to utilize its resources in the pursuit of national goals and objectives;
3. as norm-shaping factors affecting the predispositions of the nation's leaders as to where and how they utilize the nation's resources.

It is entirely possible for a given national attribute to affect foreign policy in more than one way.

The assumption underlying the first category is that resources in some form or another are necessary for any type of national activity. It follows, then, that limitations on the amount of resources available to a nation will of necessity set severe restrictions on the effectiveness with which that nation can pursue certain courses of action. Variables such as amount of territory, amount of arable land, size of military force, and population are all examples of national attributes conceptualized in terms of amount of resources. It is the compelling nature of this assumption that accounts for at least a portion of the appeal and importance of this entire perspective.

The amount of resources available to a nation, however, may not always be as important as the manner in which those resources are utilized. For example, consider the ability of the Israelis in the 1960s to maintain a dominant position in the Middle East against the Arab world. This point of view suggests the next category of means by which national attributes affect foreign policy behavior. This second category taps the ability of a nation to convert resources into forms appropriate to its foreign policy tasks. For example, it is not sufficient for a nation merely to possess resources; it must have the capacity to extract, develop, train, manufacture, and deliver these resources. Variables measuring such things as a nation's level of economic development, the educational level of its populace, its level of technology, and its organizational capacity are all examples of indicators of the processes by which national attributes affect foreign policy.

The third category of national attribute effects is perhaps the most complex. The focus is on the means by which these attributes affect the way policy makers allocate resources within the realm of foreign affairs. An example is the ethnic composition of a nation. The foreign policy leaders of a nation with a large ethnic population might well have a predisposition toward close relations with other nations having similar ethnic populations. This third category differs from the other two in one very important respect—national attributes directly affect the nation's goals and objectives as defined by the leaders. In the first two categories a nation's goals and objectives are considered as "givens," existing independently of the nation's attributes.

To summarize this overview, we have suggested three distinguishing characteristics of national attributes, and we have examined three means by which these attributes affect foreign policy. National attributes operate as factors affecting the amount of resources a nation has for pursuing national goals and objectives. They are also those factors that affect the nation's ability to utilize the resources it has. Finally, national attributes can be factors that affect the leaders' predispositions as to where and how resources are to be utilized.

RELATION TO PREVIOUS STUDIES

In reviewing the literature relevant to this perspective, it is clear that national attributes measuring the amount of resources in a nation have received the most attention from both foreign policy specialists and lay people alike. That aspect of research called capabilities analysis is particularly relevant here. Many scholars have examined various national attributes in order to assess capabilities and their impact on foreign policy behavior. Morgenthau (1967) is primarily concerned with a nation's "power" and how it is related to various national attributes. Organski and Organski (1961) present an excellent discussion of population as a national attribute and how it relates to foreign policy behavior. Knorr (1956) discusses military capabilities, particularly nuclear weapons, and relates this factor to national behavior. A nation's geographic features, including both natural resources and topography, are factors discussed in relation to foreign policy by Sprout and Sprout (1962).

National attributes that affect a nation's ability to convert resources and to utilize them are considered by several authors. One of the better recent discussions is by Puchala (1971: 178-179), who argues that "one cannot always directly associate a state's 'bigness' with its capacity to act in international politics.... [W]hat counts most ... is the immediate availability of resources for the service of foreign policy." He goes on to list industrialization, educational level of the population, and efficiency of societal organization as factors that affect a nation's ability to control and to utilize resources. Similarly, K. W. Deutsch (1968: 27), writing about the problem of inferring a nation's power potential from amount of resources alone, uses the image of a charging elephant to make his point. The animal is capable of smashing down large obstacles but is incapable of threading a needle because it cannot control its behavior sufficiently. Deutsch suggests that something similar holds for nations—their power potential is based on both the amount of resources *and* the ability to control, to convert, and to allocate resources.

Choucri and North (1975) are among those who have argued that national attributes can affect the general predispositions of a nation's leaders to act in certain ways in foreign affairs. According to their conceptual framework, nations characterized by a certain combination of national attributes—an increasing population, advanced levels of technology, and a diminishing resource base—will tend to exhibit lateral pressure, which is the process of expanding a nation's activities beyond its national boundaries. Puchala (1971: 184-185), after discussing the various ways in which a nation's goals and objectives determine resource requirements, argues:

> There is, however, another important dimension to the relationship between goals and resources. *This is that resource availability may influence or even determine a state's choice of international political goals.* Not only are government demands for resources adjusted to match goals, but goals too are often adjusted to match resources available to governments.

We must also consider briefly the notion of "will," or the V complex, suggested by Wilkinson (1969) because at first glance it appears that this factor is quite similar to the other factors that affect predispositions. In Wilkinson's framework, will and the V (for volition) complex comprise one of three main factors used in explaining foreign policy and are second in importance only to a capabilities factor. However, it is clear from the description of this factor that Wilkinson considers it to be a characteristic of the political leadership of a nation and *not* a characteristic of the national entity as a whole. For this reason, the V complex does not seem to qualify as a national attribute. Factors quite similar to Wilkinson's are considered elsewhere in this volume, either as characteristics of individual political leaders (chapter 3) or as the orientations of particular political regimes (chapter 5).

Turning to empirical research findings, what has been discovered about the relationship between national attributes and foreign policy behavior?

This is a difficult question to answer for several reasons. First, as we have noted earlier, the concept of national attributes is used so broadly that it includes many different kinds of variables. Second, as will be noted below, the empirical analyses using these diverse variables have produced mixed and conflicting results. Third, there has been little empirical research that has attempted to deal with national attributes as a *class* of variables rather than as one or two individual variables used in a research design. However, there are several works that do attempt to analyze national attributes, and we shall turn to them now.

Rosenau (1966) generated considerable theoretical interest in national attributes and their influence on foreign policy behavior when he presented his pre-theory of foreign policy. In that pre-theory, he proposed a typology of nations that was created from three variables: magnitude of size, level of economic development, and degree of political accountability. He argued that the foreign policy behaviors of different types of nations would differ and that the behaviors of nations of similar types would be similar. At least two of the three variables used by Rosenau, size and economic development, clearly fit our conceptual definition of national attributes. The third, political accountability, has been considered by some to be an unstable measure, subject to too rapid and frequent change to be a national attribute (Salmore, 1972; Kean and McGowan, 1973).

In that same article, Rosenau also presented a schema for categorizing all factors influencing foreign policy into one of five variables clusters: idiosyncratic, role, governmental, societal, and systemic. The major task posed by his pre-theory was to examine the relative potency of each of these clusters for explaining foreign policy across the typology of nations; for example, he argued that systemic factors would be more important in accounting for foreign policy behavior in small states as compared to large states. A closer examination of Rosenau's five variables clusters reveals that at least two of them—governmental and societal—include variables that may meet the criteria for national attributes. Although there have been several attempts to test various aspects of the Rosenau pre-theory (Moore, 1970; Salmore, 1972), none has focused directly on a comparison of national attribute variables with other types of variables.

East and Gregg (1967) attempted to determine the relative potency of internal versus external variables in accounting for international conflict and cooperation behavior. Although their set of internal variables—economic development, political stability, political freedom, and ethnic heterogeneity—may not fit the definition of national attributes in all respects, their findings indicate that these internal variables were not as important as external variables in accounting for variance in either international conflict or cooperation.

The work of Rummel (1969) has also focused on national attributes as factors affecting foreign policy behavior. In their attempts to discover the underlying dimensions of nations' foreign policy behavior, Rummel and his colleagues have consistently identified several factors that can be considered to be national attributes. Economic development and size factors have been identified as important national attributes in studies by Sawyer (1967), Russett (1968), and Rummel (1969) among others.

In 1968 Rummel published an article in which he argued that national attribute variables had very low correlations with foreign conflict behavior. On the basis of his previous empirical work with factor analyses, as well as the work of others, Rummel (1968: 312) argued that:

> the hypothesized correlates of foreign conflict behavior [i.e., national attributes] acting singly or in combination or with the effect of other variables controlled are little related to a nation's foreign conflict behavior.

This was the basis from which Rummel developed his *field* theory of international politics in opposition to *attribute* theory. He argued that the lack of correlations between attributes and foreign conflict behavior was due to the fact that only the *magnitudes* of attributes were being considered in attribute theory, whereas it was the *relative distances* between nations on these dimensions that influenced their behavior. In field theory, the relative distances between nations are assumed to be the principal dynamic factor in the theory.

Rummel's challenge to the national attributes perspective can be responded to in several ways. First, it seems unwarranted to throw out the national attributes perspective on foreign policy because of a set of low correlations between individual attributes and foreign conflict behavior. Conflict is only one form of foreign policy behavior. If one were to analyze a wider range of behaviors, national attributes might well be highly correlated with other dimensions of behavior.

Second, Rummel's early research was not based on any theoretical conceptualization of national attributes and how these might affect foreign policy. This research used a wide variety of internal variables as the independent factors in analyses of one or two selected aspects of foreign policy behavior. The choice of both the national attribute and the foreign policy behavior variables can only be characterized as unsystematic.

In brief, our position is that the rejection of the national attributes perspective is premature. There seems to be room in the repertoire of the foreign policy analyst for both the national attributes perspective and the various field theory models that were originally offered by Rummel and that have since been modified by Gleditsch (1970) and Vincent (1974).

McGowan and Shapiro (1973), in their survey of empirical comparative foreign policy studies, have compiled a list of propositions relating various types of factors to foreign policy behavior. They also indicate those propositions that they "have confidence in," which means those that have been successfully replicated or those for which one can find support from different but comparable research designs. Propositions in their governmental, economic, societal, and cultural categories generally meet the criteria for national attribute propositions.

The only proposition in the governmental category in which McGowan and Shapiro "have confidence" is as follows: "There is a positive relationship between the military power of a state and its foreign conflict behavior" (McGowan and Shapiro, 1973: 95). But even after noting that they have confidence in this proposition, they cite studies by Rummel (1968) and Weede (1970) that contradict it. Summing up the research included in their governmental category, McGowan and Shapiro (1973: 105) note:

> There are many competent studies in this section, but the very small amount of replication forces us to withhold judgment on their validity . . . the diversity of the variables used limits our confidence. Until each of those variables is placed in a separate proposition, which is then confirmed by several studies, the usefulness of the research surveyed here will remain limited.

Under the category of economic variables, McGowan and Shapiro (1973: 107-116) identify several propositions in which they have confidence. Propositions relating type of economic system and the economic capacity of a system to war involvement have considerable support. Moreover, level of economic development has been shown to relate to a nation's voting behavior in the United Nations, with economically developed nations exhibiting a voting pattern that is less supportive of the UN. There is also a strongly supported proposition that indicates a positive relationship between a nation's economic development level and the frequency with which its representatives are elected to UN offices. Finally, there is a strong positive relationship between a nation's international trade and its involvement in other kinds of international activity.

Societal variables are defined by McGowan and Shapiro (1973: 40) as "aspects of the social structure, broadly defined, of national societies." They list only two propositions involving societal variables that seem to have strong empirical support. "There is a positive relationship between a nation's size and the general level of its foreign policy activity. . . . There is a positive relationship between population size and changes in size and a nation's foreign conflict behavior" (McGowan and Shapiro, 1973: 118). They go on to comment on the lack of research involving societal variables other than those which are population related and thus easy to measure.

Regarding propositions relating cultural variables to foreign policy, McGowan and Shapiro list none in which they have confidence. They suggest that the reason for this is the lack of work done in this field, although they do point to a number of isolated studies employing variables such as religious values, ideology, nationalism, language similarity, communications, and the like.

In summarizing the literature relevant to the national attributes perspective, we find first that there have been only a few studies that attempt to deal, either theoretically or empirically, with national attributes as a class of variables. Those that do so do not provide conclusive evidence about the importance of national attributes for explaining foreign policy. Second, the survey of empirical studies indicates that there are two general types of national attribute variables that seem to be important: (1) variables measuring the general power base of a nation (population size, military power, economic capacity) and (2) variables measuring the level of socioeconomic development of the nation (GNP per capita, degree of industrialization, telephones per capita). These two types of variables correspond quite closely to the first two categories of national attributes identified in the preceding section. We shall consider these further as we continue to develop the national attributes perspective.

DEVELOPMENT OF THE PERSPECTIVE

Our task now is to elaborate on the explanatory logic by which we relate national attributes to foreign policy. In our review of empirical research findings, we noted that two types of national attribute variables have been found to relate to foreign policy behavior: (1) variables measuring the general power base of a nation and (2) variables measuring aspects of a nation's general level of socioeconomic development. These two types of variables acting together comprise a nation's capacity to act in foreign affairs. In other words, a nation's capacity to act is a function of its amount of resources (general power base) and its ability to utilize the resources (general level of socioeconomic development). The concept of capacity to act will be discussed in greater detail below, but it is introduced here because it is necessary for understanding the general explanatory logic of the perspective.

The relationships that are assumed to exist between national attributes and foreign policy behavior are displayed in Figure 6.1. Note that national attributes affecting amount of resources and ability to utilize resources combine to form capacity to act, while attributes affecting the predispositions of national leaders are linked to the choices of foreign policy goals

Figure 6.1

The Relationship of National Attributes to Foreign Policy Behavior

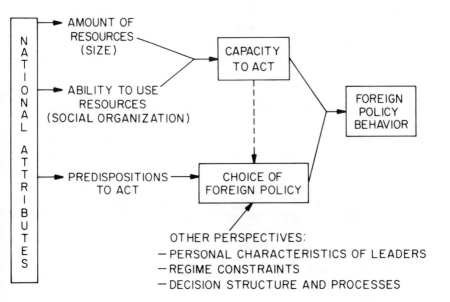

and objectives. The allocation of capacity to act to various tasks combines goals and capacity to act to directly affect a nation's foreign policy behavior. The broken arrow from capacity to act to choice of foreign policy goals represents the relationship between a leader's perceptions of his nation's capacity to act and the foreign policy goals chosen. Figure 6.1 also depicts the way in which other theoretical perspectives affect the choice of foreign policy goals and objectives.

To briefly summarize, there are two conceptually distinct, but related, causal mechanisms through which national attributes can affect foreign policy behavior: capacity to act and choice of foreign policy goals and objectives. Although a persuasive case can be made for including both causal mechanisms in our development of the national attributes perspective, we shall confine our attention to capacity to act. There are both practical and theoretical reasons for doing so. Practically, the distinctly different nature of these two causal mechanisms makes it difficult to deal adequately with both within the confines of this chapter. From a theoretical point of view, we assume that national attributes affect the choice and formation of a nation's foreign policy goals and objectives through the leaders' perceptions of their nation's capacity to act and, thus, act in conjunction with factors from other theoretical perspectives that affect perceptions. In other words, to the extent that national attributes do affect a nation's goals and objectives, the effects will be channeled through purposive human actors who are, in turn, political leaders, members of a bureaucracy, or component members of the nation's political regime (cf. Sprout and Sprout, 1965). In order to understand the factors operating on political leaders in their choice of foreign policy goals and objectives, we need to take into account more than one theoretical perspective. Because the purpose of this chapter is to examine foreign policy from a *single* perspective, we have chosen to concentrate on capacity to act.

Before we can proceed, it is necessary to have a more precise idea of what is meant by "capacity to act." This theoretical construct represents the resources available for national use in foreign affairs and the ability to utilize these resources in the service of various foreign policy goals and objectives. The term "resources" is a key concept. It is used here in its broadest sense, referring to human as well as material (nonhuman) factors. When we speak about resources, it may be helpful to note that this term can refer to any one of the following:

1. the total amount of resources existing in a national society;
2. the resources in the society that can be controlled, converted, and allocated for the pursuit of national (as opposed to sub-national or private) objectives, both domestic and international;
3. the resources in the society available for use by the government in pursuit of foreign policy goals and objectives.

These three statements stand in a hierarchical relationship. Theoretically, and in terms of capacity to act, it is the third level of resources that we are most concerned with. But the perspective may be clarified and the empirical referents made more obvious if we begin by looking at each level in succession.

National attributes tapping the first level of resources will be referred to as size factors. Such factors directly affect the capacity to act of a nation by setting the limits on its resource base. Examples of measures tapping size include total population, total GNP, total land area, and military manpower. These measures have also been referred to as measures of the "power base" or "power potential" of a nation (K. W. Deutsch, 1968), and they are similar, if not identical, to the variables that load highly on factors labeled "size" in various factor analytic studies. Rummel (1969) indicates such variables as GNP, population, national income, and population times energy production load highly on a size (power) factor. Russett (1968), in a study of international regions, identifies a size factor on which the following variables load highly: total population, GNP, area, defense expenditures as a percentage of GNP, and foreign trade as a percentage of GNP (which loads negatively). A similar size factor also appears in studies done by Berry (1960), Cattell and Gorsuch (1965), and Sawyer (1967).

The second and third levels of resources are generally similar since they both focus on the degree to which the total resources of the society can be controlled and converted. The process of converting and controlling resources is dependent upon what we shall refer to as the level of social organization of the national society. Social organization, in turn, consists of two dimensions: level of modernization and level of societal stress. The modernization dimension taps the ability of the nation's leadership to allocate and redistribute resources to different national tasks. It is assumed to be positively related to capacity to act. Modernization involves the second level of resources referred to above. The societal stress dimension includes those persistent problems in the society that the government must deal with but that are difficult to resolve in the short run. Stress is assumed to be negatively related to capacity to act. Insofar as high levels of societal stress will divert resources from foreign affairs to domestic affairs, this dimension refers to the third level of resources noted above.

Modernization as a dimension of social organization is broader than economic development and includes much of what K. W. Deutsch (1961) referred to as social mobilization. In terms of national attributes, modernization can be tapped by measures of economic development, levels of technology, communication levels in the society, educational level of the populace, organizational level of the society, size of the bureaucracy, and so forth. In general, then, nations with higher levels of modernization will have the potential for greater control over their resources and a greater degree of adaptability in determining where and how these resources will be used. More modernized nations will have a greater ability to utilize resources in pursuit of foreign policy and, hence, a greater capacity to act.

The second dimension, societal stress, has a negative impact on social organization. Examples of the types of measures that might tap this dimension include chronic inflation, substantial unemployment, widespread hunger and disease, and persistent and high levels of domestic violence. Stress is negatively related to social organization (and ultimately to capacity to act) because of two factors. First, the existence of high levels of societal stress means that intrasocietal relationships are not operating effectively and efficiently and, thus, may reduce the nation's capacity to produce goods and services. Second, societal stress requires the government to allocate more resources—more time, more attention, more material goods—to the management of these societal problems, which decreases the resources available for utilization in foreign affairs.

In summary then, a nation's capacity to act is a function of two general factors, size and level of social organization. Size taps the total resources potentially available in a nation. Social organization taps the nation's ability to control, convert, and allocate resources for use in foreign affairs. It is comprised of two dimensions: (1) modernization, which relates positively to social organization and (2) societal stress, which relates negatively to social organization.

What is the explanatory logic that relates capacity to act to foreign policy behavior? As noted above, capacity to act is comprised of two separate dimensions, size and social organization. Both are positively related to capacity to act, although each operates through a different causal mechanism. For purposes of further discussion we shall assume that these two dimensions combine additively, which means that nations ranked high on size and social organization have the greatest capacity to act and nations ranked low on size and social organization have the least capacity to act. Low size/high social organization nations and high size/low social organization nations have moderate capacity to act. These differences in capacity to act levels will be manifested in differences in foreign policy behavior in three ways: (1) differences in the substantive content of foreign policy behavior, (2) differences in the style of statecraft and the techniques used to pursue foreign policy objectives, and (3) differences in the processes by which foreign policy is made.

First, one can expect to find differences in the substantive content of the foreign policies of nations with high and low capacity to act because the very fact of having little capacity to act means that certain types of tasks and problems must be attended to. The lack of capacity to act is due to small amounts of resources or low levels of social organization or both. Under these conditions, it can be reasonably argued that the foreign policy behavior of such nations will reflect great concern for and interest in issues that might have an effect on their already low capacity to act. Issues and problems relating to economic growth and development will be particularly salient. Nations will seek out relationships with those other international actors that are most likely to increase their capacity to act. Examples might include signing trade agreements, joining a cartel, seeking foreign investment, applying for international grants and loans, and the like.

A similar type of argument can be made with regard to the style and techniques used in executing a nation's foreign policy. Looking again at nations with a low capacity to act, we can argue that because of their low capacity to act, they are more likely to utilize techniques of statecraft which will be "low cost," that is, those that will consume the fewest resources, whether human or nonhuman. The best illustration of this is the tendency for smaller nations to utilize international organizations and other multilateral (as opposed to bilateral) settings for carrying out much of their foreign policy activity (Azar, 1973; East, 1973a). International organizations, whether global or regional, offer smaller nations the opportunity to hear and to be heard by many nations at a cost which is little greater than that necessary to send a delegation on a mission to meet bilaterally with another nation.

The processes of foreign policy decision making are also likely to differ in high and low capacity to act nations. For low capacity to act nations, we can expect the foreign policy-making organization to be smaller and to have a lesser degree of internal specialization. These factors can lead to severe problems and limitations—for example, in monitoring foreign affairs issues. Low capacity to act nations are not likely to be able to monitor effectively all issues and areas of interest to them. Nor will they be able to be represented at all international conferences that might be important to them or in all the national capitals that they would wish. Therefore, decisions are likely to be made on the basis of less complete information; foreign policies are likely to be made in international bodies and as a result of collective multinational actions rather than as a result of deliberations in national bodies. Furthermore, because of the importance of economic issues in low capacity to act nations, the foreign ministry is likely to play a less prominent role in foreign affairs, often taking a secondary position to one or another of the ministries responsible for economic issues such as trade, agriculture, finance, and the like.

SELECTED ASSUMPTIONS

Having presented the general explanatory logic relating differences in capacity to act to differences in foreign policy behavior, we can move to the task of abstracting and discussing a few of the central assumptions underlying the national attributes perspective. By doing so, we hope to be able to review and clarify several major aspects of the perspective.

ASSUMPTION 6.1: *Limitations on a nation's resources will place limitations on the foreign policy activities of that nation.* With this assumption we make the connection between the concept of resources and foreign policy behavior. This is a form of the "conservation of energy" principle, acknowledging the fact that resources are necessary for the undertaking of any activity.

ASSUMPTION 6.2: *Given any level of resources, the nation with the highest level of social organization will be able to convert and control its resources most effectively.* This assumption highlights the mechanism underlying our conceptualization of social organization and its relationship to capacity to act.

ASSUMPTION 6.3: *Nations with high capacity to act will tend to use their capacity in foreign policy.* A nation's total resources cannot be allocated to foreign policy activities since a substantial proportion of resources must be utilized in meeting the domestic needs and demands of the nation's people. It is not our assumption that nations will allocate equal proportions of their resources to domestic and foreign affairs, but we do assume that there will be a correspondence across nations between their total resources and their capacity to act in foreign affairs.

ASSUMPTION 6.4: *Foreign policy decision makers will attempt to utilize their nation's capacity to act in a manner that will maximize the achievement of their foreign policy goals.* This is a form of the "rationality" assumption with regard to foreign policy behavior. The assumption does not say anything about what the nation's foreign policy goals are or should be. It just assumes that whatever the goals, the foreign policy decision makers will make every effort to move toward a realization of their goals.

In summary, these four assumptions represent a partial listing of those that underlie the national attributes perspective on foreign policy analysis. The basic thrust of this perspective can be stated thusly: differences between nations in their national attributes (as reflected in capacity to act) will account for differences in their foreign policy behavior. Using these assumptions and this general statement of the perspective, we can now offer a set of illustrative propositions relating capacity to act to various aspects of foreign policy behavior.

ILLUSTRATIVE PROPOSITIONS

The propositions listed below are presented with the hope that they will give the reader sufficient additional information about the national attributes perspective so that he or she will be able to generate additional propositions relating national attributes to aspects of foreign policy.

PROPOSITION 6.1

A nation's capacity to act is positively related to the amount of foreign policy activity generated by that nation.

Here we are hypothesizing that the nation with the greatest capacity to act will, in fact, engage in the most foreign affairs activity. The rationale for this proposition rests on our assumption that limitations on resources will limit foreign policy activity. No attempt is made here to differentiate among types of activity. Rather we are interested in the total number of foreign policy events generated by a nation, as shown by foreign policy events data (e.g., McClelland and Hoggard, 1969; Burgess and Lawton, 1972; C. F. Hermann et al., 1973). The hypothesis might also be tested by relating national attributes to factor scores for nations on a participation dimension such as the one identified by Rummel (1966).

PROPOSITION 6.2

The lower a nation's capacity to act, the higher its proportion of foreign policy behaviors related to those substantive problem areas involving economic matters.

Because of the importance of economic questions to nations with a lower capacity to act (as noted above), we would expect economic matters to comprise a higher proportion of their substantive activity in the foreign affairs sector. If the nation is less modernized, for example, the major goals of the political leaders might be to raise the economic development level, to bring additional foreign capital and investment into the country, and to attend to those international problems and situations that may affect the nation's economic well-being. As a less-developed nation, it is very likely that the economy is greatly penetrated by other nations and other transnational units, e.g., multinational corporations, banks, intergovernmental economic organizations.

A similar argument can be made with regard to more highly modernized nations that have a small resource or power base. Here, economic matters are still of critical importance because such nations do not have the resource base necessary for sustained growth to meet the ever increasing demands of the domestic sector in a more modernized nation. So issues of economic growth are paramount for these nations, too. Furthermore, one can argue that the smaller, more modernized nation is likely to be very dependent on (or interdependent with) other nations for some vitally needed goods or services.

PROPOSITION 6.3

The lower a nation's capacity to act, the narrower the scope of action (both substantively and geographically) of its foreign policy behavior.

This proposition assumes that the lack of capacity to act will be reflected in a reduced organizational capability to monitor and react to foreign affairs. There will be fewer persons employed in the foreign policy bureaucracy; therefore, it will be impossible to attend to all of the relevant issues arising in the international system or to direct attention to all geographic regions. This lack of organizational capacity will be manifested in foreign policy by such indicators as the smaller number of different issues that are dealt with by the foreign affairs bureaucracy and the smaller number of different nations to which foreign affairs activity is directed.

PROPOSITION 6.4:

The lower a nation's capacity to act, the larger the proportion of foreign policy behavior taking place in a multilateral setting.

This proposition builds on the assumption that nations act in such a manner as to maximize the achievement of their goals. Nations realizing their limited capacity to act are more likely to engage in multilateral foreign affairs activity. Such low capacity nations will probably initiate much of their foreign policy activity in the context of international organizations because these organizations both provide a means of maximizing their exposure and increase the likelihood of mobilizing support for their positions. Insofar as we are able to measure the degree to which nations act unilaterally or in concert with one another, we would expect to find low capacity nations initiating actions in concert more frequently than high capacity nations.

PROPOSITION 6.5:

The lower a nation's capacity to act, the greater the proportion of high commitment and high negative affect in its foreign policy behavior.

At first glance, this proposition strikes one as counter-intuitive. The more obvious prediction would seem to be the opposite—that low capacity nations would engage in *less* high commitment and *less* high negative affect behavior in order to reduce the risks and the costs involved. But the process that is assumed to underlie this proposition has to do with the nation's ability to monitor and react to foreign affairs. Since low capacity nations have either limited resources to allocate to monitoring foreign affairs or a poorly organized and ineffective governmental agency assigned to carry out this task, in many instances these nations may not perceive issues in international politics that impinge on their own vital interests until these issues have been developing for some time, often in directions undesired by the low capacity nation. One might also argue that even if such issues were perceived at an early stage, the small state would not have the personnel or skills to influence these early deliberations or perhaps even to participate in them. Therefore, issues vital to the nation are often likely to develop and to be formulated without effective input from the low capacity nation. Thus, when the issue is finally perceived and when the nation does have to act, it can no longer utilize low commitment, low affect, or cooperative behaviors. The low capacity nation is faced with a situation where it must deliver a very strongly worded statement expressing its opposition to the issue as it has been formulated, or it must utilize threats or other high affect actions in order to influence the outcome.

SUMMARY

In this chapter we have focused on a set of factors—national attributes—that have held a prominent place in the analysis of foreign policy for a long time. Factors such as land area, population, natural resources, and the economy have always been considered important when analyzing and attempting to predict a nation's foreign policy behavior. Despite the frequency with which these various factors are discussed individually in the literature, there has been very little theoretical or empirical work done on what we have called the national attributes perspective. In this perspective, it is assumed that the class of variables defined as national attributes is a major source of variation explaining differences in foreign policy behavior. Therefore, it was necessary to begin by clarifying what we meant by the term national attributes and to outline how national attributes are related theoretically to foreign policy behavior. The concept of capacity to act was introduced as a means of integrating the numerous ways national attributes might affect foreign policy. Examples were given of how capacity to act might affect three aspects of a nation's foreign policy: (1) its substantive content, (2) the techniques or style of statecraft, and (3) the processes and structures for making foreign policy decisions. Finally, capacity to act was separated into its two component dimensions, size and social organization, and the relationship of each of these dimensions to foreign policy was examined. A listing of selected assumptions was drawn from the perspective, and a set of illustrative propositions was presented.

This perspective on foreign policy can also be related to other theoretical perspectives. We will note at least three such linkages. First of all, the national attributes perspective assumes that national political leaders act in foreign affairs in the name of the government. These persons will be influenced in their actions by numerous psychological and personality characteristics (see chapter 3). The leaders' perceptions of their own nation's capacity to act will depend on such factors as experience in foreign affairs, interest in foreign affairs, need for power, and beliefs in self-efficacy as a political leader.

A second linkage involves regime characteristics (see chapter 5). A nation's ability to utilize its resources is clearly a function of the degree to which the regime is constrained by various political factors. Even though a national government may have legal access to and control over a large proportion of a society's total resources, as would be the case in a nation with a highly centralized economy, such access and control would be of little use in foreign affairs if the regime was paralyzed due to a stalemate in the governing coalition.

Finally, the national attributes perspective can be related to the decision structures and processes of the nation (see chapter 4). The organizational format adopted by the leaders for dealing with foreign policy tasks can affect the manner in which resources are allocated in the foreign policy sector. For example, in a nation with high levels of social organization (i.e., highly modernized), a strong national leader acting with staff and associates may be able to acquire very tight control of the foreign policy machinery, whereas in a nation with a lower level of social organization, there may be no effective foreign policy machinery for a leader to control.

In closing, we want to stress again that the primary purpose of this chapter has been to explicate a single perspective for foreign policy analysis—the national attributes perspective. However, there are many relationships between this perspective and the others in this book. We feel that this explication of single perspectives is a necessary but preliminary step that must be completed before moving to the task of creating multicausal, multivariate explanatory models of foreign policy behavior using all of the perspectives presented in this book.

7

THE INTERNATIONAL SYSTEM PERSPECTIVE AND FOREIGN POLICY

Maurice A. East

The international system perspective on foreign policy focuses attention on the most macro level of analysis. The central concern is with changes in the broad contextual characteristics of the international environment in which nations pursue their foreign policy goals and objectives. This perspective can generally be characterized in the following manner: as aspects of the international system change, there will be changes in the foreign policy behavior of the individual nations comprising that system.

In this chapter, we begin by defining an international system and by distinguishing international system variables from other types of variables that have often been confused with them. Then the general explanatory logic of the perspective relating international system variables to foreign policy is developed. This is followed by a discussion of five aspects of change in the international system that are assumed to be important for the analysis of foreign policy behavior. Finally, the basic assumptions of the perspective and several illustrative propositions are presented.

AUTHOR'S NOTE: Members of the University of Kentucky comparative foreign policy group have contributed greatly to this chapter, especially Pat Callahan, Jim Harper, and Tom Lairson. In addition, this chapter has benefited from close scrutiny by Stephen Salmore and from numerous discussions with other colleagues from the CREON Project.

OVERVIEW OF THE PERSPECTIVE

The *concept* of international system is certainly not new in the study of international politics or foreign policy. However, an international system *perspective* for the study of foreign policy is a relatively new development. As noted in the introductory chapter, a perspective can be described as a general orientation that posits the importance of some specified set of variables for explaining foreign policy and then provides an explanatory logic relating these central variables to foreign policy. Although some analysts have included the concept of international system in their list of variables to be examined when studying foreign policy, few have considered the international system as the central focus. As a result, the theoretical framework for linking international system variables to foreign policy is not very well developed. Before presenting our attempt to develop such a framework, it will be useful to examine briefly the concept of international system.

The literature of international politics and foreign policy is replete with references to international system. Historians have used this concept when writing about the diplomacy of many different eras. For instance, one type of international system—the bipolar system—was used by Thucydides to discuss the Peloponnesian Wars (see Fliess, 1966). Another type—the balance-of-power system—is examined in many diplomatic histories of eighteenth- and nineteenth-century Europe (for example, Gulick, 1955). International system is also a widely used concept in the international relations writings of political scientists in the 1960s and 1970s.

The way that these writers use the international system concept, however, does not coincide in all respects with the way it is used in this chapter. Therefore, let us make clear at the outset how we intend to use this concept. In defining a system, we turn to Hall and Fagan (1968: 18) who state: "A system is a set of objects together with relationships between the objects and between their attributes." After considering this definition and many others, Young (1968a: 15) discerned several general characteristics of systems that are present in virtually all definitions:

> Each definition embodies the idea of a group of objects or elements standing in some characteristic structural relationship to one another and interacting on the basis of certain characteristic processes.

Building on the Hall-Fagan definition of a system and Young's characteristics of that term, what additional defining characteristics must a system have before it can be considered an *international* system? It must be a system whose components include, but are not necessarily limited to, the most comprehensive territorially based political entities. Thus, an international system refers to the patterns of interactions and relationships among the major territorially based political actors existing at a particular time. In the contemporary era, it is generally agreed that the modern nation-state is the principal type of political actor in world politics (see, e.g., K. W. Deutsch, 1968; Nye and Keohane, 1971). In other historical periods, other types of political entities were the dominant actors in the international system. Examples would include the warring feudal states in ancient China, the city-states of classical Greece, and the Italian state system of fifteenth-century Europe (see Bozeman, 1960; K. J. Holsti, 1972). Even though we recognize the dominance of the modern nation-state at the present time, we also recognize that there are other types of entities playing significant roles in the contemporary international system—entities such as universal and regional intergovernmental organizations (IGOs), transnational guerrilla and terrorist groups, multinational corporations (MNCs), and a rapidly growing number of nongovernmental organizations (NGOs) operating in a wide variety of functional areas. In our definition of an international system we include these entities along with nation-states as components of the system.

With this understanding of how the concept of international system will be used, we turn our attention to outlining the basic characteristics of the international system perspective for studying foreign policy. In general this perspective is concerned with how changes in the international system affect the foreign policies of nations in that system. One important feature is that international system variables must focus on patterns of interactions and relationships among all the major entities in the international system. In other words, the perspective is holistic and considers the system as a single unit.

This requirement that the international system perspective be holistic distinguishes it from two other relatively common approaches. One is concerned with various geographic regions of the world considered as systems of action (Russett, 1967; Berton, 1969; Cantori and Spiegel, 1970). The second approach includes studies that isolate particular systems of activity involving two or three or a few entities that interact frequently regardless of geographic proximity. A good example is Russett's (1963) study of the United States and the United Kingdom, in which he assumes that these two nations constitute a system of action and then proceeds to analyze various patterns of activity within that assumed system. Although these two approaches may be useful, they do not focus on the international system as we have conceptualized it. The types of "systems" that are central to these approaches are conceptualized in the international system perspective as sub-systems *within* the international system. In our perspective it is possible to ask questions about the relationships between and among such sub-systems and the international system (for example, see Binder, 1958). This concern for how sub-systems are affected by the international system of which they are a part is a unique characteristic of the international system perspective.

There are two other aspects of the international system perspective that must be noted. The first concerns the dimension of time. The effect of a change in an international system variable can only be analyzed over time. In most cases when one wants to examine the effect of some variable on foreign policy behavior, the analysis is carried out in one of two ways: (1) by looking at changes in the variable over time with regard to some unit of observation or (2) by looking at change in terms of the variation found when comparing values across numerous units of observation at the same moment in time. These are often referred to as diachronic and synchronic analyses, respectively. The holistic nature of the international system perspective makes it impossible to carry out synchronic analysis because at any given point in time there is only one unit of observation, one international system to be examined.[1] Therefore, analyses of the effects of changes in the international system on foreign policy must be diachronic or cross-time in design.

The other important aspect of the international system perspective we need to note is that international system variables are distinguishable from what are referred to elsewhere as external variables (Rosenau and Hoggard, 1974; Harf et al., 1974). External variables are those attributes of a nation that require reference to some external entity in order to give the variable meaning. "Distance in air miles from the USSR" is one example of an external variable. "Number of formal alliance partners" is another. Both of these variables require one to make reference to an external entity, in one case the USSR and in the other allies. Furthermore, external variables are variables on which nations can be compared at the same point in time. Recalling the previous point about the importance of the time dimension to the international system perspective, we have a critical distinction between external and international system variables. As Harf et al. (1974: 236) put it:

> At any one moment the number of external data points is equal to the number of units in the system, usually the number of nations in existence, whereas there exists only one *systemic* data point at any given moment in time.

Given the importance of this distinction between external and international system variables, perhaps another example would be helpful. When considering intergovernmental organizations from the external perspective, the nation is the unit of observation and one possible *external* variable is the number of IGOs of which the nation is a member. Theoretically each nation in the system could belong to a different number of IGOs. Viewing intergovernmental organizations from the international system perspective, the system becomes the unit of observation and one possible *systemic* variable is the total number of IGOs in the international system at a given point in time.

To briefly summarize, we have presented our definition of an international system, and we have noted three characteristics of the international system perspective. First, the perspective is holistic—international system variables refer to the entire system as a single unit and not to sub-systems within it. Second, the time dimension is a crucial element in the perspective because the international system must be analyzed over time in order to discern changes in the system. Finally, international system variables are distinguishable from external variables, allowing us to recognize the unique contribution of the system perspective to foreign policy analysis.

Having placed these conceptual boundaries on the perspective, we can continue our overview by outlining briefly the possible theoretical linkages between international system variables and foreign policy. As Jones and Singer (1972: 13) note, an ecological orientation is basic to an international system perspective in "that the behavior and interaction of the nations are more influenced by [the] system than vice-versa." There are two ways systemic variables can affect foreign policy. First, a change in the system can lead to similar changes in the foreign policy behavior of nations in that system. Second, a change in the system can produce *differential* changes in the foreign policy behavior of nations in that system. Such differential reactions can result from the interaction of systemic variables and other nonsystemic variables that may differ from nation to nation such as national attributes, regime constraints, and personal characteristics of the leaders. Or differential reactions can occur because nations comprising the system perform different functions and play different roles in that system—balancer, ally, bloc leader, and the like. We suspect that nations having different roles in the international system will react differently to changes in that system. Both of these ways of relating international system variables to foreign policy will be examined in greater detail below.

We conclude our overview by raising a question about the importance of international system variables to foreign policy leaders of nations. Why should foreign policy decision makers be interested in systemic variables? We feel that from the decision maker's point of view, two general aspects of the international system are important—the complexity of the system and the availability of various resources within it. These two will be discussed more fully below; at this point it is only necessary to note that complexity and availability of resources are both important factors that must be considered by leaders making decisions on how to act and interact

TABLE 7.1
Dimensions Tapping Complexity and Availability of Resources

	Dimensions
Complexity	1. Number and type of components in the system
	2. Number and type of issues being dealt with in the system
	3. Structure of interaction among the components in the system
Availability of Resources	4. Patterns of resource distribution in the system
	5. Degree of organization in the system

effectively in the international system. In developing the perspective, complexity and availability of resources will be tapped by five dimensions of the international system as shown in Table 7.1. We argue that changes in any one of these five dimensions of the international system will lead to changes in the foreign policy behavior of nations in that system.

RELATION TO PREVIOUS STUDIES

As we have noted, the concept of international system is referred to frequently in both the theoretical and empirical literature of international studies. In this section, we shall offer an assessment of this body of literature insofar as it is relevant to an international system perspective on foreign policy. Anticipating the general thrust of this section, it is our conclusion that much of the international system literature is only indirectly relevant to this perspective. Nevertheless, it is instructive to consider some of this work in greater detail.

In one of the earliest theoretical analyses of international systems, M. A. Kaplan (1957) argues that the foreign policy behavior of nations will be affected by the type of international system in which they are operating. He states in one example that in the relatively stable balance-of-power type of international system, nations with great decision latitude pay about equal attention to domestic and foreign considerations when determining their foreign policy. But when the system changes to a much less stable, tight bipolar one, these nations pay much more attention to foreign or external considerations. Such nations also pay more attention to external considerations than do nations with little decision latitude. The logic underlying Kaplan's argument is that nations with great decision latitude have considerable control over the allocation of attention by the government to either external or domestic concerns. Nations with great decision latitude are able to shift more of their attention to external factors as the international system becomes less stable.

Despite this promising early effort by Kaplan, the thrust of much of the literature has been in a different direction. Many studies have been essentially descriptive in nature, attempting to determine and then map the salient dimensions of the international system (see Burns, 1957; Rosecrance, 1966; Young, 1968b; Modelski, 1974). These studies do not try to relate systemic factors to foreign policy or any other sort of behavior. Moreover, the research that goes beyond the descriptive level generally focuses on relationships between one set of systemic variables and another. These studies primarily involve correlational analyses of systemic variables with other systemic variables. The study by Singer and Small (1968) is an excellent example of this type of research. They tested for the existence of a relationship between alliance aggregation (a structural attribute of the international system) and the amount of war in the system. Studies of the relationship between status discrepancy in the system and amount of war (M. Wallace, 1971; East, 1972) are also examples of the "system explaining system" research. Although these studies are very suggestive of ways in which systemic variables can affect foreign policy, they cannot be considered examples of the international system perspective because no attempt has been made to provide a theoretical link between systemic variables and the actions of individual nations comprising the system.

Many discussions of international system variables have been marred by the failure to maintain the distinction between systemic and external variables. For example, Rosenau (1971: 109) includes both systemic and external variables in a category he calls systemic in his pre-theory of foreign policy.

> As for systemic variables, these include any nonhuman aspects of a society's external environment or any actions occurring abroad that condition or otherwise influence the choices made by its officials. Geographical "realities" and ideological challenges from potential aggressors are obvious examples of systemic variables. . . .

Both of Rosenau's examples are in fact external variables that can vary from nation to nation at a given point in time, and his discussion provides no other criteria for distinguishing systemic from external variables. In a footnote in a later article (Rosenau and Hoggard, 1974), Rosenau recognizes the need to distinguish between the two, but this distinction has not appeared in his subsequent work. McGowan and Shapiro (1973) also fail to make this distinction in their framework for categorizing empirical, comparative foreign policy studies. Quoting from the first paragraph of their chapter on systemic variables (McGowan and Shapiro 1973: 161):

> The second of the two sets of variables which influence foreign policy from outside the nation-state are characteristics of the inter-national system such as geographic location [external], degree of integration of a nation into the system [external], status rank within the system [external], the characteristics of international organiza-tions [probably systemic depending on the variable], and the level of violent conflict in the system [systemic]. [insertions not in original]

In spite of this tendency to group external and systemic variables together, we hope that this chapter will demonstrate the value of maintaining this distinction and of using the international system perspective for analyzing foreign policy.

In summarizing this review of the literature, we conclude that a large proportion of the work that has been done using international system variables to date is of marginal relevance to our concern with the inter-national system perspective on foreign policy. Few, if any, empirical studies that attempt to relate international system variables to foreign policy behavior have been carried out. However, much of the research relating system variables to one another is suggestive of dimensions of international system change that might be used in analyzing foreign policy from the system perspective.

DEVELOPMENT OF THE PERSPECTIVE

As we noted in the overview of this perspective, there are two ways that international system variables can affect the foreign policy behavior of nations. Changes in the international system can produce similar reactions among nations or differential reactions among nations. Both types of relationships require cross-time analysis to identify changes in the interna-tional system. Both types of relationships assume that changes in the international system are perceived relatively accurately and similarly by the foreign policy makers of the nations in the system. In its most general form this assumption says that national political leaders are able to perceive the major changes and trends in the international environment and that they perceive these relatively accurately. If some such assumption is not made, it becomes virtually impossible to distinguish theoretically between international system effects on foreign policy and the congeries of other factors also affecting foreign policy. On another level, one can also argue that over time national leaders must have a relatively accurate perception of the international system if their nations are to continue to exist as components of the system. We shall now turn to a closer examination of these two types of relationships. Perhaps the most obvious way that international system variables can affect foreign policy behavior is through a direct relationship between changes in the system over time and similar reactions to these changes by the nations in the system. In positing this type of relationship we assume that changes in the system cause nations to change their foreign policy behavior in *similar* ways. Singer (1961: 81) suggests the relevance of such an assumption to the international system perspective in his oft-quoted article on levels of analysis:

> [The international system] level of analysis almost inevitably requires that we postulate a high degree of uniformity in the foreign policy operational codes of our national actors. By definition, we allow little room for divergence in the behavior of our parts when we focus upon the whole.

If we relax the assumption that all nations will react similarly to perceived changes in the system while still assuming that changes in the system are perceived relatively accurately and similarly by decision makers in the nations of the system, international system changes can lead to differential reactions among nations. The *reactions* of leaders to these perceptions of system change can vary and, hence, national behavior can vary. The perceptions of systemic change held by the leaders in various nations, even though assumed to be virtually the same, will set in motion a process whereby other nonsystemic factors that vary from nation to nation will affect the way in which the leaders react. These nonsystemic factors—e.g., national attributes, constraints on the regime, personal characteristics of the leaders—will interact with systemic variables differently in each nation, thus resulting in different reactions to relatively similar perceptions of the international system. One good example is the interaction of regime constraint variables and systemic variables described by M. A. Kaplan (1957) and noted above in the literature review section. Regimes with great decision latitude react to increased instability in the international system by allocating more attention to foreign affairs, whereas regimes with little decision latitude are not able to shift attention from domestic to foreign affairs so easily. As a result, we would expect to find a difference in the foreign policy behaviors of high constraint versus low constraint regimes as the international system changes from a more to a less stable system.

Another reason nations may vary in their reactions to systemic change is because their responses are, in part, a consequence of the roles they have in the system. A brief examination of M. A. Kaplan's (1957) models of international systems reveals that, regardless of the particular configuration, every system is comprised of components—nations as well as other entities—that perform different functions and assume different roles. For example, Kaplan's balance of power system is comprised of entities performing such roles as balancer, bloc member, and bloc leader. In the loose bipolar system, there are bloc leaders, nonbloc members, bloc members, and universal organizations. The unit veto system is comprised of entities assuming the roles of nuclear powers, protectors, mediators, and universal organizations. Nations performing different roles in an international system are likely to react differently to changes in the system. In a loose bipolar system, bloc leaders and nonbloc members have different roles that would lead them to react differentially if the configuration of that system began to change in the direction of a tight bipolar system. The bloc leader nations would probably welcome and support moves to strengthen their control over members of their bloc, whereas the nonbloc members would oppose this shift because the pure tight bipolar system does not include nonbloc members.

Let us briefly summarize the development of the international system perspective thus far. There are two ways of linking systemic variables and foreign policy behavior. One assumes that nations react similarly to perceived systemic changes; the other assumes that there will be differential reactions by nations to systemic changes. These differential reactions are caused either by the interaction of systemic variables with nonsystemic variables that may vary from nation to nation or by the fact that nations have different roles in the international system, roles that generate different reactions to systemic changes.

Now our attention turns to the problem of dimensionalizing the international system. What dimensions of the international system are most salient for explaining the foreign policy behavior of the nations in that system? From the viewpoint of the foreign policy decision maker, what aspects of the international system are likely to have the greatest consequences for the success or failure of a nation's foreign policy? Five dimensions of the international system have been selected for further discussion because we believe they tap two general aspects of the system that have profound consequences for a nation's foreign policy—system complexity and the availability of resources within the system.

COMPLEXITY

Complexity refers to the number and variety of components in the international system and the intricacy of the relationships between and among those components. Foreign policy leaders are concerned with the complexity of the international environment because it determines to a large extent the degree to which they can control the destiny of their nation. The more complex the system, the more difficult it is for a nation to control and manipulate the effects of that system on itself. The ability to manipulate or even predict the consequences of one's actions or the actions of others is dependent on the complexity of the system. Changes in complexity can be tapped by three dimensions of the international system.

1. **Number and Type of Actors.** This dimension refers generally to the size of the international system and the number of different types of entities that comprise it. These variables are likely to relate directly to the ease with which nations can act effectively within the international environment. One example of the sort of problem that might be caused by an increase in the number and type of actors concerns communications. As the number of nations in the system increases, there will be a need for new forms of communication; bilateral diplomatic channels become increasingly ineffective as the number of actors in the system increases. Moreover, as the size of the system increases, it will be increasingly difficult to monitor the behavior of actors in the system. Minor powers and Third World states may find this advantageous, although major powers may find it a distressing limitation on their ability to influence or control activities in the system.

2. **Number and Type of Issues.** International systems, by virtue of being systems, can be thought of as performing certain tasks (Modelski, 1961), including the task of coping with or "processing" various substantive issues. The more issues being processed by the system and the greater the variety of issues, the more complex the system. Clearly not every foreign policy issue considered by a nation is an issue processed by the system. In this regard it might be helpful to conceive of international system issues as those broad substantive concerns (1) that are most prominent in the deliberations of international organizations and international conferences and (2) to which the largest amount of attention and resources are committed by the actors in the system in their bilateral and multilateral activities. Once again, we expect that different types of nations are likely to react differently to changes in the number and type of issues processed by the system. For example, major powers might favor an increase in the number of issues being processed by the system because an increase would provide a richer menu of issues to be used in negotiating

with other powers, making possible such strategies as side payments, tradeoffs, and old-fashioned bargaining.

3. **Structure of Interaction.** This dimension taps the pattern of relationships between and among components of the system as they interact on issues. By way of illustration, we shall focus here on the structure of conflict relations as one of the more important forms of interaction. Polarity can be considered a measure of the structure of conflict in the system. Polarity can be assessed in two ways: (1) by the number of centers (poles) around which conflict takes place, and (2) by the degree to which actors cluster around or adhere to polar positions in a conflict. If we measure polarity in these ways, we can differentiate, for example, between the conflict structures of tight and loose bipolar systems as well as between bipolar and multipolar systems.

The structure of conflict bears directly on system complexity, a unipolar or tight bipolar system being the least complex and a loosely structured, multipolar system being the most complex. However, looking at the structure of conflict in terms of system complexity does not help us arrive at any consensus on the question of which conflict structure is more conducive to peaceful, cooperative relations. Note the debate between Waltz (1964) and Deutsch and Singer (1964) on precisely this issue. Regardless of how this controversy is ultimately resolved, the point still remains that the structure of conflict in the international system is of crucial importance to foreign policy leaders.

AVAILABILITY OF RESOURCES

This aspect of the international system affects to a large extent where the leaders of a nation direct their foreign policy actions if they want to pursue national goals and objectives most effectively. It is necessary to be aware of the availability of resources in the system in order to take advantage of them. Here we are concerned not only with material resources that can be exchanged among nations—such as petroleum, agricultural products, and investment capital—but also with resources that can only be attributed to nations—such as prestige, political influence, and organizational effectiveness. By being aware of changes in the location and distribution of such resources over time, political leaders can act more effectively in implementing their nation's foreign policies.

4. **Distribution of Resources.** This dimension refers to the distribution of goods, services, capabilities, and values throughout the system. We are not interested here in the exact location or amount of resources in various nations. This information is relevant to the national attributes perspective or, perhaps, the external variables perspective. From the system perspective, we are concerned with the *distribution* of these resources and changes in distributions over time. For example, foreign policy leaders probably

become concerned if there is a great proliferation of nuclear weapons to other nations in the system, because this proliferation represents a profound shift in the distribution of destructive capabilities regardless of whether or not it is also an increase in total destructive power in the system. As the distributions change over time, the foreign policies of nations in the system will also change, with leaders adapting to the new "realities."

The nuclear proliferation example illustrates again the way in which a change in the international system can generate differential reactions from different types of nations. Nuclear powers are most likely to react very negatively to any proliferation of nuclear weapons, whereas nonnuclear powers, particularly those that have the technological capacity to support nuclear weapons, may see this systemic change as an opportunity to start acquiring their own nuclear arsenal.

5. **Degree of Organization.** This final dimension taps the degree to which the international system is arranged in a manner that facilitates the processing of international system issues. A highly organized system has the capacity to cope effectively with issues. This dimension is important to foreign policy decision makers because the organizational capacity of the international system is a resource that can be used by nations in the pursuit of their foreign policy goals and objectives. An increase in the organizational capacity of the system increases the availability of resources for use by nations. This sort of change is likely to result in changes in the foreign policy behavior of nations as they begin to take advantage of these newly available resources. Measures that could tap this dimension include such variables as the number of intergovernmental organizations in the system, the amount of overlapping of memberships in these organizations, the degree to which nations are represented diplomatically in one another's capitals, and the amount of resources available for allocation by international as opposed to national institutions.

In summarizing our discussion of dimensionalizing the international system, we have argued that international system variables affect foreign policy by providing foreign policy decision makers with information about the complexity of the international environment in which they must operate and about the availability of resources in the system. Five specific dimensions were discussed, each one tapping some aspect of systemic complexity or availability of resources. Changes in any of these dimensions will lead to changes in the foreign policy behavior of nations in the system.

SELECTED ASSUMPTIONS

Underlying the international system perspective, there is a set of assumptions or statements of "givens" that are necessary for generating testable hypotheses. Some of the central assumptions of this perspective are discussed next.

ASSUMPTION 7.1: *In the contemporary era, the international system is comprised of all the nation-states in the world.* The thrust of this assumption is to recognize the global nature of the international system at the present time. Although we clearly recognize that nations differ in the degree to which they relate to or are a part of the global system, nevertheless they are assumed to be components in the global system. This assumption in no way denies the validity of studying less than global groupings of nations, but it does make clear that such studies are not part of the international system perspective.

ASSUMPTION 7.2: *The patterns of relationships and interactions between and among the components of the international system are sufficiently stable to make it meaningful to talk about attributes of the system.* Although the international system is constantly changing over time, this assumption permits political leaders and academic analysts alike to conceptualize the system in terms of relatively stable patterns.

ASSUMPTION 7.3: *Political leaders are concerned about various dimensions of the international system as factors that must be taken into account when making foreign policy decisions.* It is this assumption that links the perceptions of systemic change by political leaders to foreign policy behavior. In developing the perspective we suggested that it is the complexity and availability of resources in the system that political leaders are concerned about when considering the international system.

ASSUMPTION 7.4: *Changes in the international system are perceived relatively accurately by the political leaders of the nations comprising the system.* As we argued above, this assumption is a critical one for the perspective. It allows us to theoretically isolate the effects of systemic variables and to distinguish them from other factors influencing foreign policy.

ILLUSTRATIVE PROPOSITIONS

The propositions presented here include one example from each of the five dimensions of the international system described earlier. They are all examples of international system variables that change over time, thereby affecting the foreign policy behavior of nations in the system.

PROPOSITION 7.1

As the level of organization in the international system increases, a greater proportion of a nation's scope of action will be directed toward international organizations.

Recall from Chapter 2 that scope of action is the distribution of behavior among some class of recipients. The present proposition indicates a systemic condition that increases the proportion of a nation's distribution of behaviors which have internal organizations as recipients. The rationale for this proposition rests on the assumption that nations will direct their foreign policy behavior toward those entities that represent resources in the system. The existence of effective systemic institutions, such as international organizations, will mean that nations will increasingly interact with them, seeking their support and a share of any material resources they have to distribute. Nations with little capacity to act are likely to interact with such international organizational entities because they represent a forum in which the collective weight of the lesser nations can be felt and because these organizations may have at their disposal much needed economic and technical assistance. Nations with the capacity to act will see these institutions as a forum for dealing with some of the serious problems that cannot be handled effectively in bilateral or sub-systemic interactions, problems such as food production and distribution, population control, environmental quality control, and international economic welfare issues.

PROPOSITION 7.2

As the distribution of economic wealth and productive capacity in the international system becomes more unequal, a greater proportion of all the substantive problem areas attended to in the foreign policy behavior of nations in the system will be concerned with economic affairs.

Because of the extreme importance to all nations of economic growth and development, issues relating to this substantive problem area will become highly salient as the distribution of economic capacity becomes more unequal. The "have not" nations will constantly attempt to acquire a greater share of economic goods and services through the use of foreign policy activities. "Have" nations will become quite concerned with economic matters, trying to make certain that any actions taken will neither substantially reduce their position of economic advantage nor negatively affect their prospects for future growth and development. As the distribution of economic capacities shifts, issues such as trade regulations, increases in multilateral economic assistance, rates of development, and international financial arrangements will become increasingly important foreign policy issues for all nations.

PROPOSITION 7.3

As the structure of conflict in the international system moves toward a loosely organized multipolar configuration, the foreign policy behavior of nations will become more independent rather than interdependent.

As the structure of conflict shifts in the predicted direction, the complexity of the international system will tend to increase. When the conflict structure becomes more multipolar and, as a consequence, blocs become less cohesive, external constraints on the behavior of nations are reduced. In a tight bipolar conflict structure, for example, a nation that is a subordinate member of one of the two blocs is highly constrained in its foreign policy behavior. Frequently such a nation reacts only to directives from the superordinate bloc leader, or its behavior is passive in the sense that it generally follows the policy lines laid down by the bloc leader, often acting jointly with the leader and other members of the bloc in interdependent behavior. In contrast, the loosely multipolar conflict structure allows individual nations more opportunity to act alone and more opportunity to take initiatory action on various matters without risking either the wrath of a bloc leader or the possibility of setting off interbloc conflict. This tendency for initiatives and solitary action was characterized in Chapter 2 as independent behavior.

PROPOSITION 7.4

As the number and type of actors in the international system increase, the proportion of a nation's foreign policy behavior involving diplomatic instrumentalities will increase.

The rationale here is that as the size of the international system increases, complexity increases. With increased complexity there is an increased need for diplomatic and protocol behavior in order to maintain even a minimal level of communication and interaction within the system. Clearly, increases in the number of actors in the system does not necessarily result in a corresponding increase in all types of activity in the system. Some of the nations that have recently become independent are marginal participants, at best, on many issues. Nevertheless, it is important that a minimal level of interaction and communication be maintained simply to assure that the channels remain effective and do not atrophy. If efforts are not made to maintain this minimal level, then such channels will not be operative or effective if and when they are needed to cope with some crisis in the future.

PROPOSITION 7.5

As the number of issues processed by the international system increases, the proportion of issue-specific bargaining and coalition-formation behavior will increase and the use of that type of pro-

*motive instrumentality involving ideological rhetoric in foreign
policy behavior will decrease.*

An increase in the number of issues being processed in the system increases
the number of possible issues on which bargaining and negotiation can
take place. Nations will value various outcomes differently on different
issues. As a result, there will be increased opportunity for bargaining and
mobilization of collective support. Moreover, we can expect to find a
decrease in the proportion of non-issue-specific ideological rhetoric that
often is used as an instrument of statecraft. In this regard, we can contrast
the rhetoric of the Cold War days of the 1950s with the types of behavior
that characterize the foreign policy activities of the major powers today.

SUMMARY

The major purpose of this chapter has been to present an international
system perspective for the study of foreign policy. This perspective can be
differentiated from the great bulk of other literature discussing international systems by its focus on the linkage between international system
variables and foreign policy behavior. We have argued that systemic variables are important to foreign policy makers because these variables reflect
the broad contextual characteristics of the international environment in
which foreign policy behavior takes place. The complexity of that environment and the availability of resources in it are two aspects that are of
considerable concern to national political leaders.

It is both accurate and appropriate to note at this juncture that
international system variables are probably the most remote from foreign
policy in terms of what McGowan and Shapiro (1973: 48) call the "social
distance of causal variables from actual policy choice." However, they still
do have an effect on foreign policy. Given the remoteness of this causal
connection, it is very likely that systemic variables interact with variables
from other perspectives before impacting on foreign policy. We have
alluded to some of these possible linkages already, but they should be
mentioned again, if only to highlight the relationship of this perspective to
others.

The degree to which political leaders recognize opportunities or limitations represented by the perceived changes in the system is likely to be
affected by various personal characteristics of those leaders (chapter 3).
For example, how leaders react to systemic changes will most likely be
affected by the training and experience of those leaders in foreign affairs.

The political constraints under which a regime operates (chapter 5)
form another variable that is likely to affect the way in which national

leaders react to international system changes. For instance, even if a political leader considers a particular systemic change as an opportunity for the nation to strike out in a new foreign policy direction, that leader's predisposition to act may be affected by the constraints on his regime.

National attributes of nations (chapter 6) can be related to international system variables in a similar way. A nation's capacity to act, determined by its national attributes, will affect a leader's predisposition to act. If a nation has a low capacity to act, the leaders of that nation may not be able to take advantage of opportunities presented by changes in the system.

These three examples of relationships between the international system perspective and the other perspectives are merely illustrations of the types of interrelationships that seem to exist among the various perspectives. However, suffice it to say in closing that these interrelationships become clearer as the individual perspectives are developed.

NOTE

1. It should be noted that, given our conceptualization of an international system, two or more international systems could exist at the same time. In fact, in earlier historical eras this was the case, with a Chinese system and a European system existing simultaneously with virtually no contact at all. Another international system, or perhaps several, may well have existed in the Western hemisphere at the same time. However, since the early 1960s, when large numbers of Asian and African nations gained independence, it seems reasonable to assume a holistic nature for the international system. In other words, in the contemporary era, international system variables by definition must refer to patterns of relationships that encompass virtually all nations.

8

PRIOR BEHAVIOR AS AN EXPLANATION
OF FOREIGN POLICY

Warren R. Phillips

Throughout this volume, by treating foreign policy behavior as purposive, the authors have assumed that it is a considered response to a prior stimulus. Although the source of the stimulus need not itself be external to the actor, the most common activators of externally directed behavior are the foreign policy actions of other nations. This perspective contends that the foreign policy behavior of a nation can be effectively explained by considering both the types and amounts of foreign policy behaviors that the nation receives from other nations as well as the nation's own prior foreign policy behavior. More specifically, this approach is based upon the belief that the behavior of one nation toward another is a function of its previous experience in dealing with that nation. Nations develop routines or standardized procedures for dealing with each other, routines of reciprocity and inertia. Other forces that affect the exchanges between two nations strengthen or weaken the effect of one or the other of these two routines.

AUTHOR'S NOTE: The author wishes to express his gratitude to the Advanced Research Projects Agency (ARPA 2345-3D20, DAHC15 73 C 0197, RF 3527-A1), to the National Science Foundation (GS-3117), to the Mershon Center of the Ohio State University, and to the Ohio State University Instruction and Research Computer Center for their support during the preparation of this paper. In addition, special thanks belong to Robert Crain for assistance on related papers.

OVERVIEW OF THE PERSPECTIVE

The international environment in which nations exist is an interactive one. The behaviors of one nation toward another, that is, a nation's foreign policy, are responses to the prior actions of other nations. The actions of each nation involve efforts to influence who the leaders of other nations will be, what decisions they will take, and how they will define their relations with other nations. A nation, as an actor in the international system, will largely base its actions with a second nation on the nature of the last or last several actions that the other nation has directed toward it. Furthermore, we expect that nations will generally return behavior similar to that received. Put more directly, we are suggesting that behavior begets behavior. Stated as a working hypothesis: An actor's behavior toward a specific object is a function of the behavior that it received from the object.[1] This principle that a nation's behavior toward another nation is determined by the patterns of action received from that nation we shall refer to as reciprocity.

But international relations must certainly be more than a tennis match in which each actor merely returns his object's service. Forces at work over time within a nation insure that specific strategies are employed when dealing with specific object nations. As Halperin (1974: 99) suggests: "Most of the actions taken by bureaucracies involve doing again or continuing to do what was done in the past. In the absence of some reason to change their behavior, organizations keep doing what they have been doing." Bureaucratic inertia, as an explanation of performance in organizations, leads to another working hypothesis that a nation's behavior in foreign policy results, in part, from its own prior patterns of action (in contrast to the prior behavior of others). Stated more formally: A given nation's behavior toward a specific object is a function of its previous behavior toward that object.[2]

We can combine these two processes of reciprocity and bureaucratic inertia to form a single statement that can be used to explain a nation's foreign policy behavior: The foreign policy dynamics of a nation are influenced by both bureaucratic inertia (its own prior behavior toward an object) and reciprocity (the prior behavior received from an object).[3] But the processes of reciprocity and bureaucratic inertia may sometimes call for different foreign policy responses to a received stimulus. For example, consider the relationship between Cuba and the United States from the perspective of Cuba. For a period of time, American behaviors directed at Cuba were infrequent and generally hostile. Cuba responded to those behaviors with its own hostile rhetoric toward the United States. After a time, bureaucratic inertia became reinforcing as both drew on prior experience involving few behaviors—all of them unfriendly. Assume that at some point the United States or Cuba begins to signal that it desires some change in the relationship and, accordingly, initiates a series of behaviors that occur more often and are orchestrated to signal a cautious but nonhostile tone. After receipt of a few such messages, the reciprocity basis for behavior toward the other partner no longer conforms to bureaucratic inertia (e.g., Cuba's own previous actions concerning America). Foreign policy decision makers in the recipient nation face a choice between conflicting grounds for decision. Whether they use reciprocity or inertia as the basis for their new responses depends on how much information they have about the intent of the initiator of change and the manner in which this information is interpreted.

The problem before us, therefore, is to specify the conditions under which reciprocity or inertia will predominate. Using theoretical concepts derived from information theory, we will attempt to differentiate between periods in which bureaucratic inertia, on the one hand, and reciprocity, on the other, will tend to best explain foreign policy behaviors.

McClelland (1961) suggests that the workings of a modern foreign office resemble the day-to-day operations of a well-run industrial plant. Many cables and other communications, often detailed and technical, are received each day by a nation's foreign ministry. To cope with this complexity, experts are assigned responsibility for monitoring the exchanges with specific countries. The ability of the experts to deal with their assigned tasks is in part a function of their understanding of the intent underlying the patterns of behavior that have been received from object nations in the recent past. In order to decide on an appropriate response to make to an object nation, the experts must be able to understand clearly and unambiguously the messages that they have been receiving from the object. As Halperin and Kanter (1973: 40) suggest:

> Nations affect the actions of one another less by physically compelling changes in behavior than by acting on one another's perceptions and expectations; interaction among nations is primarily a matter of threats, promises, and warnings designed to influence behavior by persuasion. Accordingly, the primary vehicle for the exercise of international influence takes the form of "signals" among international actors. Actions—the outputs of the national security bureaucracy—are "signals," designed to persuade another nation to alter its behavior in the preferred direction.

Thus, every act of a nation can be considered as a potential piece of information communicating to other nations the desires or dislikes of the acting nation.

The amount of information being conveyed in any period of time must depend upon both the number and variety of signals transmitted between nations. Variety of signals is important as long as they are reinforcing. We shall argue that it is the variety or heterogeneity of signals received from a specific other nation that determines the policy analyst's ability to reliably interpret incoming information. We contend that during periods when incoming signals are reliably and accurately interpreted the process of reciprocity will determine the recipient nation's responses. Conversely, when the stream of incoming signals conveys little information and, therefore, cannot be readily interpreted, the process of bureaucratic inertia will dominate.

RELATION TO PREVIOUS STUDIES

One of the earliest advocates of the international interaction approach was McClelland (1961, 1966). For him, interaction analysis has as a primary concern tracing patterns of demand and response between nations. He suggests that nations have access to only a limited inventory of responses in coping with the situations produced by system disturbances. How the government of the nation tends to select types of actions from the inventory to meet different kinds of nonroutine international situations provides evidence of the government's operational code in international politics.

Other theorists have also underscored the importance of considering the interactions of nations, especially those between antagonists. Burton (1968) asserts that the progression toward war depends upon equal contributions from both sides, each being governed by perceptions of threat. Holsti et al. (1968) argue that war may occur in a number of ways, but the chances of its occurrence are increased in the crisis atmosphere generated by the hostile joint exchanges of the parties involved. Zinnes (1968) has been concerned with the expression of hostility, with its perception, and with the ensuing responses. These authors all emphasize the process of exchange that assumes the equal importance of both participants and actions. Thus, we see that the flow of foreign policy as exchanges between nations has been the topic of discussion, debate, and analysis. It has infrequently, however, been the subject of formal theoretical development.

Although many of our current problems stem from the lack of formal explanation of the patterns of interactions between nations, it must be pointed out that the difficulty has not been becasue we have lacked a basis for making formal explanations. Several international relations scholars

(M. Deutsch, 1953; McClelland, 1967; Phillips, 1973) have proposed the possibility of using the international communications literature, which is rich in suggestions, for formulating formal theories. Wright (1955: 269) has defined international communications in the following manner: International communications involve the

> art of using symbols to express, to inform, to formulate, or to influence the opinion and policy of groups on matters of importance for international relations. In a narrower sense, it is the art of using symbols to influence other nations. As a discipline it is the philosophy guiding that art and the science analyzing international communications, determining their purposes, and measuring their effects.

In fact, we can view the entire political process as a process of mutual modification of images through feedback in communication (see Boulding, 1956).

Some writers have explicitly utilized the notion that behavior begets behavior in explaining the interactions between nations. Richardson (1960) contends that the rate of change in hostility of one nation toward a second depends upon the level of hostility that the second harbors toward the first.[4] This idea of a relationship between the actions of one nation and the past behavior of the object nation has been generalized by Pruitt (1969: 392) with the introduction of the concept of reciprocity. "Change in one party's level of output on a given dimension often produces *reciprocation*, . . . i.e., a resulting change in the other party's level of output on the same or another dimension." Azar (1970), Leng (1972), and Tanter (1972) have also considered the hypothesis that an actor's behavior toward another nation results from the patterns of actions received from that nation.

Several difficulties are encountered in applying international communications to the study of the interactions of nations. One critical issue concerns the question: Does the receiver nation actually receive the message as the sender intended or does interference in the channel distort or garble the message? An excellent review of this issue can be found in A. Whiting's (1969) discussion of the problems the United States faced during its bombing of North Vietnam. The United States had to convince the Chinese that its aircraft did not intend to cross the Chinese border. Whiting points out that many statements and subsequent actions were repeated to insure that the Chinese correctly understood the intentions of the United States. The perspective that we are presenting is an attempt to make explicit the conditions under which decision makers can reliably interpret incoming messages and thereby respond appropriately.

DEVELOPMENT OF THE PERSPECTIVE

Central to understanding when a nation's foreign policy behavior will be determined by a process of reciprocity or one of bureaucratic inertia is the quality of information a nation has received from the signals sent by the object. It is this information that will determine the nature of the response. Techniques have been developed to measure and account for both the variety of signals transmitted and the amount of information transmitted. The heterogeneity of these signals—that is, the variety of basic patterns at any point in time—is a measure of the uncertainty that would attend any attempts to specify the sender's selection process (Cherry, 1957; Shannon and Weaver, 1949; Ashby, 1952). For instance, a nation that repeatedly and exclusively sends verbal accusations to another nation leads analysts in the recipient nation to expect accusations. These analysts have very little uncertainty in expectation about the type of act likely to be received next from the sender. On the other hand, nations that send a variety of signals lead analysts in the receiver nation to be less certain about the likely next signal. When it arrives such a signal conveys more information in the sense that it helps to reduce the uncertainty created by the prior reception of heterogeneous signals. Therefore, we can measure the amount of information in a series of signals by ascertaining the effect on the recipient's uncertainty. The higher the uncertainty, the more information there is in the new signals. The problem, then, is to measure uncertainty. Information theory provides an excellent measure of the uncertainty, H, present in a set of signals:

$$H = \sum_{i=1}^{N} - P_i \log_2 P_i$$

P here is the independent probability of the occurrence of signal type i; there are N types of signals. Thus, from the probabilities, P_i, of different types of signals occurring in a given time period (e.g., same month), the uncertainty associated with the score for that period can be ascertained. If all outputs are equally likely, uncertainty is at a maximum. It is common to divide the actual uncertainty by the maximum value, deriving as a result the percentage of this maximum uncertainty, (H_{rel}), that is comparable across sources with differing sets of signals.

Let us consider two examples. In the first case a particular nation chooses to send to a particular object eighty foreign policy behaviors (or signals) in a given time period. The distribution of these behaviors is such that each of eight types of behaviors is used ten times. Notice that the actor has chosen to send an equal number of each type of signal to the object. By way of contrast, consider a second case involving another nation that sends the same object eighty behaviors in a similar time period, but they are all of the same type. The relative uncertainty figure for the distribution in the first example would be 1.00 and that for the distribution in the second example would be 0.00. The implications of these examples and of uncertainty are that in the equal probability instance there is no way to judge if further occurrences will be more likely to fall in one category rather than another. However, in the second example we can see that the object nation is more likely to expect to receive the same act it has been receiving in the last eighty sequences. Thus, the recipient reduces its uncertainty concerning the likely behavior of the actor. In other words, the smaller the H_{rel} figure, the more likely a nation is to choose a particular activity.

McClelland (1968, 1972) has carried out several analyses with this uncertainty measure (H_{rel}) in order to establish how it functions in crisis and noncrisis periods. He has demonstrated that the mix of behavior in a crisis does indeed change toward greater variety. The basic results are these (McClelland, 1972: 92-93):

1. With occasional exceptions, an H_{rel} of .700 or higher is associated with crisis months and only with crisis months.

2. If we operationalize the beginning and duration of an international crisis with an H_{rel} of .700 or higher, we are able to state when a particular crisis began and how long it lasted.

3. All noncrisis periods, with rare exceptions, have monthly H_{rel} figures below .700.

Several students of communications in international relations argue that in periods of crisis system overload occurs and actors display a reduced ability to interpret foreign policy inputs (Holsti, 1965; Burton, 1968). This observation would suggest that for dyads in periods of high relative uncertainty, usually crises, nations are less able to respond reciprocally to their object nation's activities.

However, it seems to be the case that in periods less uncertain than crises, nations are capable of responding more appropriately when they understand more fully the object nation's behaviors. This point needs further development. Burton (1969: 54-55) has suggested that one of the "tricks" in negotiation is that actors should send frequent and reinforcing responses if they wish to communicate changes in their perceptions of the situation. He also suggests that the process of resolution of conflict is in part a process of testing whether or not information is received as it was transmitted. If a communication is not correctly interpreted by the recipient, additional communications expressing the same intent in other ways should be dispatched. Thus, when nations are sending multiple types of signals it would appear easier for other nations to respond with what they judge to be appropriate behaviors. We are arguing that the simple repetition of the same behavior does not convey intent nearly as well as a combination of different behaviors all aimed at reinforcing the intent of the actor. For example, nations can more easily persuade others that they will fulfill treaty obligations if they employ a variety of signals—such as both words and deeds (which serve to reinforce each other)—rather than simply repeating a single signal—e.g., verbal claims.

Nations that are interacting frequently must consider how they can make the other nation understand the intent of their communications. If a nation wishes to orchestrate its foreign policy behaviors to facilitate understanding, it must design and deliver messages in a way that will gain and hold the attention of the intended object. The signals must refer to past experience between actor and object. Further, the communicator must choose actions to match and reinforce his verbal statements so that the message is convincing. Finally, the communicator must be able to interpret responses to his actions as signals that the receiver either does or does not understand the intent.

To summarize the perspective to this point: Provided that the communications channel is not overloaded, the more heterogeneous and reinforcing the signals sent from one nation to another in a given time period, the more certain the recipients are the response they choose is appropriate.

Extrapolating from this discussion, we propose that when one nation sends another nation homogeneous signals (that is, when the redundancy in signals is high) the recipient nation will identify less clearly the intent of the actor and will act on its own inertia. For periods of time in which there is a heterogeneity of mutually reinforcing signals and, thus, a greater amount of information, recipient nations are more certain about the implications of the actor's behaviors. In these periods of time, reciprocity should exert a stronger influence than inertia on foreign policy behaviors. Hence, recipient nations adjust to another actor's strategies more readily in periods of high uncertainty (i.e., information variety) and tend to continue doing what they had done in the past during periods of low uncertainty. Stated more formally, we can assert that in periods of high relative uncertainty, reciprocity is a better predictor of foreign policy behavior of a nation than is inertia, whereas in periods of low uncertainty, inertia is a better predicter than is reciprocity.

The pattern of interaction between two nations, however, is often more complex than simple alternatives of periods of inertia and reciprocity. Complex patterns of reciprocity are likely to develop, especially if nations interact on a frequent and consistent basis. Consider the example of the well-run foreign office. Such an office is composed of country analysts who monitor, categorize, sort, and interpret incoming signals and who develop routines for converting the signals received into different information to serve specialized purposes. Because of shared experiences in dealing with each other, when two nations with such foreign offices interact, an ordered pattern of understanding is likely to develop. The country analysts, who filter and interpret the information on which each nation relies, become increasingly adept at processing greater amounts and more complex information. They also gain a greater ability to respond to more heterogeneous patterns of behavior as each gains experience in dealing with the other. The ability to choose reciprocal response patterns is a function of incoming signals. But it is also a function of experience. This experience develops as a result of the interaction between the two nations and, as argued here, this development is facilitated by feedback indicating that one nation has correctly or incorrectly interpreted the signals it has received from the other. It is to be expected that reciprocity begins as a simple stimulus-response sequence but, as both nations gain experience in dealing with each other, more and increasingly complex chains of action and reaction are reciprocally linked together. Relatively frequent and consistent exchanges between two nations are likely, therefore, to result in the development of complex patterns of reciprocal behavior.

SELECTED ASSUMPTIONS

ASSUMPTION 8.1: *The foreign policy behavior of a nation is a function of its own and other nations' prior behavior.* This is a central assumption of this perspective—one which distinguishes it from other perspectives presented in this volume. The influence of factors located within the acting nation and differences between object nations are specifically not taken into account in this perspective. This assumption, however, can be relaxed, and, as we suggest in the concluding section of this chapter, it is perhaps necessary to consider factors other than prior behavior in order to provide a more complete explanation of foreign policy behavior.

ASSUMPTION 8.2: *A nation will attempt to respond in kind, or reciprocally, to behaviors received from other nations.* This assumption expresses the idea that behavior begets behavior and has been referred to as the process of reciprocity.

ASSUMPTION 8.3: *Reciprocal actions will be possible only if a nation clearly understands the meaning of the behaviors directed toward it.* This qualification that the meaning of incoming signals must be comprehended leads to our next assumption.

ASSUMPTION 8.4: *If the behaviors of a sending nation cannot be correctly interpreted by the receiving nation, it will repeat its prior pattern of behavior toward the sending nation.* This is the process of bureaucratic inertia.

ASSUMPTION 8.5: *The more heterogeneous the signals sent from one nation to another in a given time period, provided they are reinforcing, the more information these signals will give to the receiving nation.* The more accurate the information, the more certain the receiving nation is that the responses it chooses are appropriate.

ILLUSTRATIVE PROPOSITIONS

Because we have argued that high relative uncertainty in a set of signals is an indicator of high information content, we can, therefore, propose the following propositions.

PROPOSITION 8.1

In periods of low relative uncertainty, inertia is a better predictor of the foreign policy behavior of a nation than is reciprocity.

PROPOSITION 8.2

In periods of low relative uncertainty, inertia is a better predictor of foreign policy behavior of a nation than is reciprocity.

PROPOSITION 8.3

Complexity in patterns of reciprocity will be greater in dyads that exhibit frequent exchanges than in dyads that interact only infrequently.

The concepts of inertia and reciprocity used in these propositions can be related to many of the other dimensions of foreign policy behavior enumerated in Chapter 2. For example, if, with respect to a certain target or set of targets, a government has in its past behavior expressed low commitment, negative affect, or any of the other noted dimensions of behavior, then we would expect its current behavior toward that target to manifest those same characteristics. Similarly, if another entity's prior behavior toward the present actor was marked by low commitment, negative affect, or other behaviors mentioned in Chapter 2, then we would expect those same characteristics to appear in the present actor's response provided that reciprocity applied.

SUMMARY

In the development of this perspective, a tentative explanation has been offered. But foreign policy exchanges should not be considered an unchanging interplay in which all actors are governed exclusively by identical restraints placed upon them through the processes of inertia and reciprocity. A number of other forces are operating, both within the nation and in the nation's environment, that influence the degree to which a nation reciprocates behavior received or chooses to continue past behavior. Some of these forces that are at work in determining foreign policy behavior have been identified in the theoretical perspectives presented in other chapters. In addition, other elements considered important by some students of foreign policy but not fully explicated in the chapters of this book are of particular relevance in elaborating the approach we have outlined.

Certainly the pressure of domestic events would seem to act as an important instrument or force in influencing a nation to over-respond or under-respond to the behavior received from other nations (see Phillips, 1973). During periods of intense domestic activity, key decision makers must devote energies to solving or controlling the internal situation. To the degree that their time is consumed with domestic events, their ability to orchestrate foreign policy is minimized. Because this is the case, we would expect an increased tendency for over-response or under-response to an opponent's moves during periods of intense domestic activity. One way in which domestic events and international situations may interact to create pressures upon the choice of routines being employed is by changing the level of decision makers involved in a decision. For simplicity we can divide decision makers into two groups—working level bureaucrats and senior political officers. Domestic crises ought to draw senior level decision makers' attention away from foreign affairs. On the other hand, international crises ought to draw senior political officers into the decision process.

Third-party actions also influence the action and reaction model that has been set out here. Hermann and Salmore (1971) point out the need for considering the indirect object of a behavior as a means of investigating third-party actions. Phillips and Hainline (1973) have studied the secondary impact of behaviors in stimulus-response models developed for a triad consisting of the Soviet Union, the United States, and China. Phillips and

Callahan (1973) have attempted to formalize this framework to account for the indirect effects of third parties on the behavior of dyads.

The perspective presented in this chapter provides a rationale for looking at the exchanges between nations. We have posited that nations attempt to achieve reciprocity by matching their foreign behaviors to the inputs that they receive. This consistency of inputs and outputs is a function of their goals and the information, or feedback, that they receive from previous successes and failures. What must follow is an attempt to expand upon these ideas and to identify those forces that make the process a dynamic one with more fluctuations than simple matching routines would suggest.

NOTES

1. Mathematically, this statement is represented by the following equation:

$$B_{nq,m,t} = \sum_{m=1}^{P} \alpha_m B_{qn,m,t}$$

where $B_{nq,m,t}$ is the behavior of nation n directed toward nation q on dimension m at time t. $\sum_{m=1}^{P} \alpha_m B_{qn,m,t}$ is the weighted sum of each of nation q's behaviors toward n as measured, respectively, along the P dimensions of behavior. The weights (α's) used in computing the sum indicate the relative importance of nation q's behavior in influencing the behavior of nation n on dimension m.

2. Mathematically, this statement can be translated into the linear equation: $B_{nq,m,t} = \alpha_m B_{qn,m,t-1}$ where the symbolization is identical to the first equation and t-1 is a time period earlier.

3. The two approaches can be combined to form a single equation:

$$B_{nq,m,t} = \alpha_m B_{qn,m,t-1} + \sum_{m=1}^{P} \alpha_m B_{qn,m,t}.$$

The meanings of the individual terms remain the same as in the two preceding equations.

4. "This theory is about general tendencies common to all nations; about how they resent defiance, how they suspect defense to be concealed aggression, and how they respond to imports by sending out exports; about how expenditure on armaments is restrained by the difficulty of paying for them; and lastly, about grievances and their queer irrational ways, so that a halting apology may be received as though it were an added insult" (Richardson, 1960 : 13).

THE SITUATION AND FOREIGN POLICY

Linda P. Brady

The attention that scholars have given to such international events as the outbreak of World War I, the Cuban missile crisis, and the Yom Kippur War suggests the importance of the situation in research on foreign policy. But these three situations represent only a small fraction of the total number of situations that have been studied or could be studied. In making foreign policy, decision makers continuously respond to situations created by stimuli in the international environment. In this chapter we will argue that characteristics of these situations influence both the process by which foreign policy is made and the substance of foreign policy behavior.

Stimuli from the international environment become situations when they are perceived by decision makers. Generally, stimuli are perceived if they have the potential to affect the goals of a government or, in other words, if they pose a problem for a government. When faced with a problem, decision makers define the nature of that problem. Although specific perceptions of the situation may vary from individual to individual, there appear to be some common characteristics in most decision makers' definitions of the situation. One set of characteristics concerns the nature of the problem: its impact on a government's goals, its complexity,

AUTHOR'S NOTE: The author wishes to thank the other contributors to this volume, Patrick Callahan, and Carter Phillips for their comments on earlier drafts of this chapter.

the skills that it requires, the time pressures that it places on a government, and the importance of the source of the situation to a government. A second set of characteristics focuses on the match between the stimulus and its interpretation, that is, on the accuracy or fidelity between the stimulus and the decision. makers' perceptions of it. Both sets of characteristics affect the way a government makes foreign policy and the nature of its foreign policy behavior.

As in the other chapters, in this chapter we will present the intellectual underpinnings of this situational perspective as it relates to foreign policy making; we will also elaborate the explanatory mechanism that links the dimensions of the situation to foreign policy behavior, introduce selected assumptions of the perspective, and suggest illustrative propositions that relate the dimensions of the situation to foreign policy behavior.

OVERVIEW OF THE PERSPECTIVE

Three things have to occur before a situation exists for a foreign policy decision maker. There has to be a stimulus, a perception that the stimulus creates a problem, and an interpretation of the nature of the problem. We have labeled these latter two processes "occasion for decision" and "definition of the situation." When a stimulus is perceived to precipitate a problem, there is an occasion for decision. Interpretation of the nature of the problem involves the decision maker in ascertaining a definition of the situation. Let us examine these three constructs in more detail.

STIMULUS

The foreign policy decision-making process is activated by a stimulus. The stimulus may involve the behavior of another nation or an international entity; for example, the Soviet placement of missiles in Cuba during the early fall of 1962 provided a stimulus for American decision makers. Or a stimulus may result from environmental changes not initiated by specific human actors, e.g., floods and earthquakes. Stimuli set the stage for foreign policy making; they indicate what is happening in the international environment. As such, stimuli are objective phenomena that can be described independently of decision makers' perceptions.

OCCASION FOR DECISION

Unlike the stimulus, the occasion for decision is a subjective phenomenon and addresses the question of why some stimuli are perceived and others ignored by decision makers. Decision makers perceive or attend to a stimulus when that stimulus creates a problem for their government.

A stimulus creates a problem when it suggests a discrepancy between existing conditions and conditions that are desired by the government, i.e., a government's goals. We assume that foreign policy makers have goals and that they engage in foreign policy in an effort to achieve these goals. When events occur that interfere with progress toward these goals, then a problem is created for decision makers. Moreover, when events occur that present the possibility of accelerated progress toward these goals, a problem is also created. In the latter case decision makers are faced with the problem of taking advantage of the opportunity to move closer to their goals.[1] In either case, the decision makers attend to the stimulus. When decision makers perceive that a stimulus precipitates a problem for their government, there is an occasion for decision.

Let us return to our example of the Soviet deployment of missiles in Cuba in 1962 to illustrate the difference between stimulus and occasion for decision. Soviet actions created an occasion for decision for American decision makers because the Kennedy Administration could not accept a Soviet military presence in the western hemisphere. It was not the Soviet actions per se but American perceptions of the problems that such actions caused that led to the occasion for decision. The Soviet military presence, according to members of the Kennedy Administration, created problems in America's dealings with her European and Latin American allies and damaged the credibility of other defense commitments abroad.

DEFINITION OF THE SITUATION

Once there is an occasion for decision, decision makers formulate their definition of the situation. They seek out a description of the problem and put it in perspective. Some of the questions decision makers may pose in defining the situation are: Who is the source of the problem? What are our previous relations with the source? What are the time constraints for action? What kinds of skills are required to deal with the problem? In the example of Soviet missiles in Cuba, American decision makers defined the situation as a Soviet threat to defense and security values. Moreover, they perceived that there was little time in which to act. Similar to the occasion for decision, the definition of the situation is subjective.

Decision makers' definitions of the situation can be examined in two different ways. One can focus on the fidelity between the decision makers' perceptions of the situation and the stimulus or one can examine how the decision makers characterize the problem. By focusing on the fidelity between perceptions and stimulus, we are interested in information transmission. Every stimulus transmits information about the environment. The question becomes how close a match is there between the objective characteristics of the stimulus and decision makers' perceptions of these characteristics. The hypothesis can be advanced that the more closely related objective reality and perceived reality are, the more effective the information transmission process is. In theory, we should be able to test this hypothesis by comparing observers' descriptions of the stimulus with policy makers' descriptions of the stimulus and then noting the correspondence between the two. As an illustration of this type of analysis with our Soviet missile threat example, we observe that there is a debate among experts on whether or not the missiles the Soviets placed in Cuba in the fall of 1962 were any more offensive than the weapons they had already given Cuba early in 1962. American decision makers, however, perceived the earlier weapons as defensive while the missiles were viewed as offensive (cf. Hermann, 1969a).

In analyzing decision makers' definitions of the situation, we can also focus on how they characterize the problem that they perceive to be facing their government. In other words, we can examine the content of the decision makers' definitions of the situation or the nature of the problem as they perceive it. Although there are many ways to characterize a problem, we have selected five for consideration because of their significance in the explanation of foreign policy: (1) psychological distance, (2) impact on goals, (3) problem complexity, (4) skills required, and (5) time pressure.

1. **Psychological distance.** Psychological distance refers to feelings of remoteness or separation from an object and need not be identical to actual physical distance. Two individuals may be close physically (e.g., next-door neighbors) but feel distant psychologically if their relationship is not characterized by a tradition of frequent interaction. A similar phenomenon may occur in the relations between governments. American policy makers probably feel closer to British officials than to their counterparts in Cuba, although the United States is geographically much closer to Cuba. Stated differently, psychological distance taps the relevance or salience of the stimulus actor to the national government whose behavior we seek to explain. The more relevant or salient the behavior of the stimulus actor is to the responding government, the closer psychologically the two groups of decision makers can be considered to be.

2. **Impact on goals.** A second characteristic of the problem is its perceived impact on policy makers' goals. Does it facilitate or interfere with goal achievement? If the problem facilitiates goal achievement, then it presents decision makers with an opportunity. On the other hand, if the problem interferes with goal achievement, then it presents decision makers with a threat. As one element of the definition of the situation, threat/opportunity describes the decision makers' perception of the impact of the stimulus on their goals.

3. **Problem complexity**. Problem complexity, a third characteristic, focuses on the number and the difficulty of the intellectual operations that decision makers perceive are required to solve the problem. The greater the number and the greater the difficulty of these operations, the greater the complexity of the problem confronting decision makers. Problem complexity is not defined by the number of objective sub-tasks that can be identified, but by decision makers' perceptions of their ability to cope with the problem. If policy makers perceive well-developed capabilities within the decision-making unit, then they are likely to perceive the problem as less complex than if they do not perceive these capabilities.

4. **Skills required**. Related to problem complexity is the characteristic skills required. Skills required indicates whether decision makers perceive that creative or routine intellectual processes are required to solve the problem. Of interest here is the difference between planning and operations within bureaucracies. Planning tasks require the formulation of innovative, forward-looking alternatives, whereas operations generally require the application of established rules to current problems. In effect, planning involves a future time orientation while operations involve a present time orientation.

5. **Time pressure**. Time pressure is the fifth characteristic. It refers to the temporal relationship between the stimulus and the actor as perceived by the decision maker. By temporal relationship we mean the extent to which policy makers feel that they have little time to make a decision. Time pressure indicates decision makers' perceptions of the time frame within which they must formulate a response.

Let us examine the Soviet deployment of missiles in Cuba through the eyes of American decision makers to illustrate these five problem characteristics. With regard to psychological distance, the Cuban situation was salient to the United States both in geographical and in goal-related terms. The presence of missiles only ninety miles from the eastern coast created a situation that American policy makers could not ignore. Moreover, the tradition of American involvement in Latin America increased the relevance of the Soviet and Cuban actions. As these statements suggest, American decision makers perceived the Soviet action as a direct threat to American goals both in the western hemisphere and in the larger global context. The situation interfered with American goal achievement. In terms of problem complexity, the Soviet missiles in Cuba presented American decision makers with a fairly circumscribed problem—as President Kennedy indicated, "to get the missiles out." The major question that the Kennedy Administration discussed was how to get the missiles out, thus highlighting operations rather than planning skills. Clearly, with regard to time pressure, American decision makers perceived that they had little time in which to act—only until the missiles became operational, which they believed could happen in a matter of days.

Certainly there are more than five aspects to a problem in a decision maker's definition of the situation. We have included these five because they form an integral part of the explanatory mechanism that links definition of the situation to foreign policy behavior. That mechanism will be developed in an elaboration of the relationship between the situational perspective and foreign policy following a review of previous studies.

RELATION TO PREVIOUS STUDIES

As we noted in the beginning of this chapter, scholars have produced numerous case studies focusing on specific situations. Crises and other high threat situations have received the largest portion of such attention. Analyses of the Cuban missile crisis abound (Abel, 1966; Allison, 1971; Kennedy, 1969; Holsti et al., 1969) as do studies of the outbreak of World War I (O. Holsti, 1965, 1972; Holsti and North, 1966; Zinnes et al., 1972). However, there are exceptions to this trend toward studying crises. Besides the analysis of responses to more routine situations, some scholars have attempted to develop both theoretical and empirical approaches to a wider range of situations (see Hermann, 1969b; Brewer, 1972; Brady, 1974a).

In addition to the case studies there is a growing literature that examines the three aspects of a situation we have proposed—the stimulus, occasion for decision, and definition of the situation—as they affect foreign policy. Such research suggests the difference between the objective and subjective components of a situation, emphasizing the importance of the subjective component. For example, the Sprouts (1965, 1971) in their discussion of the "milieu" within which foreign policy decisions are made separate the environment into objective (operational) and subjective (psychological) components. The occasion for decision and the definition of the situation represent the psychological environment of decision makers in that they describe decision makers' perceptions of their environment. The stimulus is part of the operational or objective environment. Snyder et al. (1969: 202) note that a foreign policy maker's action "flows from his definition of the situation." Studies also indicate the relevance of images to a situational explanation of foreign policy. Robinson and Snyder (1965), for instance, suggest a relationship between the situation and policy makers' images: the occasion for decision influences whose images "count" in the policy-making process as well as the substance of those images. A similar perspective is advocated by Pruitt (1965). Policy makers' definitions of the situation result from their images of other governments.

That is, definitions of the situation include images of other governments, perceptions of the relationships between these governments and one's goals, and expectations concerning appropriate behaviors to be directed at other governments.

The theoretical efforts of Jervis (1970, 1976) and Boulding (1962, 1969) may represent the best of this situational tradition. Their most important contribution probably lies in their conceptualization of images as both long-term and more immediate influences on foreign policy. Images can be treated as descriptions both of the general context within which nations are located and of the more immediate situation to which policy makers respond. For example, Jervis (1969) distinguishes long-term images (such as the actor's beliefs about the domestic political system, his previous experiences, and his image of international history) from dimensions of the more immediate situation confronting decision makers (such as the tendency to view other states' behaviors as more centralized, disciplined, and coordinated). The latter images more appropriately fit our concept of definition of the situation. On the basis of his analysis of conflict and conflict resolution, Boulding (1962: 311) concludes that "a prerequisite to reconciliation is flexibility in the images, and especially in the value images, of the parties concerned." Underlying this conclusion is Boulding's assumption that the transitory images held by decision makers may decidedly influence the outcomes of conflict situations.

Although studies that adopt a situational perspective to explain foreign policy behavior are both numerous and varied, few studies make explicit the explanatory mechanism that links the definition of the situation to foreign policy behavior. In our overview of the perspective we presented the concepts that denote the presence of a situation. Next we will elaborate the relationships that exist among these concepts and further develop the explanatory mechanism.

DEVELOPMENT OF THE PERSPECTIVE

Fundamental to the relationship between the situation and foreign policy is the assumption that policy makers' definitions of the situation affect not only foreign policy behavior but also the structure of the foreign policy decision-making unit and the process by which foreign policy choices are made. It is the definition of the situation and not the occasion for decision per se that influences the foreign policy process. The decision maker's perception that there is a problem in the environment is not sufficient to predict his nation's foreign policy process or response. If, however, we learn how decision makers characterize or define the problem, we can suggest who will participate in working on that problem, what procedures they will use, and what foreign policy behavior will result. Let us examine each of the characteristics of the problem mentioned earlier to see how they influence who participates, the procedures used, and the resultant foreign policy behavior.

CHARACTERISTICS OF THE PROBLEM

1. **Psychological distance.** As defined in our overview of the perspective, psychological distance refers to the relevance or the salience of the source of the stimulus for the national government whose behavior we seek to explain. If the source is highly salient, then high level policy makers will probably participate in the decision-making process. The salience of the source suggests that the current stimulus may have long-range implications for the government and, thus, prompts the attention of decision makers with extensive responsibilities for the formulation of foreign policy. Moreover, standard operating procedures and routines are less likely to be used if decision makers are psychologically close to the source of the stimulus. Such procedures do not permit the flexibility in response that high level policy makers may feel is required to deal with the highly salient source.

With regard to foreign policy behavior, we expect that psychological closeness promotes frequent interaction with the source. In fact, the more salient the source of the stimulus, the more likely the stimulus is to be perceived in the first place as an occasion for decision. Communication links with the source provide a means for stimuli to be perceived. Furthermore, there is probably an inverse relationship between psychological distance and intensity of behavior. Decision makers tend to direct more intense behaviors at nations that they perceive to be psychologically close. If the salient source is an enemy, it will receive the most hostile behavior. If the salient source is an ally, behavior will probably include strong commitments of material and support.

2. **Impact on goals.** The impact that the stimulus is perceived to have on the actor's goals is probably one of the more significant elements of the definition of the situation. We have assumed that governments engage in foreign policy behaviors in order to achieve either short- or long-term goals in the international arena and have proposed that stimuli become occasions for decision when they are perceived to have an impact on a government's goals. Moreover, we have suggested that stimuli can be perceived as facilitating goal achievement (producing an opportunity) or as interfering with goal achievement (denoting a threat). Both threats and opportunities influence the nature of the foreign policy decision unit and the foreign policy decision-making process. Many and high level policy

makers tend to comprise the decision unit under conditions of threat. This seems reasonable because decision makers want to make effective use of their resources in response to threatening situations. Moreover, threats encourage an intense period of communication among the participants in the decision unit. Although opportunity situations encourage the same degree of participation as threatening situations, opportunities result in low level rather than high level participation. The absence of impending harm to desired values makes less crucial the involvement of high level officials. One of the consequences of the participation of many low level participants is less effective communication within the decision unit.

The substance of foreign policy behavior also varies for threats and opportunities. For instance, if decision makers define the situation as threatening, they are likely to engage in hostile responses. Moreover, these responses will be intense. In contrast, opportunities, while leading to intense responses, encourage cooperative rather than hostile reactions. Cooperative responses to opportunities move the acting government closer to the achievement of its goals. In effect, opportunities facilitate multiple, cooperative actions across time while threats encourage single, hostile responses.

3. **Problem complexity.** Problem complexity refers to the number and the degree of difficulty of the intellectual operations that policy makers perceive in a specific problem. Decision makers assess problem complexity by noting the capabilities within a decision-making unit that can be brought to bear on the problem. The complexity of the problem influences who participates in the decision-making process. If the problem is perceived as complex by decision makers (that is, it needs to be broken down into a series of sub-tasks), then there is often extensive bureaucratic involvement in the decision-making process. The standard operating procedures and routines that characterize bureaucracies are especially suited to handling specific sub-tasks. Such extensive bureaucratic involvement slows down decision making, increasing the time needed for taking action. As a result, the chances of there being a general response are often reduced. When a response occurs, it is less likely to be innovative if the problem is perceived as complex. There is a tendency to view the complex problem as a series of discrete problems rather than as one opportunity to implement a major change of direction in foreign policy.

4. **Skills required.** This problem characteristic indicates whether the problem requires creative (planning) or routine (operations) intellectual processes in its solution. Does the problem demand the generation of new ideas and approaches or does it involve the implementation or translation of ideas into practice? For problems that require creative intellectual processes, many and high level officials are likely to comprise the decision

unit, whereas for problems that require more routine intellectual processes, fewer and low level officials are likely to participate. High level policy makers are less likely to accept or be asked to accept routine problems. Moreover, high level policy makers move beyond their formal role requirements and, thus, can more easily engage in creative enterprises.

If the problem requires the development of new ideas, then interbureaucratic communication and the generation of alternatives will be encouraged. The reverse is probably the case for problems involving routine intellectual processes. Such problems encourage decision makers to fall back on their standard operating procedures, which suggests—according to much research on bureaucratic behavior (e.g., Allison, 1971; Destler, 1972)—that decision makers will engage in little interbureaucratic communication and will neglect the development of alternatives. Because creative problems tend to generate multiple alternatives, they often result in innovative foreign policy responses.

5. **Time pressure**. Time pressure refers to decision makers' perceptions of the time that is available to them for taking action. Just as relations between individuals are constrained or facilitated by the presence or absence of time pressure, so relations within a decision unit are affected by the time frame that decision makers perceive to be operating. When decision makers perceive the situation to involve short time, the decision unit tends to include few participants from one rank within the administrative structure. In contrast, extended time situations allow the participation of many decision makers drawn from varying ranks within the administrative structure. Short time situations also discourage interaction and communication among participants, often resulting in the generation of fewer alternatives within the decision unit. Communication within and between decisional ranks and the formulation and evaluation of alternatives are more likely to occur when decision makers perceive that there is extended time for action.

With regard to foreign policy behavior, short time situations place obstacles in the path of high commitment behaviors by making it difficult to complete the planning activities often required for commitment. Moreover, those behaviors that occur when time is perceived as short tend to be status quo or conservative rather than innovative. Contrast these behaviors with those undertaken when there is a perception of extended time for action. Extended time facilitates high commitment responses and encourages innovative policy.

Figure 9.1 summarizes the relationship between situation and foreign policy that we have been describing. When a stimulus from the international environment is perceived by decision makers to cause a problem for achievement of their government's goals, it precipitates an occasion for

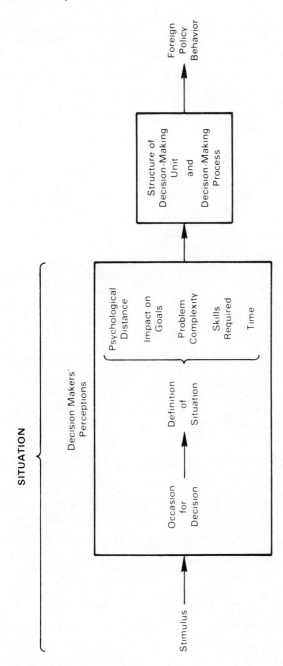

Figure 9.1. Summary of relationship between situation and foreign policy.

decision. Policy makers formulate a definition of the situation, ascertaining at least five characteristics of the problem—i.e., psychological distance from the source of the stimulus, the nature of the problem's impact on the government's goals, the complexity of the problem, the skills required for dealing with the problem, and the time allotted for a decision. How decision makers define the situation influences the nature of the foreign policy decision unit and the foreign policy-making process. The structures and processes, in turn, affect foreign policy behavior.

ACCURACY OF DEFINITION OF THE SITUATION

The accuracy or fidelity with which decision makers define the situation can also have an impact on the foreign policy-making process and foreign policy behavior. If decision makers accurately perceive the stimulus, then information concerning the environment has been transmitted efficiently. That such is often the exception rather than the rule is evidenced by explanations of the outbreak of World War I (O. Holsti, 1972), of American decisions to escalate the Korean War (Paige, 1968), and of the Vietnam conflict (Janis, 1972) that rely on misperception as a primary explanatory variable. In particular, misperception appears to influence the impact or consequences of foreign policy behavior. For example, misperception of the psychological distance between the actor and the source of the stimulus can lessen the consequences of some actions while increasing the level of negative feedback on others. Misperception of a threat can result in fewer and lower ranking policy makers participating in the decision than would be warranted given a more objective perception of the stimulus. Misperception of the time available for response can result in the less effective implementation of decisions that require extensive commitment of resources.

Accuracy in defining the situation is influenced by two other types of variables that affect decision makers' perceptions—characteristics of the decision structure and process and decision makers' own personal characteristics. The impact of decision structure and process on the definition of the situation is documented in chapter 4 of this volume as well as by Allison (1971), Halperin (1974), and Brady (1976). This effect is summarized by Allison's statement that "where you stand depends on where you sit." With regard to the decision makers' own personal characteristics, it seems inevitable that policy makers' beliefs or views of the world will influence their definitions of the situation (see chapter 3 in this volume as well as Bonham, 1975). A policy maker who views the international environment as generally conflictful will probably define more situations as threats than a policy maker who views the international environment as generally cooperative. Here is certainly an area for possible integration of several of the perspectives discussed in this book.

In this section we have suggested how situational variables relate to foreign policy. Next we attempt to make explicit some of the guiding assumptions of this perspective.

SELECTED ASSUMPTIONS

The process of making explicit one's assumptions is always difficult; at the same time it is a task central to the development of theory. The assumptions introduced in this chapter, although they may not represent all the necessary conditions for formally deriving the situational perspective, illustrate the kinds of assumptions on which that perspective is based.

ASSUMPTION 9.1: *Foreign policy behaviors of nations are discrete actions of decision makers that are taken in response to an occasion for decision created by the prior actions of domestic or foreign entities.* This assumption is basic to the situational perspective since it identifies a stimulus to which decision makers respond. That stimulus may occur in the domestic as well as the foreign environment.

ASSUMPTION 9.2: *A stimulus becomes an occasion for decision when it creates a problem for decision makers in achieving their government's goals.* This assumption suggests which stimuli will be perceived by decision makers and generate an occasion for decision.

ASSUMPTION 9.3: *Because authoritative decision makers initiate foreign policy actions in the name of their nation and officially commit that nation's resources in the international arena, it is their perceptions and behaviors that must be understood in order to explain the decision and action components of foreign policy.* By focusing on authoritative decision makers we assume that foreign policy may best be explained from their perspective. By authoritative decision makers we mean those public officials (whether elected or appointed) who have formal responsibility for decision making and who actively participate in the decision-making process (see Hermann, 1972a). Although we acknowledge that nongovernmental individuals and groups have a role to play in the day to day flow of people and nonhuman resources across national boundaries, only authoritative decision makers have the power to officially commit their country's resources in the pursuit of national goals.

ASSUMPTION 9.4: *If an occasion for decision is perceived by decision makers, then various characteristics applicable to any situation—but which may have different values in different situations—will be perceived by virtually all decision makers exposed to that occasion for decision.* Although situations are unique both in the sense of occurring at a particular point in time and in being composed of a unique set of circumstances, general characteristics for defining situations can be identified. We have suggested that psychological distance, impact on goals, problem complexity, skills required, and time pressure represent some of these general characteristics. Policy makers' perceptions of the relationship between the situation and their goals or objectives appear in many decision-making analyses of situational influences. For example, Hermann (1972b), Lentner (1972), Paige (1972a), and Schwartz (1972) identify threat to desired goals as a necessary component of crisis situations. Moreover, the presence or absence of time pressure on decision makers has also received attention. O. Holsti (1972), Hermann (1972b), and Paige (1968) identify short time as a necessary characteristic of crisis situations. One of the significant consequences of being able to identify multiple general properties of situations is that multidimensional typologies of situations can be constructed. Such multidimensional typologies help to provide more complete descriptions of the situational context within which behavior occurs.

ASSUMPTION 9.5: *Differences may emerge in perceptions of the situation from one decision maker to another because situations reflect the values, goals, past experiences, and general images regarding international affairs of the individual decision maker, his or her organizational context, and his or her nation.* Decision makers' perceptions in any specific situation are influenced by their images of international affairs (Boulding, 1969; Jervis, 1970) as well as by the differences among the organizational units in which they find themselves (Allison, 1971) and the larger context within which the situation occurs (Kelman, 1955). When policy makers "define" a situation they ascribe meaning to the stimulus on the basis of their personal images and experiences. Put differently, definition of the situation results in a valuation by policy makers (Snyder, 1958: 17). Moreover, the decision-making process occurs within an organizational context and, often, the interaction of competing national, organizational, and personal goals leads to variations in perceptions of the situation (Jervis, 1970; Allison, 1971). Furthermore, because each situation can be located in the larger context of ongoing relations between nations, interpretation of each situation depends on the relationship between the situation and the general level of interaction with the source of the stimulus (Kelman, 1955: 51). As a consequence of these varying influences on perceptions of the situation, the definition of any specific situation may differ from one decision maker to another.

ASSUMPTION 9.6: *If within the decision-making unit there exists a consensus concerning the occasion for decision and definition of the situation, then governmental attention to the problem is more likely.* This assumption suggests that a problem must be perceived by decision makers before it can be acted upon. Moreover, concerted and effective action is more likely if decision makers have similar perceptions of the problem. In the absence of agreement, foreign policy actions tend to be random and undirected, if they are undertaken at all.

ILLUSTRATIVE PROPOSITIONS

In this section we present a set of propositions that link definition of the situation variables with foreign policy behavior. The rationale for most of these propositions has already been presented in some detail and will only be alluded to briefly here.

PROPOSITION 9.1

The less the psychological distance perceived between the decision makers' nation and the source of the stimulus, the more likely there is a high amount of activity between the two entities.

The logic for this proposition is straightforward. When in two governments decision makers consider the other salient to goal achievement, they will encourage repeated interactions, thus accounting for the high amount of activity between them. Regardless of the friendly or hostile nature of such interactions, decision makers in both governments perceive that they cannot ignore the other and, in fact, that their goals are best served by constant monitoring and evaluation of the other's foreign policy behavior.

PROPOSITION 9.2

When decision makers are faced with threats to their government's goals, their foreign policy responses are likely to exhibit high negative affect.

Decision makers respond to impending harm by trying to prevent the threat from being carried out. Generally such actions are hostile. Studies on the outbreak of World War I (O. Holsti, 1965, 1972), the American decision to enter the Korean conflict (Paige, 1968), and the Berlin Wall episode (McClelland, 1969) lend support to this proposition.

PROPOSITION 9.3

When decision makers are faced with opportunities to make progress toward their goals, they are likely to engage in high positive affect responses.

This proposition follows from Proposition 9.2. Opportunities result when a stimulus is perceived as facilitating goal achievement. Given an opportunity, decision makers are more likely to make progress on their goal if they respond cooperatively. Cooperative responses tend to elicit subsequent cooperative behavior (Pruitt, 1969), thus moving the nation ever closer toward the decision makers' professed goals.

PROPOSITION 9.4

The greater the perceived complexity of the problem, the greater will be the specificity of any foreign policy behavior dealing with that problem.

Problem complexity leads to involvement of a wide variety of bureaucratic units, if for no other reason than that the task can be broken down into sub-problems, and sub-problems tend to fit standard operating procedures (Steinbruner, 1974: 69). The results of this process are specific actions that involve a commitment to the solution of individual problems.

PROPOSITION 9.5

When the situation primarily requires the use of creative (planning) rather than routine (operations) intellectual processes, foreign policy behaviors result that have high external consequentiality, that is, far-reaching consequences both for specific other nations and for the international system as a whole.

Creative intellectual processes lead to the generation of multiple alternatives, some of which can represent major changes of policy direction, goals, and commitments. Other things being equal, behaviors that represent a new direction are more likely than behaviors that repeat standard goals and policies to be noticed in the international arena and, consequently, to have a major impact in that arena. As noted in Chapter 2, such high impact behavior has been designated external consequentiality. Thus, a government's behavior is likely to be consequential if that behavior results from creative intellectual processes. Note, for example, the impact of the Marshall Plan in Europe following World War II.

PROPOSITION 9.6

When decision makers perceive only a short time period in which to make a decision, they tend to engage in low commitment behavior and, conversely, when extended decision time is perceived, decision makers engage in high commitment behaviors.

When constrained by short decision time policy makers rely on their previous experiences, images, and belief systems to define the situation and to evaluate alternative responses. It has been demonstrated that the range of alternatives narrows when policy makers are forced to deliberate under severe time constraints (Hermann, 1969a; O. Holsti, 1972). Moreover, the preparations that tend to precede high commitment behavior require time and, thus, are unlikely to be made under conditions of short decision time.

Extended as compared with short decision time provides decision makers with a longer period for deliberation. As a consequence, decision makers tend to consider a larger number of alternatives and a wider range of policy options (Downs, 1966; Hermann, 1969a). Moreover, decisions made in extended time situations permit the extensive planning and evaluation of alternatives and the mobilization of resources and implementation of behaviors that high commitment policies generally require.[2]

SUMMARY

In this chapter we have examined how the situation affects foreign policy. By focusing on such concepts as the occasion for decision and definition of the situation, we have suggested that the interpretation that a decision maker puts on a stimulus can influence foreign policy behavior. Foreign policy behaviors represent responses to perceived stimuli. Decision makers' perceptions are affected by many factors and herein lies an important aspect of the situational perspective. In explaining foreign policy from a situational perspective, one must necessarily include other types of variables such as decision structures and processes or decision makers' personal characteristics. If we consider past experience as setting the context within which the stimulus occurs, then other types of variables like those in the national attributes or international system perspectives also can influence decision makers' definitions of the situation. In short, the situational perspective suggests one basis on which to integrate the various perspectives in explaining foreign policy.

What other interesting and theoretically important questions about foreign policy behavior can the situational perspective address? One such question is the level of analysis problem in international relations (see Singer, 1961; Sondermann, 1961). Situations link actions (foreign policy behaviors) and interactions. If Nation A acts toward Nation B and Nation B's decision makers perceive the action, then a situation is created for Nation B. When Nation B's decision makers respond to that situation, they can create a situation for Nation A. Nation A's decision makers, if they perceive this counter-action, respond to Nation B's action, potentially creating a second situation for Nation B, and so on. What situations allow us to do, then, is to describe a series of interactions between nations. Behavior creates an occasion for decision, the occasion leads to a definition of the situation, and that definition, in turn, determines subsequent occasions for decision, definitions of the situation, and behavior. Thus, the situational perspective encompasses both actions and interactions, an important linkage for the explanation of international politics.

Not surprisingly, the situational perspective also encourages a linkage between domestic and foreign policy. There has been much research, represented both by quantitative and nonquantitative efforts, on the domestic/foreign policy linkage. The relevance of the situational perspective to this research is twofold. In the first place, stimuli in both the domestic and international environments create occasions for foreign policy decisions. Moreover, the five problem characteristics of the definition of the situation are applicable to both domestic and international situations.

Quite obviously, certain kinds of situations (such as crises) have serious potential consequences for both national units and the future of the international system. In a century overshadowed by the possibility of nuclear war, the impact of crises on foreign policy behavior deserves considerable study. Often accompanied by stress, crises can hamper decision makers' ability to cope with the situation. As Holsti (1976) argues, this condition can interfere with the usual decision processes and result in irrational foreign policy choices. Decision makers tend to overreact or underreact to the actions of other nations. Under extreme stress the decision process may collapse, preventing any form of response. Given the possibility that their reactions might result in a nuclear exchange, the behavior of decision makers in crises should be studied with the aim of increasing their ability to cope adequately with stress. Janis (1972), Milburn (1972), and Holsti and George (1975) include similar statements in their rationales for the study of crises and other high stress situations.

Thus, in addition to its explanatory potential, the utility that the situational perspective has for policy makers encourages further theoretical and empirical development. This chapter has attempted to lay the foundations for such future analyses.

NOTES

1. This use of the concept "problem" may not conform to accepted practice. In this chapter a problem does not necessarily represent a difficulty, but rather a task that decision makers must confront. Thus, both threats and opportunities create problems for decision makers.

2. We have not considered the interaction of problem characteristics in this chapter. Certainly we might develop propositions that link joint variations in two or more problem characteristics to variations in a single measure of foreign policy behavior. For example, under conditions of threat and short time we might expect more high commitment behaviors than under conditions of opportunity and short time. See Brady (1974a) for additional illustrations.

10

CONCLUSION: TOWARD INTEGRATING THE PERSPECTIVES

Stephen A. Salmore, Margaret G. Hermann,
Charles F. Hermann, and Barbara G. Salmore

The previous chapters have identified seven perspectives that may aid in developing explanations of the foreign policy behaviors of nations. We have considered how the personal characteristics of political leaders, decision structures and processes, aspects of political regimes, national attributes, properties of the international system, prior foreign behavior, and transitory qualities of the situation influence foreign policy behavior. Each perspective provided a partial list of necessary assumptions, contained an underlying rationale or explanatory logic that connected variables from that perspective to foreign policy behavior, and indicated some illustrative propositions for testing the linkages between the perspective and foreign policy behavior. In effect, the previous chapters have tried to show how each of the seven perspectives *by itself* plausibly accounted for selected foreign policy behaviors.

Probably the natural tendency at this point is to state a preference for one or two of the perspectives, thinking that the selected ones provide the most adequate explanations of foreign policy behavior. At least, there may be a temptation to ask the questions: Which perspective best explains foreign policy behavior? Under what conditions will one perspective do better at explaining foreign policy behavior than the others? As the introduction to this book indicated, however, such questions do not reflect the orientation of the CREON Project. We do not see the explanation of foreign policy behavior as a rivalry between competing theoretical perspectives but rather we are interested in how the perspectives combine to explain foreign policy behavior. In other words, we believe the appropriate question to ask upon completing the material on the various perspectives is: How can the variables and rationales advanced in the discussions of the separate perspectives be integrated to provide more comprehensive, multicausal explanations of foreign policy behaviors?

In the introduction (chapter 1) we mentioned that part of the CREON orientation involved the use of multicausal explanations. Having reviewed each of the theoretical perspectives separately, it now seems appropriate to suggest the reason for this commitment. Our indirect observations of foreign policy making suggest that it is a complex process, even in relatively small, preindustrial nations. As the seven theoretical perspectives in this book indicate, there are many potentially influential variables at work in the making of foreign policy. Given the diversity in these perspectives and the fact that arguments can be made associating each perspective to foreign policy behaviors, it seems unlikely that examining the relationships between a single perspective and foreign policy behaviors will produce an adequate explanation of these external behaviors.

The authors of the previous chapters often have found it necessary to involve variables from other perspectives in developing the rationale or assumptions for their perspective. For example, the personal characteristics of political leaders are viewed as affecting foreign policy behavior only under certain situations and in particular decision structures; the explanatory logic for the situational perspective is highly dependent on knowledge about the personal characteristics of the leaders as well as decision structures and processes; systemic variables seem to shape the national attributes that are relevant to foreign policy at any one point in time. In effect, there is an awareness in these chapters of the interdependencies among the perspectives even as each author tries to develop the solitary utility of his or her perspective. In this sense, the chapters have already presented some ways of integrating the perspectives.

In short, we believe that examining one perspective at a time—as has been done in the preceding chapters—is a necessary intermediate step for improving our understanding of each perspective's major variables, its explanatory logic, and its basic assumptions. However, we expect that one probably cannot fully comprehend the forces determining foreign policy behavior by only examining the direct effects of each perspective's variables or behavior. What we propose in this chapter, therefore, is to discuss in more detail several ways in which variables from the seven perspective have been interrelated in the previous chapters and to present two model.

that begin to integrate the perspectives in explaining foreign policy behavior.

STRATEGIES USED IN
INTERRELATING THE PERSPECTIVES

The perspectives are interrelated in three ways in the previous chapters. 's. The three include the use of common and conflicting assumptions, the introduction of variables from other perspectives as mediating or contextual variables, and the recognized interaction of variables from several perspectives. Let us explore each of these strategies in more detail.

One means by which the theoretical perspectives presented in the different chapters are interrelated is in terms of the assumptions. In some instances, different authors appear to have identified the same conditions as necessary for the relationships hypothesized between selected variables in the perspective and certain foreign policy behaviors. Compare, for example, the second assumption on political regimes and the first assumption of the national attributes perspectives. Both interpret foreign policy as sharply influenced by the nature of the resources available to the government. Similarly, the third assumption in the chapter on the situational perspective refers to the "perceptions and behaviors" of authoritative decision makers, and the third assumption in the chapter on the personal characteristics perspective refers to the "political leaders' views of the world." Assuming that world views are partially determined by the individual's perceptions, then there may be important elements of commonality in these assertions about influences on foreign policy behavior.

In addition to the presence of common or similar assumptions as a means of relating the separate theoretical perspectives, we can find necessary conditions stated in one perspective that appear to be contrary to those in another. As an illustration, notice the explicit introduction of a form of rationality calculation in the political regime and national attributes assumptions in contrast to the use of motives, beliefs, perceptions, images, and experiences in the chapters on situations and personal characteristics. From the information provided it is not clear that the assumptions are directly contradictory about the origins or rules that guide individual behavior. If they are, however, the realization provides a basis for searching for an overarching or "switching" assumption that might accommodate both assertions under different circumstances. Alternatively, an exploration might be launched to determine the consequences of substituting the alternate assumption into a perspective that had not previously considered it. In this manner, seemingly contradictory assumptions between perspectives can be used in an integration strategy along with those assumptions that theoretical perspectives have in common.

The second strategy for integrating the perspectives revealed in this volume is more direct than focusing on assumptions. It involves the use of variables from other perspectives as mediating or contextual variables. This strategy results when an author recognizes that variables from other perspectives affect the relationship between the perspective under study and foreign policy behavior. By mediating variable we mean a variable that intervenes in time *between* the perspective being examined and foreign policy behavior, thus influencing the relationship between the perspective's variables and foreign policy behavior. For example, in the chapter on the situational perspective the author notes that decision structure and process variables intervene between the government's definition of the situation and its foreign policy behavior. How the situation is defined influences the type of decision unit that will be used and the decision unit, in turn, affects the government's foreign policy behavior.

Contextual variables refer to variables that "set the stage" for the relationship between the perspective under consideration and foreign policy behavior. In effect, contextual variables establish conditions under which an hypothesized relationship is likely to occur. The personal characteristics perspective contains an example of contextual variables. The author suggests that the relationship between political leaders' personal characteristics and foreign policy behavior is stronger under certain circumstances. One of these circumstances involves the leader's scope of action. If a leader operates in a government in which he or she has a broad scope of action, such as in an unconstrained regime, the leader's personal characteristics will be more salient in foreign policy making. Here a regime variable sets part of the context or specifies one condition for the relationship between a leader's personal characteristics and foreign policy behavior.

To a certain extent, the distinction between mediating effects and contextual effects depends on which perspective is being used to explain foreign policy behavior. Consider the previous example. From the point of view of the personal characteristics perspective, a variable from the political regimes perspective specifies the "context" in which a leader operates on foreign policy behavior. If the same relationship is viewed from the regime perspective, the type of leader "mediates" the effect that regime constraints have on foreign policy. The important thing to remember about this way of integrating the perspectives, however, is that variables from other perspectives alter the relationship between variables in the perspective under study and foreign policy behavior.

A third way in which the perspectives are related involves interaction effects. Two perspectives may simultaneously interact to change the effect on foreign policy behavior that each would have when operating alone. In other words, when acting alone, a given explanatory variable may be observed to have one type of effect on foreign policy, but when it operates concurrently with other variables the results may be quite different. The multiple variables may combine to increase the effect exponentially over what would be expected if they acted separately. Alternatively, the net result may be the reverse of the separate outcomes. An example of an interaction between variables from different perspectives is found in the national attributes chapter. The author indicates that a change in the perspective's impact on foreign policy behavior occurs when the policy maker's goals are combined with the government's capacity to act. When considered in isolation, increases in a government's capacity to act are seen as expanding its participation in foreign affairs. Suppose one also considers the goal structure of the political leaders—a variable dependent upon such personal characteristics as belief systems and motives that, in turn, produce the leader's world view. Governmental increases in capacity to act *and* a leader with a world view that gives high priority to goals that are realized through foreign behaviors will lead to increased foreign affairs participation. In this case the anticipated result is exactly the same as the expectation from the bivariate relationship. But if the leader's goal structure is altered or if a leader with a different goal structure emerges, then a different interaction effect occurs. Given a leader with a world view that results in an emphasis on domestic goals, increases in capacity to act might yield no increases in foreign affairs participation. In fact, increases in capacity to act might even result in reductions in foreign affairs participation if the new capacity brings previously unobtainable domestic goals within reach provided a concerted effort is made.

Several implications for relating the theoretical perspectives into multicausal explanations of foreign policy behaviors emerge from the illustrations drawn from the preceding chapters. First, the perspectives appear to affect one another as well as the relationships between a specific perspective and foreign policy behavior. Some of the most critical relationships may, in fact, turn out to be between variables in different perspectives rather than between a single theoretical perspective's explanatory variables and behavior directly. Thus, it seems important to explicate the nature of the relationships between variables in different perspectives. Second, the variables from the various perspectives will probably not combine in a simple additive manner to provide substantial increases in our ability to explain foreign policy. The presence of mediating, contextual, and interactive effects suggests more complex interplay between the variables from the theoretical perspectives than does a simple additive model. Third, there are within the descriptions of the perspectives implicit first-approximation models for integrating the perspectives. Building on these implicit integrative statements from the previous chapters, we will present two multi-causal models of foreign policy behavior. These two models remain at a fairly simple and general level but will provide some idea of what we mean by a multicausal explanation. Before we turn to the models, however, we need to clarify what it is about foreign policy behaviors that we wish to explain.

DIFFERENTIATING FOREIGN POLICY BEHAVIORS TO FACILITATE EXPLANATION

In chapter 2 we distinguished foreign policy from foreign policy behavior and noted our preference for the latter as a more discrete, observable unit of measurement. We defined foreign policy behavior as purposive action directed at some external entity(ies) and initiated by individuals who are authoritative governmental decision makers or their representatives. The twenty-two types of behavior properties illustrated in the second chapter and the variations introduced in the propositions in subsequent chapters indicate the diversity of classifications and scales of behavior that are possible. Given this wide variety of possible foreign policy behaviors and classification schemes, it is by no means clear that the explanation for one type of behavior will be adequate for another type of behavior. It would appear that a necessary task in any integrative effort is to specify the types of behaviors to be explained.

For the purposes of the present integrative exercise, we will not use distinctions involving different types or dimensions of foreign policy behavior such as those introduced in chapter 2. Instead we will introduce two alternative ways of thinking about foreign policy behaviors. One alternative will be called pattern behavior; the other will be discrete behavior. The basic distinction between these two depends on whether one wishes to explain behavior aggregated across some substantial period of time (e.g., a number of years) or to explain the likelihood of a particular behavior in a specific incident. An analogy from meteorology will illustrate the difference. One type of meteorological question might be: Why has the mean temperature for a given geographical location increased substantially over the past twenty years? A different type of question would be: What is the probability of higher temperatures (or rain, or the like) in a given geographical location tomorrow?

Pattern behavior in foreign policy is equivalent to the mean temperature change over 20 years in the meteorological example. By pattern behavior we mean the aggregation of foreign policy behavior over an extended, standardized unit of time—say, a year or more. The number of economic transactions per year constitutes an illustration of a pattern behavior. Pattern behaviors can be expressed in a variety of descriptive statistics, e.g., averages, ratios, variances, gini indices. Pattern behaviors depend on aggregation for their meaning and in measurement terms cannot be decomposed to assign independent values for each occurrence of the behavior. Further examples of pattern behaviors based upon variables mentioned in the propositions of previous chapters include annual amount of foreign policy activity, the frequency of reciprocity with a given entity per year, and the yearly geographical distribution of recipients of a government's foreign policy initiatives.

A discrete behavior characterizes a single foreign policy action. There is no aggregation over time. Any means of conceptualizing foreign policy behavior that gives a distinct meaning to each occurrence of the action is a discrete behavior. In measurement each discrete behavior must have an independently derived scale value or must be independently located in a nominal category. Explanations of discrete behaviors that are not unique historical accounts usually involve conditions that affect the probability of a given behavior. In this sense they are comparable to the earlier meteorological example in which one uses knowledge of the atmospheric conditions expected to prevail tomorrow at a certain location to forecast the probability of rain. In the propositions advanced in previous chapters such variables as commitment, independence of action, specificity, and goal statements could be treated as discrete behaviors.

It seems likely that different theoretical perspectives and explanatory mechanisms will be involved in explaining pattern behaviors and discrete behaviors. Because pattern behaviors represent the aggregation of a nation's foreign activities over a period of time, perspectives that specify variables having relatively stable or slow changing values are likely to be most appropriate. On the other hand, an explanation of discrete actions will probably demand variables from perspectives that take different values for different discrete actions. Therefore, we will describe in some detail two models that build on the integrative statements derived from the previous chapters; one model seeks to explain pattern behaviors and the other attempts to explain discrete behaviors.

TOWARD EXPLAINING PATTERN BEHAVIORS

One possible multicausal model explaining pattern behaviors is found in Figure 10.1. This model is offered as a broad sketch of the way in which

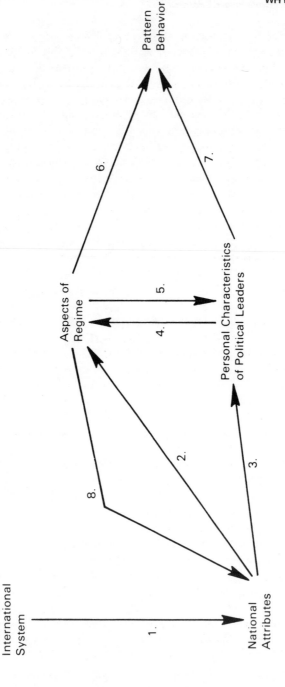

Figure 10.1. Multicausal model (Model 1) proposed as one way of integrating CREON perspectives to explain pattern behavior.

the perspectives whose variables are relatively stable over time can be integrated to explain pattern behavior. As presented, the model is not directly testable. To be testable, operationalized variables for which observed values could be obtained would have to be specified. After discussing the general model we will select a particular pattern behavior and variables for the perspectives to illustrate how the model might operate at the individual variable level.

Let us proceed now to describe the rationale behind the relationships in the general model (designated Model 1) in Figure 10.1. When we are examining pattern behavior we are interested in explaining a government's foreign policy behavior over a given period of time. The unit of analysis is the government. The question of interest in Model 1 is what variables are important for understanding the pattern behavior that the government is exhibiting in its foreign policy. Model 1 suggests that variables from the international system, national attributes, regime, and personal characteristics of political leaders' perspectives influence pattern behavior.

Arrow 1 of the model indicates that properties of the international system impact on the national attributes of a nation. Variables comprising the international system perspective usually exhibit the least variation over short periods of time of all the perspectives examined in this book. Changes in the international system are likely to be slow. As a result, system variables set the stage or context in which a government acts. These variables define the nature of the world in which the government must operate and the government's place or position in that world. In effect, system variables help to place national attributes in perspective. Thus, the knowledge that one's nation is relatively small or large, centrally or peripherally located in global interactions, developed or underdeveloped is acquired by knowing such system variables as number of actors, structure of conflict, and distribution of resources in the system.

Arrow 2 in Model 1 suggests that national attributes can influence the nature of the regime or government in power. For example, the attribute of modernization appears to be related to regime accountability (cf. Dahl, 1971). Hypothetically, highly accountable or democratic governments are less probable in countries that are plagued by persistent problems of social unrest (i.e., stress) or that have not achieved high levels of economic development (i.e., modernization). Here national attributes act as context-setting variables for the regime perspective. This arrow also may be interpreted as indicating that variables from the regime perspective mediate the relationship between national attributes and foreign policy behavior. As an illustration, the regime variable, "constraint," has implications for how much of a nation's resources can be used for foreign policy. In other words, constraint affects a nation's capacity to act. Highly constrained regimes seem less able to use their resources for foreign policy. In sum, arrow 2 suggests an interdependency between variables from the national attributes and regime perspectives in the explanation of pattern behavior. National attributes set the limits within which a regime operates and, in turn, the regime affects how national attributes are involved in foreign policy making.

National attributes also affect the personal characteristics of political leaders as denoted by arrow 3 in Model 1. National attributes can influence the kind of leaders who come into power. Thus, for instance, developing nations may be hypothesized as producing nationalistic, independent political leaders. Personal characteristics of political leaders can, in turn, affect how national attributes are defined and utilized in shaping foreign policy. Consider, for example, the proposition that the political leader with little interest in foreign policy may fail to perceive or be indifferent to ways of using his or her nation's resources in foreign affairs.

The relationships between regime variables, political leaders' personal characteristics, and pattern behavior—indicated by arrows 4, 5, 6 and 7—are more complex than those described to this point. Not only do variables from the regime and personal characteristics perspectives influence one another, but variables from each perspective mediate the other's influence on foreign policy behavior. Some illustrations are in order. The personal predispositions of political leaders can affect the leadership style of a regime. Likewise certain types of regimes are likely to produce certain types of leaders, e.g., independent leaders are likely to arise in less constrained regimes. An illustration of the mediating effect appears in chapter 3 on the personal characteristics of political leaders. That chapter contains the hypothesis that the less constrained the regime, the greater impact a political leader's personal characteristics can have on the government's foreign policy behavior. In turn, how "rational" a particular regime's strategy is in foreign affairs is dependent on the personal characteristics of the political leaders.

Arrows 4, 5, and 8 suggest another aspect of Model 1. It has the potential for being dynamic, that is, accounting for change over time. Through the feedback loops indicated by these arrows, the foreign policy behavior of a government can change as a result of internal changes in the relationships between these component variables. Thus, for instance, a regime is hypothesized as being able to successfully increase the level of economic development of the nation (arrow 8) that, in turn, affects the types of leaders selected. These leaders may, then, moderate the regime's orientation toward the need for more rapid economic development. Changes of this type appear to have occurred within the Soviet Union during the past two decades and have been accompanied by general changes in that nation's foreign policy behavior.

Now that we have described the general relationships in Model 1, let us identify a particular type of foreign policy pattern behavior and individual variables from the perspectives to show more specifically how the model might work. The pattern behavior that we will examine is the annual level of commitment of a government's resources to other nations. Commitment can range from talking about using one's resources (e.g., proposal of trade or aid) to the irreversible use of one's resources (e.g., actual trade or aid). The variables that we will relate to commitment from the theoretical perspectives are degree of organization in the international system (international system perspective), capacity to act (national attributes perspective), regime constraint (regime perspective), and nationalism of political leaders (personal characteristics perspective). The relationships between and among these variables are diagrammed in Figure 10.2.

Arrow 1 suggests the hypothesis that the greater the degree of organization in the system, the greater a nation's capacity to act in foreign affairs. Increases in the organization of the international system mean increases in such mechanisms as global institutions, established procedures, and communication networks that are accessible to all individual nations within the system. Thus, the organizational facilities augment each nation's resources and enable the members of each society, including the government, to act more ably in activities outside their country (see chapters 6 and 7).

Arrow 2 reflects the proposition that constrained regimes are more likely in economically developed as opposed to underdeveloped nations. By constraint we mean the degree of coherence or unity in the regime, the nature and extent of the regime's accountability in the domestic political process, and the degree to which the regime represents the wider society (refer to chapter 5). Moreover, constraint acts as a mediating variable for the relationship between capacity to act and annual level of commitment. We speculate that highly constrained regimes are less able to use their resources for foreign policy and, thus, are less able to commit their resources irreversibly to other nations.

As denoted in arrow 3 nationalistic leaders are hypothesized to be more likely to rule in nations with low capacity to act (the developing countries) than in nation's with a large capacity to act. Nationalism here refers to a strong attachment and identification with one's nation and a belief in the need to maintain the nation as a separate entity (see chapter 3). Nationalism mediates the relationship between capacity to act and commitment. Our hypothesis is that the capacity to act is more likely to affect commitment the less nationalistic the leader. Nationalistic leaders are unlikely to act in any way that will limit the independence of their nation.

Arrows 4 and 5 stem from the propositions that high constraint regimes are less likely to produce nationalistic leaders and, in turn, that nationa-

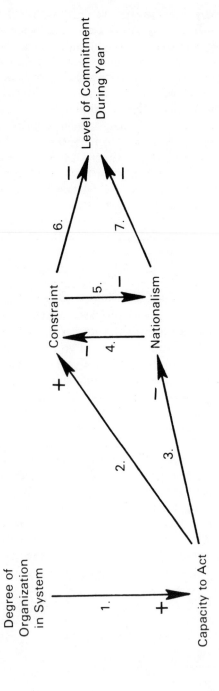

Figure 10.2. An illustration of Model 1.
(Plus and minus signs indicate direction of relationships.)

listic leaders work to reduce the constraints on the regimes of which they are a part. Two qualities which the nationalistic leader usually has—high need for power and distrust of others—are unlikely to endear him or her to the selectors in the political process of a high constraint regime. Moreover, such traits lead the nationalistic leader to adopt a maximalist, expansionist orientation toward rule and resource change while in office (see chapter 5 for more detail on these two dimensions of leadership style).

Constraint and nationalism mediate each other's relationship with commitment (arrows 6 and 7). Constraint is hypothesized to affect commitment more when the leaders are low in nationalism. Given rule by leaders with little nationalism, high constraint regimes will evidence lower annual levels of commitment of their nation's resources to other nations than will low constraint regimes. According to our hypothesis, nationalistic leaders are less likely—as indicated by arrow 4—to perceive accurately the distinction between high and low constraint. They will probably act as if there were little constraint. For the less nationalistic leaders, the distinction is a real one. Nationalism, however, is more likely to be related to commitment when constraint is low. In low constraint regimes, the more nationalistic the leadership is, the lower the government's level of commitment to other nations. The personal characteristics of political leaders (such as the degree of nationalism) are more able to impact on foreign policy the more control they have over the formation of that policy. Low constraint regimes permit such control.

In sum, according to Model 1 pattern behavior is the result of complex interrelationships among the variables from four perspectives—properties of the international system, national attributes, aspects of the regime, and personal characteristics of political leaders. System variables provide the context in which any government acts, defining a nation's position in the system based on its national attributes. National attributes, in turn, affect the types of regimes and leaders that nations have. Regimes and leaders play upon the national attributes of their nation and the characteristics of one another in determining pattern behavior.

TOWARD EXPLAINING DISCRETE BEHAVIORS

The second type of foreign policy behavior that we are interested in explaining in this chapter is discrete behavior. Of interest here is the answer to the question: What is the probability of a government responding in a particular way to a specific type of occasion for decision? For example, how likely it is that the Soviet Union will initiate war when threatened militarily by China? This type of exploration is quite interesting to policy makers and others concerned with particular types of events. To the extent that a discrete behavior is a function of certain identifiable and recurrent properties and relationships, it can be of use in forecasting. This type of explanation, however, is one of the most difficult to construct adequately because it requires accurate information on pattern behavior (like that from Model 1) *and* knowledge about numerous variables that can change from one foreign policy task to another. Two of the theoretical perspectives described in this book focus on variables that are measured at the event level—variables that change with each discrete behavior. These two perspectives, situation and decision structure and process, provide the core of Model 2, which is diagrammed in Figure 10.3. As with Model 1, we will first discuss the model in general. Then we will select a particular type of discrete behavior and specific variables from each of the perspectives to illustrate how the model might operate at the individual variable level.

A stimulus perceived by policy makers as posing a problem for their government is the trigger for activating Model 2. Policy makers define the situation. This definition can be influenced by several types of variables as noted in arrows 1, 2, and 3 in Figure 10.3. The prior relationship between the policy makers' government and the apparent source of the stimulus can affect how the situation is defined. For instance, British destroyers within twelve miles of the U.S. coast would probably be viewed with less alarm than would Soviet trawlers. The personal characteristics of the leaders may also influence how the situation is defined. The leaders responsible for defining the situation may differ across events (e.g., secretary or assistant secretary of state in one event, ambassador in another, intelligence officer in a third, and so on). As a result, different personal characteristics will be involved depending on the situation. Moreover, the leaders involved may be more or less sensitive to their environment. If the stimuli are novel or ambiguous, how the leaders view the world may affect their interpretations. Along with variables from the prior behavior and personal characteristics perspectives, variables from the decision structure and process perspective can affect how the situation is defined. Delegates from diverse governmental bureaucracies may see the situation quite differently than do the head of state and his personal staff. Which type of decision structure plays the primary role in shaping the definition of the situation can be important.

The relationship between variables from the situation perspective and the decision structure and process perspective is one of mutual influence (see arrows 3 and 4). We have described how decision structures and processes can influence the definition of the situation. How a situation is defined can, in turn, affect the decision structures and processes that

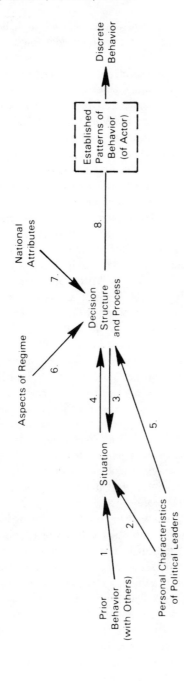

Figure 10.3. Multicausal model (Model 2) intended to explain discrete foreign policy behavior.

result. For example, a situation defined as a crisis will probably result in a different kind of decision structure from a situation defined as routine and nonthreatening.

Variables from three other perspectives also impact on decision structures and processes. Arrows 5, 6 and 7 denote these relationships. Leaders' personal characteristics, regime characteristics, and national attributes affect decision structures and processes. Variables from these perspectives indicate what kinds of decision structures and processes will be preferred by the government. Thus, the leader with a high need for power will assume an authoritative role in the decision process and participate more in foreign policy making. The more constrained the regime, the more likely decision processes are to involve extensive bargaining. The lower a nation's capacity to act, the smaller its foreign policy bureaucracy. These three propositions illustrate the nature of the relationships between variables from these perspectives and decision structures and processes.

Arrow 8 in Model 2 indicates the relationship between decision structures and processes and discrete behavior. This relationship is mediated by the acting government's own established pattern of behavior. In other words, its general propensity or predisposition to use certain kinds of behavior must be reconciled with its disposition for certain action emerging in the immediate set of circumstances. The general tendency and immediate predisposition may reinforce one another, in which case the government reponds in the particular instance with its usual or typical behavior. On the other hand, the demands of the present situation may run counter to the typical response. Under such conditions, the resulting discrete behavior may depend on such variables as the importance of the situation to the government, the specific issues being addressed, and the continuity of the government's prior pattern behavior toward the source of the stimulus. These are the types of variables that are activiated when the tendency toward action in the present situation and the previously established behavior pattern are contradictory.

Not depicted in Model 2 is the feedback from this model to pattern behavior in Model 1. Of course, one isolated behavior is unlikely to alter the nation's accumulated pattern of behavior. But if a number of discrete actions occur that deviate from the prior pattern, then the aggregated pattern of behavior will begin to shift as surely as the individual deposits in the Colorado River change the configuration of the Grand Canyon.

Let us now examine Model 2 using specific variables rather than the undifferentiated theoretical perspectives. To show the parallelism between Models 1 and 2, we will use our illustrative type of discrete behavior the level of commitment in a government's response. Here we are interested in the degree of commitment of a nation's resources that a government

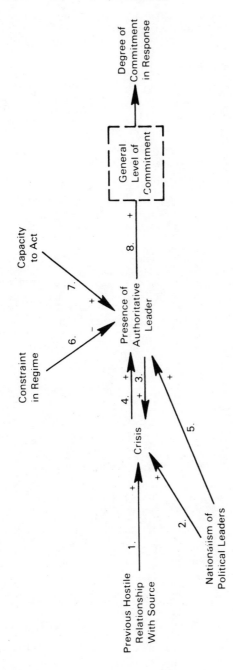

Figure 10.4. An illustration of Model 2.
(Plus and minus signs indicate direction of relationships.)

makes in a single action. The particular variables to be used from the theoretical perspectives plus their interrelationships and their impact on commitment are found in Figure 10.4. Most of these variables have already been defined in our discussion of Model 1.

The stimulus triggering our example of Model 2 is a threatening action from another nation that gives the acting government little time in which to respond—in other words, a stimulus that has the potential for creating a crisis for the acting government (see Hermann, 1969a; Brady, 1974a). It is hypothesized that the extent to which the stimulus is perceived to be a crisis will depend on the general hostility in the government's prior relations with the apparent source of the stimulus. The more hostile the previous relations, the more crisis-like the stimulus will be perceived, that is, the more threat and the less time the policy makers will perceive (arrow 1). Policy makers are likely to expect crises from nations with whom they have had hostile relations. Also affecting the definition of the situation is the nationalism of the political leaders. One of the defining characteristics of nationalism is a tendency to perceive one's own nation as the best and to view other nations with suspicion. Thus, the hypothesis is: The more nationalistic the leaders, the more crisis-like the situation will probably be perceived to be (arrow 2). Similarly, whether or not an authoritative policy maker is present in the decision unit may influence how the situation is defined. If the leader is the head of state and assumes full authority for foreign policy making, we propose that the situation is more likely to be perceived as crisis-like than if such a leader is absent (arrow 3). Staff (the individuals most accessible for consultation on short-time decisions) are unlikely to push opinions contrary to the authoritative leader, particularly if they, too, perceive the stimulus as highly threatening. Moreover, they are unlikely to present differing information about the situation if they believe that the leader has made up his or her mind about it.

Crisis situations tend to involve high level policy makers, including the head of state (see Hermann, 1969a). Thus, it is hypothesized that the more crisis-like the situation is perceived to be, the more likely it is that an authoritative leader will be present (arrow 4). How authoritative the leader will act is in part determined by his personal characteristics. The more nationalistic the leader, the more authoritatively we believe the individual is likely to be (arrow 5). As we noted in illustrating Model 1, nationalistic leaders work hard to increase their power and authority. How restricted the formal authority of the leader is may be learned from a regime characteristic like constraint and a national attribute like capacity to act. The more constrained the regime or the lower its capacity to act (little resource capability and social organization), the more restricted a leader's formal authority is postulated to be (arrows 6 and 7). No matter how authoritative leaders may wish to be, if they are in constrained regimes or in regimes with few resources, their powers are limited.

If a fairly unrestricted, authoritative leader participates, the discrete behavior will probably involve a higher level of commitment than if the leader is absent. That is the hypothesis represented by arrow 8. The absence of an authoritative decision maker becomes important because—as was noted in chapter 4—the use or intended future use of national resources (i.e., high commitment behavior) requires the approval of an authoritative decision maker. This relationship between authoritative leader and commitment behavior is mediated, however, by the government's general pattern of commitment behavior toward the apparent source of the crisis and, perhaps more specifically, by the general pattern of commitment behavior toward the apparent source during previous crisis situations. If the general pattern has been one of strong commitment, then that tendency will reinforce the result expected in the present instance with participation of an authoritative decision maker. As a consequence, the probability of high commitment behavior is increased. If the general pattern, on the other hand, is one of weak or little commitment, then the likelihood of a high commitment behavior in this specific situation is reduced.

CONCLUSION

In this chapter we have tried to show how the theoretical perspectives described in the previous chapters can be integrated to explain foreign policy behavior. Whereas in each of the previous chapters we were concerned with examining a single perspective, here we were interested in showing how the perspectives could be interrelated to explain two approaches to the conceptualization and measurement of foreign policy behavior—pattern behavior and discrete behavior. In some sense this chapter is but an introduction to the tasks that lie ahead—such as the task of developing models of the kind presented here that account for a wide variety of pattern behaviors and discrete behaviors. Other models should be designed to explain foreign policy behaviors conceptualized in different ways. As work on these models progresses it may well be that the boundaries between theoretical perspectives will begin to fade and truly multicausal explanations of foreign policy behavior will begin to emerge. The authors of this book are committed to pursuing these tasks. This book will have achieved its objective if it has helped the reader to understand and evaluate such undertakings. We hope that some might be motivated to try this or an alternate strategy for providing better explanations of foreign policy.

REFERENCES

ABLE, E. (1966) The Missile Crisis. New York: Bantam.

ALLISON, G. T. (1971) Essence of Decision: Explaining the Cuban Missile Crisis. Boston: Little, Brown.

――― (1969) "Conceptual models and the Cuban missile crisis." American Political Science Review 63 (September): 689-718.

――― and M. H. HALPERIN (1972) "Bureaucratic politics: A paradigm and some policy implications," in R. Tanter and R. H. Ullman (eds.) Theory and Policy in International Relations. Princeton, N.J.: Princeton University Press.

ANDRIOLE, S. J., J. WILKENFELD, and G. W. HOPPLE (1975) "A framework for the comparative analysis of foreign policy behavior." International Studies Quarterly 19: 160-198.

ARON, R. (1966) Peace and War: A Theory of International Relations. Garden City, N.Y.: Doubleday.

ART, R. J. (1973) "The policy sciences and foreign policy." Policy Science 4: 467-490.

ASHBY, N. (1969) "Schumacher and Brandt: The divergent 'operational codes' of two German socialist leaders." Mimeo. Stanford University.

ASHBY, W. R. (1952) Introduction to Cybernetics. New York: Barnes & Noble.

ASPATURIAN, V. V. (1972) "Soviet foreign policy," in R. C. Macridis (ed.) Foreign Policy in World Politics. Englewood Cliffs, N.J.: Prentice-Hall.

AZAR, E. A. (1973) Probe for Peace: Small State Hostilities. Minneapolis, Minn.: Burgess.

――― (1970) "Profiling and predicting patterns of international interactions: A signal accounting model." Paper presented at the annual meeting of the American Political Science Association, Los Angeles.

――― and J. D. BEN-DAK (eds.) (1975) Theory and Practice of Events Research. London: Gordon and Breach.

――― R. A. BRODY and C. A. McCLELLAND (1972) "International events interaction analysis: Some research considerations." Sage Professional Papers in International Studies 1, 02-001. Beverly Hills, Calif.: Sage.

BARBER, J. D. (1972) The Presidential Character. Englewood Cliffs, N.J.: Prentice-Hall.

――― (1966) Power in Committees. Chicago: Rand McNally.

BENDIX, R. (1963) "Concepts and generalizations in comparative sociological studies." American Sociological Review 28.

BENNIS, W. (1973) "The doppelganger effect." Newsweek 17 (September): 13.

BERRY, B. J. L. (1960) "An inductive approach to the regionalism of economic development," in N. Ginsburg (ed.) Essays on Geography and Economic Development. Chicago: University of Chicago Press.

BERTON, P. (1969) "International subsystems—A submacro approach to studies." International Studies Quarterly 13: 329-334.

BINDER, L. (1958) "The Middle East as a subordinate international system." World Politics 10: 408-429.

BLAKE, D. H. (1969) "The identification of foreign policy output: A neglected but necessary task." Paper presented at the annual meeting of the Midwest Political Science Association, Ann Arbor, April 24-26.

BLALOCK, H. M., Jr. (1961) Causal Inferences in Nonexperimental Research. Chapel Hill: Univ. of North Carolina Press.

BLAU, P. M. (1974) On the Nature of Organizations. New York: John Wiley.

BLOOMFIELD, L. P. (1968) "The political scientist and foreign policy," in A. Ranney (ed.) Political Science and Public Policy. Chicago: Markham.

BONHAM, G. M. (1975) "Cognitive process models and the study of foreign policy decision making." Paper presented at the annual meeting of the International Studies Association, Washington, D.C.

BOULDING, K. E. (1969) "National images and international systems," in J. N. Rosenau (ed.) International Politics and Foreign Policy. New York: Free Press.

——— (1962) Conflict and Defense. New York: Harper & Row.

——— (1956) The Image. Ann Arbor: Univ. of Michigan Press.

BOZEMAN, A. (1960) Politics and Culture in International History. Princeton, N.J.: Princeton Univ. Press.

BRADY, L. P. (1976) "Bureaucratic politics and situational constraints in foreign policy." Sage International Yearbook of Foreign Policy Studies. Vol. 4. Beverly Hills, Calif.: Sage.

——— (1975) "Explaining foreign policy using transitory qualities of situations." Paper prepared for the annual meeting of the American Political Science Association, San Francisco, September 2-5.

——— (1974a) "Threat, decision time, and awareness: The impact of situational variables on foreign policy behavior." Ph.D. dissertation. Ohio State University.

——— (1974b) "Goal properties of foreign policy: Professed orientation to change and goal subject." Paper prepared for the annual meeting of the Southern Political Science Association, New Orleans, November 7-9.

——— (1971) "The international events data movement: A new approach to the identification of foreign policy output." Mimeo. Ohio State University.

BRAYBROOKE, D. and C. LINDBLOM (1963) Strategy of Decision. New York: Free Press.

BRECHER, M. M., B. STEINBERG, and J. STEIN (1969) "A framework for research on foreign policy behavior." Journal of Conflict Resolution 13 (March): 75-101.

BREWER, T. L. (1972) "Foreign policy situations: American elite responses to variations in threat, time, and surprise." Sage Professional Paper in International Studies 1, 02-006. Beverly Hills, Calif.: Sage.

BRONFENBRENNER, U. (1960) "Personality and participation: The case of the vanishing variables." Journal of Social Issues 16: 54-63.

BRZEZINSKI, Z. and S. P. HUNTINGTON (1964) Political Power USA/USSR. New York: Viking.

BURGESS, P. M. and R. W. LAWTON (1972) "Indicators of international behavior: An assessment of events data research." Sage Professional Paper in International Studies 1, 02-010. Beverly Hills, Calif.: Sage.

BURNS, A. L. (1957) "From balance to deterrence: A theoretical analysis." World Politics 9: 494-529.

BURROWES, R. and B. SPECTOR (1973) "The strength and direction of relationships between domestic and external conflict and cooperation: Syria, 1961-67," in J. Wilkenfeld (ed.) Conflict Behavior and Linkage Politics. New York: David McKay.

BURTON, J. (1969) Systems, States, Diplomacy, and Rules. Cambridge, Mass.: Cambridge Univ. Press.

——— (1968) Conflict and Communication. New York: Free Press.

BUTLER, F. S. and S. TAYLOR (1975) "Toward an explanation of consistency and adaptability in foreign policy behavior: The role of political accountability." Paper presented at the annual meeting of the Midwest Political Science Association, Chicago, April.

CALLAHAN, P. and D. SWANSON (1974) "Autonomous action properties of foreign policy: Specificity, degree of activity, and commitment." Paper presented at the annual meeting of the Southern Political Science Association, New Orleans, November 7-9.

CANTORI, L. J. and S. L. SPIEGEL [eds.] (1970) The International Politics of Regions: A Comparative Approach. Englewood Cliffs, N.J.: Prentice-Hall.

CATTELL, R. B. and R. L. GORSUCH (1965) "The definition and measurement of national morale and morality." Journal of Social Psychology 67: 77-96.

CHAYES, A. (1972) "An inquiry into the workings of arms control agreements." Harvard Law Review 85: 905-969.

CHERRY, C. (1957) On Human Communication: An Inquiry into the Foundations of Nationality. Cambridge, Mass.: MIT Press.

CHOUCRI, N. and R. C. NORTH (1975) Nations in Conflict. San Francisco: W. H. Freeman.

CHRISTIE, R. and F. L. GEIS (1970) Studies in Machiavellianism. New York: Academic Press.

COATE, R. A. (1974) "Contextual properties of foreign policy: Substantive problem-areas and over/under response." Paper presented at the annual meeting of the Southern Political Science Association, New Orleans, November 7-9.

COHEN, B. C. (1968) "Foreign policy," pp. 530-535 in D. C. Sills (ed.) International Encyclopedia of the Social Sciences. Vol. 5. New York: MacMillan.

——— and S. A. HARRIS (1975) "Foreign policy," pp. 301-488 in F. I. Greenstein and N. W. Polsby (eds.) Handbook of Political Science. Vol. 6. Reading, Mass.: Addison-Wesley.

COLEMAN, J. S. (1973) The Mathematics of Collective Action. Chicago: Aldine.

COLLINS, B. E. and H. GUETZKOW (1964) A Social Psychology of Group Processes for Decision-making. New York: John Wiley.

COLLINS, B. E. and B. H. RAVEN (1969) "Group structure: Attraction, coalitions, communication, and power," pp. 102-204 in G. Lindzey and E. Aronson (eds.) The Handbook of Social Psychology. Vol. 4. Reading, Mass.: Addison-Wesley.

COPLIN, W. D. (1974) Introduction to International Politics: A Theoretical Overview. Chicago: Rand McNally.

——— P. J. McGOWAN, and M. K. O'LEARY (1974) American Foreign Policy: An Introduction to Analysis and Evaluation. North Scituate, Mass.: Duxbury Press.

CRABB, C. V., Jr. (1972) American Foreign Policy in the Nuclear Age. New York: Harper & Row.

CURTIS, M. (1965) Western European Integration. New York: Harper & Row.

CYERT, R. M. and J. G. MARCH (1963) A Behavioral Theory of the Firm. Englewood Cliffs, N.J.: Prentice-Hall.

DAHL, R. A. (1971) Polyarchy. New Haven, Conn.: Yale Univ. Press.

——— (1963) Who Governs: Democracy and Power in an American City. New Haven, Conn.: Yale Univ. Press.

DAVIS, D. H. (1972) How the Bureaucracy Makes Foreign Policy. Lexington, Mass.: Heath.

DAVIS, J. H. (1969) Group Performance. Reading, Mass.: Addison-Wesley.

DeRIVERA, J. H. (1968) The Psychological Dimension of Foreign Policy. Columbus, Ohio: Merrill.

DESTLER, I. M. (1972) Presidents and Bureaucrats: Organizing the Government for Foreign Policy. Princeton, N.J.: Princeton Univ. Press.

De TOCQUEVILLE, A. (1945) Democracy in America. Vol. 1. New York: Knopf.

DEUTSCH, K. W. (1968) The Analysis of International Relations. Englewood Cliffs, N.J.: Prentice-Hall.

——— (1961) "Social mobilization and political development." American Political Science Review 55: 493-514.

——— and J. D. SINGER (1964) "Multipolar power systems and international stability." World Politics 16: 390-406.

DEUTSCH, M. (1953) Nationalism and Social Communications: An Inquiry into the Foundations of Nationality. Cambridge, Mass.: MIT Press.

DOWNS, A. (1966) Inside Bureaucracy. Boston: Little, Brown.

——— (1957) Economic Theory of Democracy. New York: Harper & Row.

DRIVER, M. J. (1976) "Individual differences in ideological content and conceptual structure as determinants of aggression in the Inter-Nation Simulation," in M. G. Hermann (ed.) A Psychological Examination of Political Leaders. New York: Free Press.

DRUCKMAN, D. (1976) "The person, role, and situation in international negotiations," in M. G. Hermann (ed.) A Psychological Examination of Political Leaders. New York: Free Press.

EAST, M. A. (1975) "Explaining foreign policy behavior using national attributes." Paper presented at the annual meeting of the American Political Science Association, Sept. 2-5.

——— (1973a) "Size and foreign policy behavior: A test of two models." World Politics 25: 556-576.

——— (1973b) "Foreign policy-making in small states: Some theoretic observations based on a study of the Uganda Ministry of Foreign Affairs." Policy Sciences 4: 491-508.

——— (1972) "Status discrepancy and violence in the international system: An empirical analysis," in J. N. Rosenau, V. Davis, and M. A. East (eds.) The Analysis of International Politics. New York: Free Press.

——— and P. M. GREGG (1967) "Factors influencing cooperation and conflict in the international system." International Studies Quarterly 11: 244-269.

EAST, M. A. and M. G. HERMANN (1974) "Outcome properties of foreign policy: External consequentiality, situation generation, and acceptance ratio." Paper presented at the annual meeting of the Southern Political Science Association, New Orleans, November 7-9.

EPSTEIN, L. (1964) British Politics in the Suez Crisis. Urbana: Univ. of Illinois Press.

ERIKSON, E. H. (1969) Gandhi's Truth. New York: Norton.

——— (1962) Young Man Luther. New York: Norton.

——— (1950) Childhood and Society. New York: Norton.

FIEDLER, F. E. (1967) A Theory of Leadership Effectiveness. New York: McGraw-Hill.

FLIESS, P. J. (1966) Thucydides and the Politics of Bipolarity. Baton Rouge: Louisiana State Univ. Press.

FRANK, J. D. (1968) Sanity and Survival. New York: Random House.

FRANKEL, J. (1963) The Making of Foreign Policy. New York: Oxford Univ. Press.

FROMAN, L. A., Jr. (1968) "The categorization of policy contents," in A. Ranney (ed.) Political Science and Public Policy. Chicago: Markham.

GAMSON, W. A. and A. MODIGLIANI (1971) Untangling the Cold War. Boston: Little, Brown.

GEORGE, A. L. (1974) "Adaptation to stress in political decision making: The individual, small group, and organizational contexts," pp. 167-245 in G. V. Coelho, D. A. Hamburg, and J. E. Adams (eds.) Coping and Adaptation. New York: Basic Books.

——— (1972) "The case for multiple advocacy in making foreign policy." American Political Science Review 66(3): 751-785.

——— (1969) "The 'operational code': A neglected approach to the study of political leaders and decision-making." International Studies Quarterly 13: 190-222.

——— (1959) Propaganda Analysis. Evanston, Ill.: Row Peterson.

——— and J. L. GEORGE (1964) Woodrow Wilson and Colonel House. New York: Dover.

GIBB, C. A. (1969) "Leadership," pp. 205-282 in G. Lindzey and E. Aronson (eds.) The Handbook of Social Psychology. Vol. 4. Reading, Mass.: Addison-Wesley.

GLEDITSCH, J. (1970) "Rank theory, field theory, and attribute theory: Three approaches to interaction in the international system." DON Research Report 47. University of Hawaii.

GOLEMBIEWSKI, R. T. (1965) "Small groups and large organizations," in J. G. March (ed.) Handbook of Organizations. Chicago: Rand McNally.

GREENSTEIN, F. I. (1969) Personality and Politics. Chicago: Markham.

GULICK, E. V. (1955) Europe's Classical Balance of Power. Ithaca, N.Y.: Cornell Univ. Press.

GUTERMAN, S. S. (1970) The Machiavellians. Lincoln: Univ. of Nebraska Press.

GUTIERREZ, G. G. (1973) "The 'operational code' of Dean Rusk." Paper presented at the annual meeting of the American Political Science Association, New Orleans, September 6-9.

HACKMAN, J. R. and C. G. MORRIS (1975) "Group tasks, group interaction process, and group performance effectiveness: A review and proposed integration." Advances in Experimental Social Psychology 8: 45-99.

HALL, A. and R. FAGAN (1968) "Definition of a system." General Systems 1: 18-28.

HALPERIN, M. H. (1974) Bureaucratic Politics and Foreign Policy. Washington, D.C.: Brookings.

——— (1972) "The decision to deploy the ABM." World Politics 25: 62-95.

——— and A. KANTER (1973) "The bureaucratic perspective: A preliminary framework," in M. H. Halperin and A. Kanter (eds.) Readings in American Foreign Policy. Boston: Little, Brown.

HAMMOND, P. Y. (1965) "Foreign policy making and administrative politics." World Politics 17: 657-671.

HARF, J. E., D. G. HOOVLER, and T. E. JAMES, Jr. (1974) "Systemic and external attributes in foreign policy analysis," in J. N. Rosenau (ed.) Comparing Foreign Policies: Theories, Findings, and Methods. Beverly Hills, Calif.: Sage.

HERMANN, C. F. (1974) "Decision-making properties of foreign policy: Instrumentalities and procedural issue areas." Paper presented at the annual meeting of the Southern Political Science Association, New Orleans, November 7-9.

——— (1972a) "Policy classification: A key to the comparative study of foreign policy," in J. N. Rosenau, V. Davis and M. A. East (eds.) The Analysis of International Politics. New York: Free Press.

――― (1972b) "Threat, time and surprise: A simulation of international crisis," in C. F. Hermann (ed.) International Crises: Insights from Behavioral Research. New York: Free Press.

――― (1971) "What is a foreign policy event?" in W. F. Hanrieder (ed.) Comparative Foreign Policy. New York: David McKay.

――― (1969a) Crises in Foreign Policy: A Simulation Analysis. New York: Bobbs-Merrill.

――― (1969b) "International crisis as a situational variable," in J. N. Rosenau (ed.) International Politics and Foreign Policy. New York: Free Press.

――― (1967) "Validation problems in games and simulations with special reference to models of international politics." Behavioral Science 12: 216-231.

――― and L. P. Brady (1972) "Alternative models of international crisis," pp. 281-303 in C. F. Hermann (ed.) International Crises: Insights from Behavioral Research. New York: Free Press.

HERMANN, C. F. and M. G. HERMANN (1967) "An attempt to simulate the outbreak of World War I." American Political Science Review 61: 400-416.

HERMANN, C. F. and S. A. SALMORE (1971) "The recipients of foreign policy events." Paper presented at the annual meeting of the Peace Research Society, Ann Arbor, November 15-16.

HERMANN, C. F., M. A. EAST, M. G. HERMANN, B. G. SALMORE, and S. A. SALMORE (1973) "CREON: A foreign events data set." Sage Professional Papers in International Studies 2, 02-024. Beverly Hills, Calif.: Sage.

HERMANN, M. G. (1976a) "Some personal characteristics of congressmen related to foreign aid voting," in M. G. Hermann (ed.) A Psychological Examination of Political Leaders. New York: Free Press.

――― (1976b) "Circumstances under which leader personality will affect foreign policy: Some propositions," in J. N. Rosenau (ed.) In Search of Global Patterns. New York: Free Press.

――― (1975) "Explaining foreign policy behavior using personal characteristics of political leaders." Paper presented at the annual meeting of the American Political Science Association, San Francisco, September 2-5.

――― (1974) "Leader personality and foreign policy behavior," pp. 201-234 in J. N. Rosenau (ed.) Comparing Foreign Policies: Theories, Findings and Methods. New York: Sage-Halsted.

HILSMAN, R. (1967) To Move a Nation. New York: Doubleday.

HOFFMAN, S. (1968) Gulliver's Troubles. New York: McGraw-Hill.

HOLLANDER, E. P. and J. W. JULIAN (1970) "Studies in leader legitimacy, influence, and innovation." Advances in Experimental Social Psychology 5: 33-69.

HOLSTI, K. J. (1972) "International Politics: A Framework for Analysis. Englewood Cliffs, N.J.: Prentice-Hall.

HOLSTI, O. R. (1976) "Foreign policy decision-makers viewed psychologically: Cognitive process approaches," in G. Bonham and M. Shapiro (eds.) Thought and Action in Foreign Policy.

――― (1973) "Foreign policy decision-makers viewed psychologically: A sketchy survey of 'cognitive process' approaches." Paper presented at the Conference on the Successes and Failures of Scientific International Relations Research, Ojai, Calif., June 25-28.

――― (1972) Crisis Escalation War. Montreal: McGill-Queen's Univ. Press.

――― (1970) "The 'operational code' approach to the study of political leaders: John Foster Dulles' philosophical and instrumental beliefs." Canadian Journal of Political Science 3: 123-157.

——— (1967) "Cognitive dynamics and images of the enemy." Journal of International Affairs 21: 16-39.

——— (1965) "The 1914 case." American Political Science Review 59: 365-378.

——— (1962) "The belief system and national images: A case study." Journal of Conflict Resolution 6: 244-252.

——— and A. L. GEORGE (1975) "The effects of stress on the performance of foreign policy-makers," in C. P. Cotter (ed.) Political Science Annual: Individual Decision-Making. Indianapolis: Bobbs-Merrill.

HOLSTI, O. R. and R. C. NORTH (1966) "Comparative data from content analysis: Perceptions of hostility and economic variables in the 1914 crisis," in R. L. Merritt and S. Rokkan (eds.) Comparing Nations. New Haven, Conn.: Yale Univ. Press.

HOLSTI, O. R., A. BRODY, ad R. C. NORTH (1969) "The management of international crises: Affect and action in American-Soviet relations," in D. G. Pruitt and R. C. Snyder (eds.) Theory and Research on the Causes of War. Englewood Cliffs, N.J.: Prentice-Hall.

HOLSTI, O. R., R. C. NORTH, and R. A. BRODY (1968) "Perception and Action in the 1914 Crisis," in J. D. Singer (ed.) Quantitative International Politics: Insights and Evidence. New York: Free Press.

HOLT, R. T. and J. E. TURNER [eds.] (1970) The Methodology of Comparative Research. New York: Free Press.

HOOK, S. (1943) The Hero in History. New York: John Day.

HUNTINGTON, S. P. (1968) Political Order in Changing Societies. New Haven, Conn.: Yale Univ. Press.

——— (1960) "Strategic planning and the political process." Foreign Affairs 38.

HUTCHINS, G. L. (1974) "Relational action properties of foreign policy: Affect, scope of action and independence of action." Paper presented at the annual meeting of the Southern Political Science Association, New Orleans, November 7-9.

IRISH, M. and E. FRANK (1975) U.S. Foreign Policy: Context, Conduct, Content. New York: Harcourt, Brace, Jovanovich.

JANIS, I. L. (1972) Victims of Group think. Boston: Houghton Mifflin.

JERVIS, R. (1976) Perception and Misperception in International Politics. Princeton, N.J.: Princeton Univ. Press.

——— (1970) The Logic of Images in International Relations. Princeton, N.J.: Princeton Univ. Press.

——— (1969) "Hypotheses on Misperception," in J. N. Rosenau (ed.) International Politics and Foreign Policy. New York: Free Press.

JONES, S. and J. D. SINGER (1972) Beyond Conjecture in International Politics: Abstracts of Data-Based Research. Itasca, Ill.: F. E. Peacock.

KANTER, A. (1972) "Congress and the defense budget: 1960-1970." American Political Science Review 66: 129-143.

KAPLAN, A. (1964) The Conduct of Inquiry. San Francisco: Chandler.

KAPLAN, M. A. (1957) System and Process in International Politics. New York: John Wiley.

KEAN, J. and P. J. McGOWAN (1973) "National attributes and foreign policy: A path analysis," in P. J. McGowan (ed.) Sage International Yearbook of Foreign Policy Studies. Vol. 1. Beverly Hills, Calif.: Sage.

KEGLEY, C. W., Jr. (1973) A general empirical typology of foreign policy behavior. Sage Professional Papers in International Studies 2, 02-014.

——— G. A. RAYMOND, R. M. ROOD, and R. A. SKINNER (eds.) (1975) International Events and the Comparative Analysis of Foreign Policy. Columbia, South

Carolina: University of South Carolina Press.

——— S. A. SALMORE and D. J. ROSEN (1974) "Convergences in the measurement of interstate behavior," pp. 309-339 in P. J. McGowan (ed.) Sage International Yearbook of Foreign Policy Studies. Vol. II. Beverly Hills: Sage Publications.

KELLEY, H. H. and J. W. THIBAUT (1969) "Group problem solving," pp. 1-101 in G. Lindzey and E. Aronson (eds.) The Handbook of Social Psychology. Vol. 4. Reading, Mass.: Addison-Wesley.

——— (1954) "Experimental studies of group problem solving and process," pp. 735-785 in G. Lindzey (ed.) The Handbook of Social Psychology. Reading, Mass.: Addison-Wesley.

KELMAN, H. C. (1955) "Societal, attitudinal and structural factors in international relations." Journal of Social Issues 2(1): 42-56.

KENNEDY, R. F. (1969) Thirteen Days. New York: Norton.

KIRK, E. (1974) "Organization, group and crisis decision making in United States foreign policy formulation." Unpublished doctoral dissertation, Purdue University.

KISSINGER, H. A. (1966) "Domestic Structure and Foreign Policy." Daedalus 95.

KLEIN, D. W. (1962) "Peking's evolving ministry of foreign affairs," in D. E. Pentong (ed.) China: The Emerging Red Giant. San Francisco: Chandler.

KNORR, K. (1956) The War Potential of Nations. Princeton, N.J.: Princeton Univ. Press.

KOGAN, N. and M. A. WALLACH (1964) Risk Taking: A Study in Cognition and Personality. New York: Holt, Rinehart & Winston.

KOLKO, J. and G. KOLKO (1972) The Limits of Power: The World and United States Foreign Policy, 1945-1954. New York: Harper & Row.

KRASNER, S. D. (1972) "Are bureaucracies important?" Foreign Policy 7 (Summer): 159-179.

LASSWELL, H. D. (1963) The Future of Political Science. New York: Atherton.

——— (1948) Power and Personality. New York: Norton.

——— (1930) Psychopathology and Politics. Chicago: Univ. of Chicago Press.

LEITES, N. (1953) A Study of Bolshevism. Glencoe, Ill.: Free Press.

——— (1951) The Operational Code of the Politburo. New York: McGraw-Hill.

LENG, R. (1972) "Behavioral indicators of war proneness in bilateral conflict." Paper presented at the annual meeting of the American Political Science Association, Washington, D.C., September 5-9.

LENTNER, H. (1974) Foreign Policy Analysis: A Comparative and Conceptual Approach. Columbus, Ohio: Merrill.

——— (1972) "The concept of crisis as viewed by the United States Department of State," in C. F. Hermann (ed.) International Crises: Insights from Behavioral Research. New York: Free Press.

LEONTIEF, W. (1963) "When should history be written backwards?" The Economic History Review 16: 1-8.

LIPPMANN, W. (1965) Public Opinion. New York: Free Press.

LOVELL, J. P. (1970) Foreign Policy in Perspective. New York: Holt, Rinehart & Winston.

LOWI, T. (1967) "Making democracy safe for the world: National politics and foreign policy," in J. N. Rosenau (ed.) Domestic Sources of Foreign Policy. New York: Free Press.

MACHIAVELLI, N. (1940) The Prince. Translated from original (c. 1640) by E. Dacres. London: R. Bishop.

MacINTYRE, A. (1973) "Is a science of comparative politics possible?" pp. 171-188 in A. Ryan (ed.) The Philosophy of Social Explanation. London: Oxford Univ. Press.

MACRIDIS, R. (ed.) (1976) Foreign Policy in World Politics. Englewood Cliffs, N.J.: Prentice-Hall.

——— (1972) "French foreign policy," pp. 76-118 in R. C. Macridis (ed.) Foreign Policy in World Politics. Englewood Cliffs, N.J.: Prentice-Hall.

——— [ed.] (1962) Foreign Policy in World Politics. Englewood Cliffs, N.J.: Prentice-Hall.

MARCH, J. G. [ed.] (1965) Handbook of Organizations. Chicago: Rand McNally.

——— and H. A. SIMON (1958) Organizations. New York: John Wiley.

McCLELLAND, C. A. (1972) "The beginning, duration, and abatement of international crises: Comparisons in two conflict arenas," in C. F. Hermann (ed.) International Crises: Insights from Behavioral Research. New York: Free Press.

——— (1969) "Action structures and communication in two international crises: Quemoy and Berlin," in J. N. Rosenau (ed.) International Politics and Foreign Policy. New York: Free Press.

——— (1968) "Access to Berlin: The quantity and variety of events," in J. D. Singer (ed.) Quantitative International Politics: Insights and Evidence. New York: Free Press.

——— (1967) "International communications," in International Encyclopedia of the Social Sciences. New York: Macmillan.

——— (1966) Theory and the International System. New York: Macmillan.

——— (1961) "The acute international crisis." World Politics 14: 182-204.

——— and G. HOGGARD (1969) "Conflict patterns in the interactions among nations," in J. N. Rosenau (ed.) International Politics and Foreign Policy. New York: Free Press.

McGOWAN, P. J. (1975) "Meaningful comparisons in the study of foreign policy," pp. 52-87 in C. W. Kegley, Jr., G. A. Raymond, R. M. Rood, and R. A. Skinner (eds.) International Events and the Comparative Analysis of Foreign Policy. Columbia: Univ. of South Carolina Press.

——— and H. B. SHAPIRO (1973) The Comparative Study of Foreign Policy. Beverly Hills, Calif.: Sage.

McLELLAN, D. (1971) "The 'operational code' approach to the study of political leaders: Dean Acheson's philosophical and instrumental beliefs." Canadian Journal of Political Science 4: 52-75.

MEEHAN, E. J. (1971) "The concept 'foreign policy'," in W. F. Hanrieder (ed.) Comparative Foreign Policy. New York: David McKay.

MERRITT, R. L. and S. ROKKAN [eds.] (1966) Comparing Nations: The Use of Quantitative Data in Cross-National Research. New Haven, Conn.: Yale Univ. Press.

MERTON, R. (1940) "Bureaucratic structure and personality." Social Forces 18: 560-568.

MILBURN, T. W. (1972) "The management of crises," in C. F. Hermann (ed.) International Crises: Insights from Behavioral Research. New York: Free Press.

MODELSKI, G. (1974) Word Power Concentrations: Typology, Data and Explanatory Framework. Morristown, N.J.: General Learning Press.

——— (1961) "Agraria and industria: Two models of the international system," in K. Knorr and S. Verba (eds.) The International System. Princeton, N.J.: Princeton Univ. Press.

MOORE, D. (1970) "Governmental and societal influences on foreign policy: A partial examination of Rosenau's adaptation model." Ph.D. Dissertation. Ohio

State University.

MORGENTHAU, H. J. (1967) Politics Among Nations. New York: Knopf.

NAGEL, E. (1961) The Structure of Science. New York: Harcourt, Brace & World.

NAROLL R. and R. COHEN [eds.] (1970) A Handbook of Method in Cultural Anthropology. Garden City, N.Y.: Natural History Press.

NEUSTADT, R. E. (1970) Alliance Politics. New York: Columbia Univ. Press.

NYE, J. S., Jr. and R. O. KEOHANE (1971) "Transnational relations and world politics: An introduction." International Organization 25: 329-350.

ORGANSKI, K. and A. F. K. ORGANSKI (1961) Population and World Power. New York: Knopf.

ORVIK, N. (1972) Departmental Decision-Making. Oslo, Norway: Univ. of Oslo Press.

OSGOOD, C. E. (1962) An Alternative to War or Surrender. Urbana: Univ. of Illinois Press.

PAIGE, G. D. (1972a) "Comparative case analysis of crisis decisions: Korea and Cuba," in C. F. Hermann (ed.) International Crises: Insights from Behavioral Research. New York: Free Press.

——— [ed.] (1972b) Political Leadership. New York: Free Press.

——— (1968) The Korean Decision. New York: Free Press.

PALUMBO, D. J. (1969) "Power and role specificity in organization theory." Public Administration Review 29: 237-248.

PARETO, V. (1916) Trattato di Sociologia Generale (The Mind and Society). Firenze: G. Barbera.

PARK, R. L. (1972) "India's foreign policy," pp. 367-388 in R. C. Macridis (ed.) Foreign Policy in World Politics. Englewood Cliffs, N.J.: Prentice-Hall.

PHILLIPS, W. R. (1973) "The conflict environment of nations: A study of conflict inputs to nations in 1963," in J. Wilkenfeld (ed.) Conflict Behavior and Linkage Politics. New York: David McKay.

——— and P. CALLAHAN (1973) "Dynamic foreign policy interactions: Some implications for a non-dyadic world." Paper presented at the annual meeting of the Midwest Political Science Association, Chicago, May 3-5.

PHILLIPS, W. R. and M. HAINLINE (1973) "Major power conflict exchanges in the Sixties: A triadic analysis of the Soviet, U.S. and Chinese subsystem." Mimeo. Behavioral Sciences Laboratory, Ohio State University.

PLATO (1957) Statesman. Written as *Politikos* (c. 363 B.C.). Translated by J. B. Skemp. New York: Liberal Arts Press.

PRZEWORSKI, A. and H. TEUNE (1970) The Logic of Comparative Social Inquiry. New York: John Wiley.

PRUITT, D. G. (1969) "Stability and sudden change in interpersonal and international affairs," in J. N. Rosenau (ed.) International Politics and Foreign Policy. New York: Free Press.

——— (1965) "Definition of the situation as a determinant of international action," in H. C. Kelman (ed.) International Behavior. New York: Holt, Rinehart & Winston.

——— (1964-1965) Problem Solving in the Department of State. Monograph Series in World Affairs, Social Science Foundation and Department of International Relations. No. 2. University of Denver.

PUCHALA, D. J. (1971) International Politics Today. New York: Dodd Mead.

RANNEY, A. [ed.] (1968) Political Science and Public Policy. Chicago: Markham.

RAYMOND, G. A. (1975) "Introduction: Comparative analyses and nomological explanation," pp. 41-51 in C. W. Kegley, Jr., G. A. Raymond, R. M. Rood, and R.

A. Skinner (eds.) International Events and the Comparative Analysis of Foreign Policy. Columbia: Univ. of South Carolina Press.

RICHARDSON, L. F. (1960) Arms and Insecurity. Pittsburgh: Boxwood Press.

ROBINSON, J. A. and R. C. SNYDER (1965) "Decision-making in international politics," in H. C. Kelman (ed.) International Behavior. New York: Holt, Rinehart & Winston.

ROBINSON, T. W. (1972) "Lin Piao as an elite type," pp. 149-195 in R. A. Scalapino (ed.) Elites in the People's Republic of China. Seattle: Univ. of Washington Press.

ROGOW, A. (1963) James Forrestal: A Study of Personality, Politics, and Policy. New York: Macmillan.

ROSE, R. (1971) Governing without Consensus: An Irish Perspective. Boston: Beacon.

——— (1969) "Dynamic tendencies in the authority of regimes." World Politics 21: 602-628.

ROSECRANCE, R. N. (1966) "Bipolarity, multipolarity and the future." Journal of Conflict Resolution 10: 314-327.

ROSENAU, J. N. (1975) "Comparative foreign policy," pp. 3-38 in C. W. Kegley, Jr., G. A. Raymond, R. M. Rood, R. A. Skinner (eds.) International Events and the Comparative Analysis of Foreign Policy. Columbia: Univ. of South Carolina Press.

——— (1972) "Review of Dag Hammarskjold's United Nations and the new nations in the United Nations, 1960-1967." American Historical Review 77: 1916.

——— (1971) The Scientific Study of Foreign Policy. New York: Free Press.

——— (1970) The Adaptation of National Societies. New York: McCaleb-Seiler.

——— (1968) "Private preferences and political responsibilities: The relative potency of individual and role variables in the behavior of U.S. Senators," in J. D. Singer (ed.) Quantitative International Politics. New York: Free Press.

——— (1967) Domestic Sources of Foreign Policy. New York: Free Press.

——— (1966) "Pre-theories and theories of foreign policy," in R. B. Farrell (ed.) Approaches to Comparative and International Politics. Evanston, Ill.: Northwestern Univ. Press.

——— (1964) Public Opinion and Foreign Policy. New York: Random House.

——— (ed.) (1961) International Politics and Foreign Policy. New York: Free Press.

——— and G. HOGGARD (1974) "Foreign policy behavior in dyadic relationships: Testing a pre-theoretical extension," in J. N. Rosenau (ed.) Comparing Foreign Policies: Theories, Findings, and Methods. Beverly Hills, Calif.: Sage.

ROSENBLATT, P. C. (1964) "Origins and effects of group ethnocentrism and nationalism." Journal of Conflict Resolution 8: 131-146.

RUMMEL, R. J. (1972) The Dimensions of Nations. Beverly Hills, Calif.: Sage.

RUMMEL, R. J. (1969) "Indicators of cross-national and international patterns." American Political Science Review 63: 127-147.

——— (1968) "The relationship between national attributes and foreign conflict behavior," in J. D. Singer (ed.) Quantitative International Politics. New York: Free Press.

——— (1966) "Some dimensions in the foreign behavior of nations." Journal of Peace Research 3: 201-223.

——— (1965) "A social field theory of foreign conflict." Peace Research Society Papers 4: 131-150.

——— (1963) "Dimensions of conflict behavior within and between nations." General Systems Yearbook 8: 1-50.

RUSSETT, B. M. (1970) "International behavior research: Case studies and cumulation," in M. Haas and H. S. Kariel (eds.) Approaches to the Study of Political Science. Scranton, Penn.: Chandler.

――― (1968) "Delineating international regions," in J. D. Singer (ed.) Quantitative International Politics. New York: Free Press.

――― (1967) International Regions and the International System. Chicago: Rand McNally.

――― (1963) Community and Contention: Britain and America in the Twentieth Century. Cambridge, Mass.: MIT Press.

――― and R. J. MONSEN (1975) "Bureaucracy and polyarchy as predictors of performance: A cross-national examination." Comparative Political Studies 8 (April): 5-31.

RUTHERFORD, B. M. (1966) "Psychopathology, decision-making, and political involvement." Journal of Conflict Resolution 10: 387-407.

SALMORE, B. G. and S. A. SALMORE (1975) "Regime constraints and foreign policy behavior." Paper presented at the annual meeting of The American Political Science Association, San Francisco, September 2-5.

――― (1972) "Structure and change in regimes: Their effect on foreign policy." Paper presented at the annual meeting of the American Political Science Association, Washington, D.C., September 5-9.

――― (1970) "Political accountability and foreign policy." Paper presented at annual meeting of American Political Science Association, Los Angeles.

SALMORE, S. A. (1972) "Foreign policy and national attributes: A multivariate analysis." Ph.D. dissertation. Princeton University.

SAWYER, J. (1967) Dimensions of nations; Size, wealth, and politics." American Journal of Sociology 73: 145-172.

SCALAPINO, R. A. (1967) The Japanese Communist Movement, 1920-1966. Berkeley: Univ. of California Press.

――― (1963) "The foreign policy of the People's Republic of China," pp. 549-588 in J. E. Black and K. W. Thompson (eds.) Foreign Policies in a World of Change. New York: Harper & Row.

SCHACHTER, S. (1951) "Deviation, rejection, and communication." Journal of Abnormal and Social Psychology 46: 190-207.

SCHWARTZ, D. (1972) "Decision-making in historical and simulated crises," in C. F. Hermann (ed.) International Crises. New York: Free Press.

SEARING, D. D. (1972) "Models and images of man and society in leadership theory," pp. 19-44 in G. D. Paige (ed.) Political Leadership. New York: Free Press.

SHANNON, C. E. and W. WEAVER (1949) The Mathematical Theory of Communication. Urbana: Univ. of Illinois Press.

SHAPIRO, M. J. and G. M. BONHAM (1973) "Cognitive processes and foreign decision-making." International Studies Quarterly 17: 147-174.

SHILS, E. A. (1954) "Authoritarianism: 'Right' and 'left'," in R. Christie and M. Jahoda (eds.) Studies in the Scope and Method of "The Authoritatian Personality." Glencoe, Ill.: Free Press.

SIGLER, J. H., J. O. FIELD, and M. L. ADELMAN (1972) "Applications of events data analysis: Cases, issues, and programs in international interaction." Sage Professional Papers in International Studies 1, 02-002. Beverly Hills, Calif.: Sage Publications.

SIMON, H. (1969) The Science of the Artificial. Cambridge: MIT Press.

――― (1957) Administrative Behavior. 2nd ed. New York: MacMillan.

SINGER, J. D. (1961) "The level-of-analysis problem in international relations." World Politics 13: 77-92.

——— and M. SMALL (1968) "Alliance aggregation and the onset of war: 1815-1945," in J. D. Singer (ed.) Quantitative International Politics. New York: Free Press.

SNYDER, R. C. (1958) "A decision-making approach to the study of political phenomena," in R. Young (ed.) Approaches to the Study of Politics. Evanston, Ill.: Northwestern Univ. Press.

——— and J. A. ROBINSON (1961) National and International Decision-Making. New York: The Institute for International Order.

——— H. W. BRUCK, and B. SAPIN (1969) "The decision-making approach to the study of international conflict," in J. N. Rosenau (ed.) International Politics and Foreign Policy. New York: Free Press.

——— [eds.] (1962) Foreign Policy Decision Making. New York: Free Press.

——— [eds.] (1954) Decision-Making as an Approach to the Study of International Politics. Princeton, N.J.: Foreign Policy Analysis Project.

SONDERMANN, F. A. (1961) "The linkage between foreign policy and international politics," in J. N. Rosenau (ed.) International Politics and Foreign policy. New York: Free Press.

SPANIER, J. and E. M. USLANER (1974) How American Foreign Policy is Made. New York: Praeger.

SPIRO, H. J. (1966) "Foreign policy and political style," pp. 139-148 in The Annals of The American Academy of Political and Social Science CCLXVI.

SPROUT, H. and M. SPROUT (1971) Toward a Politics of the Planet Earth. New York: Van Nostrand-Reinhold.

——— (1965) The Ecological Perspective on Human Affairs. Princeton, N.J.: Princeton Univ. Press.

——— (1962) Foundations of International Politics. New York: Van Nostrand-Reinhold.

STASSEN, G. H. (1972) "Individual preference versus role-constraint in policy-making: Senatorial response to Secretaries Acheson and Dulles." World Politics 25: 96-119.

STEINBRUNER, J. D. (1974) The Cybernetic Theory of Decision. Princeton, N.J.: Princeton Univ. Press.

STERN, G. (1968) "The foreign policy of the Soviet Union," in F. S. Nortledge (ed.) The Foreign Policies of the Powers. New York: Praeger.

STOGDILL, R. M. (1974) Handbook of Leadership Research. New York: Free Press.

SULLIVAN, D. G. (1963) "Toward an inventory of major propositions contained in contemporary textbooks in international relations." Ph.D. dissertation. Northwestern University (Univ. Microfilms no. 64-986).

TANTER, R. (1972) "International system and foreign policy approaches: Implications for conflict modeling and management." World Politics 24: 7-39.

——— (1966) "Dimensions of conflict behavior within and between nations, 1958-60." Journal of Conflict Resolution 10: 41-64.

TERHUNE, K. W. (1968) "Motives, situation, and interpersonal conflict within prisoner's dilemma." Journal of Personality and Social Psychology Monograph Supplement 8: No. 3, Part 2, 1-23.

——— and J. M. FIRESTONE (1967) "Psychological studies in social interaction and motives (SIAM), phase 2: Group motives in an international relations game." CAL Report VX-2018-6-2. Cornell Aeronautical Laboratory.

THOMAS, E. J. and C. F. FINK (1963) "Effects of group size." Psychological Bulletin 60: 371-385.

THOMPSON, J. D. (1967) Organizations in Action. New York: McGraw-Hill.

THOMPSON, K. W. and R. C. MACRIDIS (1962) "The comparative study of foreign policy," in R. C. Macridis (ed.) Foreign Policy in World Politics. Englewood Cliffs, N.J.: Prentice-Hall.

THORDARSON, B. (1972) Trudeau and Foreign Policy: A Study in Decision Making. Toronto, Canada: Oxford Univ. Press.

TUCKER, R. C. (1965) "The dictator and totalitarianism." World Politics 17: 55-83.

ULMER, S. S. (1960) "The analysis of behavior patterns in the United States supreme court." Journal of Politics (November): 629-653.

VACCHIANO, R. B., P. S. STRAUSS, and D. C. SCHIFFMAN (1968) "Personality correlates of dogmatism." Journal of Consulting and Clinical Psychology 32: 83-85.

VERBA, S. (1969) "Assumptions of rationality and non-rationality in models of the international system," pp. 217-231 in J. N. Rosenau (ed.) International Politics and Foreign Policy. New York: Free Press.

——— (1961) Small Groups and Political Behavior: A Study of Leadership. Princeton, N.J.: Princeton Univ. Press.

VINCENT, J. (1974) "Some problem areas in dyadic research as developed in social field theory." Paper presented at annual meeting of the Southern Political Science Association, New Orleans, November 7-9.

VITAL, D. (1968) Making of British Foreign Policy. New York: Praeger.

WALLACE, M. (1971) "Power, status and international war." Journal of Peace Research 8: 23-36.

WALLACE, W. (1971) Foreign Policy and the Political Process. London: Macmillan.

WALTZ, K. N. (1975) "Theory of International Relations," pp. 1-85 in F. I. Greenstein and N. W. Polsby (eds.) The Handbook of Political Science. Vol. 8. Reading, Mass.: Addison-Wesley.

——— (1967) Foreign Policy and Democratic Politics. Boston: Little, Brown.

——— (1964) "The stability of a bipolar world." Daedalus 93: 881-909.

WEEDE, E. (1970) "Conflict behavior of nation-states." Journal of Peace Research 7: 229-235.

WELLING, J. F. (1969) "Role and norm deviation." Master's thesis. University of Minnesota.

WESTERFIELD, H. B. (1963) The Instruments of America's Foreign Policy. N.Y.: Thomas Crowell.

WHITE, G. (1969) "A comparison of the 'operational codes' of Mao Tse-Tung and Liu Shao-Chi." Mimeo. Stanford University.

WHITING, A. (1969) "How we almost went to war with China." Look Magazine (April 29): 76-77.

WHITING, J.W.M. (1969) "Methods and problems in cross-cultural research," in G. Lindzey and E. Aronson (eds.) The Handbook of Social Psychology. Vol. 2. Reading, Mass.: Addison-Wesley.

WILKENFELD, J. (1969) "Some further findings regarding the domestic and foreign conflict behavior of nations." Journal of Peace Research 2: 147-56.

——— (1968) "Domestic and foreign conflict behavior of nations." Journal of Peace Research 1: 56-69.

WILKINSON, D. O. (1969) Comparative Foreign Relations: Framework and Methods. Belmont, Calif.: Dickenson.

WINTER, D. G. (1973) The Power Motive. New York: Free Press.

WOLFENSTEIN, E. V. (1969) Personality and Politics. Belmont, Calif.: Dickenson.

――― (1967) The Revolutionary Personality. Princeton, N.J.: Princeton Univ. Press.

WRIGHT, Q. (1955) The Study of International Relations. New York: Appleton-Century-Crofts.

YARMOLINSKY, A. (1970-1971) "The military establishment (or how political problems become military problems)." Foreign Policy, No. 1 (Winter): 78-97.

YOUNG, O. R. (1968a) Systems of Political Science. Englewood Cliffs, N.J.: Prentice-Hall.

――― (1968b) A Systemic Approach to International Politics. Research Monograph No. 33. Princeton, N.J.: Center of International Studies.

ZIMMERMAN, W. (1973) "Issue area and foreign policy process: A research note in search of a general theory." American Political Science Review 67: 1204-1212.

ZINNES, D. A. (1976) Contemporary Research in International Relations. New York: Free Press.

――― (1975) "Research frontiers in the study of international politics," pp. 87-198 in F. I. Greenstein and N. W. Polsby (eds.) The Handbook of Political Science. Vol. 8. Reading, Mass.: Addison-Wesley.

――― (1968) "The expression and perception of hostility in prewar crisis: 1914," in J. D. Singer (ed.) Quantitative International Politics: Insights and Evidence. New York: Free Press.

――― J. L. ZINNES, and D. McCLURE (1972) "Hostility in diplomatic communication: A study of the 1914 crisis," in C. F. Hermann (ed.) International Crises: Insights from Behavioral Research. New York: Free Press.

INDEX

ABOUT THE AUTHORS

MAURICE A. EAST is an Associate Professor of Political Science and the associate director of the Patterson School of Diplomacy and International Commerce at the University of Kentucky. He is a principal investigator on the Comparative Research on the Events of Nations (CREON) project. He is a coauthor of *CREON: A Foreign Events Data Set* (1973), a coeditor of *The Analysis of International Politics* (1972) and the author of numerous articles for such journals as *World Politics, International Studies Quarterly and Policy Sciences.*

STEPHEN A. SALMORE is presently an Associate Professor at the Eagleton Institute of Politics at Rutgers University. He received his Ph.D. from Princeton University. He has published in the *Policy Studies Journal,* Papers of the Peace Research Society, and in a number of readers on foreign policy. In addition to participating as a principal investigator of the CREON Project he is currently directing the Eagleton Poll, a quarterly survey of public opinion in New Jersey.

CHARLES F. HERMANN serves as Associate Director of the Mershon Center and Professor of Political Science at Ohio State University. With his associates on the CREON Project he has authored *CREON: A Foreign Events Data Set* and contributed to a forthcoming book on foreign policy behaviors. Among his other publications are *Crises in Foreign Policy, International Crises,* and a number of articles. He received his Ph.D. from Northwestern University and then taught at Princeton University. Before coming to Ohio State, he received a Council on Foreign Relations International Affairs Fellowship which resulted in his working on Henry Kissinger's NSC staff for a year.

MARGARET G. HERMANN is a Senior Research Associate at Mershon Center, Ohio State University. She has a Ph.D. in psychology from Northwestern University. Her research focuses on the effects of the personal characteristics of political leaders on political behavior. She is editor of *A Psychological Examination of Political Leaders.*

BARBARA G. SALMORE received her Ph.D. from Rutgers University, is an Associate Professor of Political Science at Drew University and a Faculty Associate of the Mershon Center. She has published in the *Policy Studies Journal* and several readers on political parties and linkages as well as a forthcoming reader on the validity of events data. She continues to engage in further research related to the CREON data.

WARREN R. PHILLIPS is Professor of Government and Politics at the University of Maryland where he teaches courses in the application of quantitative methods of policy planning and to international relations. He has just finished a major review of the quality of analysis in national security planning and is in the progress of completing a book on the application of catastrophe theory to crisis management. As a past manager of CACI's policy sciences division he gained experience in the application of quantitative methodologies to problems in the intelligence and planning community. He has headed several ARPA contract efforts and has spent two years as advisor to ARPA's crisis management program.

LINDA P. BRADY is Assistant Professor of Political Science and Chairman of the International Relations Program at Goucher College. She was born in 1947 in New York City, and holds an A.B. from Douglass College (1969), an M.A. from Rutgers University (1970), and a Ph.D. from Ohio State University 1974. Her publications include "Planning for Foreign Policy: A Framework for Analysis" and "Event Data and Situational Variables: The Validity Problem." Previously she has taught at Vanderbilt University.

NOTES

NOTES

NOTES

NOTES

NOTES

NOTES